BOOK 2 – INSTITUTIONAL INVESTORS, CAPITAL MARKET EXPECTATIONS, ECONOMIC CONCEPTS, AND ASSET ALLOCATION

D1444485

SCHWESERNOTES™ 2012 CFA LEVEL III BOOK 2: INSTITUTIONAL INVESTORS, CAPITAL MARKET EXPECTATIONS, ECONOMIC CONCEPTS, AND ASSET ALLOCATION

©2011 Kaplan, Inc. All rights reserved.

Published in 2011 by Kaplan Schweser.

Printed in the United States of America.

ISBN: 978-1-4277-3622-2 / 1-4277-3622-7

PPN: 3200-1736

READINGS AND LEARNING OUTCOME STATEMENTS

READINGS

The following material is a review of the Institutional Investors, Capital Market Expectations, Economic Concepts, and Asset Allocation principles designed to address the learning outcome statements set forth by CFA Institute.

STUDY SESSION 5

Reading Assignments
Portfolio Management for Institutional Investors, CFA Program Curriculum,
Volume 2 (CFA Institute, 2012)

STUDY SESSION 6

Reading Assignment
Capital Market Expectations in Portfolio Management, CFA Program Curriculum,
Volume 3 (CFA Institute, 2012)

STUDY SESSION 7

Reading Assignments
Economic Concepts for Asset Valuation in Portfolio Management, CFA Program
Curriculum, Volume 3, Level III (CFA Institute, 2012)

STUDY SESSION 8

Reading Assignments
Asset Allocation, CFA Program Curriculum, Volume 3, Level III
(CFA Institute, 2012)

Learning Outcome Statements (LOS)

Study Session 5

The topical coverage corresponds with the following CFA Institute assigned reading:

15. Managing Institutional Investor Portfolios

The candidate should be able to:

a. <u>contrast</u> a defined-benefit plan to a defined-contribution plan, from the perspective of the employee and employer and <u>discuss</u> the advantages and disadvantages of each. (page 10)

b. <u>discuss</u> investment objectives and constraints for defined-benefit plans. (page 13)

c. <u>evaluate</u> pension fund risk tolerance when risk is considered from the perspective of the 1) plan surplus, 2) sponsor financial status and profitability, 3) sponsor and pension fund common risk exposures, 4) plan features, and 5) workforce characteristics. (page 13)

d. <u>prepare</u> an investment policy statement for a defined-benefit plan. (page 41)

e. <u>evaluate</u> the risk management considerations in investing pension plan assets. (page 15)

f. <u>prepare</u> an investment policy statement for a defined-contribution plan. (page 41)

g. <u>discuss</u> hybrid pension plans (e.g., cash balance plans) and employee stock ownership plans. (page 16)

h. <u>distinguish</u> among various types of foundations, with respect to their description, purpose, source of funds, and annual spending requirements. (page 17)

i. <u>compare</u> the investment objectives and constraints of foundations, endowments, insurance companies, and banks. (page 18)

j. <u>prepare</u> an investment policy statement for a foundation, an endowment, an insurance company, and a bank. (page 45)

k. <u>contrast</u> investment companies, commodity pools, and hedge funds to other types of institutional investors. (page 31)

l. <u>discuss</u> the factors that determine investment policy for pension funds, foundations, endowments, life and nonlife insurance companies, and banks. (page 32)

m. <u>compare</u> the asset/liability management needs of pension funds, foundations, endowments, insurance companies, and banks. (page 30)

n. <u>compare</u> the investment objectives and constraints of institutional investors given relevant data, such as descriptions of their financial circumstances and attitudes toward risk. (page 32)

The topical coverage corresponds with the following CFA Institute assigned reading:

16. Linking Pension Liabilities to Assets

The candidate should be able to:

a. <u>contrast</u> the assumptions concerning pension liability risk in asset-only and liability-relative approaches to asset allocation. (page 54)

b. <u>discuss</u> the fundamental and economic exposures of pension liabilities and <u>identify</u> asset types that mimic these liability exposures. (page 55)

c. <u>compare</u> pension portfolios built from a traditional asset-only perspective to portfolios designed relative to liabilities and <u>discuss</u> why corporations may choose not to implement fully the liability mimicking portfolio. (page 58)

The topical coverage corresponds with the following CFA Institute assigned reading:

17. **Allocating Shareholder Capital to Pension Plans**

The candidate should be able to:

a. compare funding shortfall and asset/liability mismatch as sources of risk faced by pension plan sponsors. (page 63)

b. explain how the weighted average cost of capital for a corporation can be adjusted to incorporate pension risk and discuss the potential consequences of not making this adjustment. (page 63)

c. explain, in an expanded balance sheet framework, the effects of different pension asset allocations on total asset betas, the equity capital needed to maintain equity beta at a desired level, and the debt-to-equity ratio. (page 68)

Study Session 6

The topical coverage corresponds with the following CFA Institute assigned reading:

18. **Capital Market Expectations**

The candidate should be able to:

a. discuss the role of, and a framework for, capital market expectations in the portfolio management process. (page 81)

b. discuss, in relation to capital market expectations, the limitations of economic data, data measurement errors and biases, the limitations of historical estimates, *ex post* risk as a biased measure of *ex ante* risk, biases in analysts' methods, the failure to account for conditioning information, the misinterpretation of correlations, psychological traps, and model uncertainty. (page 83)

c. demonstrate the application of formal tools for setting capital market expectations, including statistical tools, discounted cash flow models, the risk premium approach, and financial equilibrium models. (page 87)

d. explain the use of survey and panel methods and judgment in setting capital market expectations. (page 99)

e. discuss the inventory and business cycles, the impact of consumer and business spending, and monetary and fiscal policy on the business cycle. (page 100)

f. discuss the impact that the phases of the business cycle have on short-term/long-term capital market returns. (page 103)

g. explain the relationship of inflation to the business cycle and the implications of inflation for cash, bonds, equity, and real estate returns. (page 103)

h. demonstrate the use of the Taylor rule to predict central bank behavior. (page 105)

i. evaluate 1) the shape of the yield curve as an economic predictor and 2) the relationship between the yield curve and fiscal and monetary policy. (page 107)

j. identify and interpret the components of economic growth trends and demonstrate the application of economic growth trend analysis to the formulation of capital market expectations. (page 107)

k. explain how exogenous shocks may affect economic growth trends. (page 109)

l. identify and interpret macroeconomic, interest rate, and exchange rate linkages between economies. (page 110)

m. discuss the risks faced by investors in emerging-market securities and the country risk analysis techniques used to evaluate emerging market economies. (page 111)

n. compare the major approaches to economic forecasting. (page 112)

o. demonstrate the use of economic information in forecasting asset class returns. (page 114)

p. <u>evaluate</u> how economic and competitive factors affect investment markets, sectors, and specific securities. (page 114)

q. <u>discuss</u> the relative advantages and limitations of the major approaches to forecasting exchange rates. (page 117)

r. <u>recommend</u> and <u>justify</u> changes in the component weights of a global investment portfolio based on trends and expected changes in macroeconomic factors. (page 119)

STUDY SESSION 7

The topical coverage corresponds with the following CFA Institute assigned reading:

19. Equity Market Valuation

The candidate should be able to:

a. <u>explain</u> the terms of the Cobb-Douglas production function and <u>demonstrate</u> how the function can be used to model growth in real output under the assumption of constant returns to scale. (page 138)

b. <u>evaluate</u> the relative importance of growth in total factor productivity, in capital stock, and in labor input given relevant historical data. (page 140)

c. <u>demonstrate</u> the use of the Cobb-Douglas production function in obtaining a discounted dividend model estimate of the intrinsic value of an equity market. (page 142)

d. <u>critique</u> the use of discounted dividend models and macroeconomic forecasts to estimate the intrinsic value of an equity market. (page 142)

e. <u>contrast</u> top-down and bottom-up approaches to forecasting the earnings per share of an equity market index. (page 147)

f. <u>discuss</u> the strengths and limitations of relative valuation models. (page 149)

g. <u>judge</u> whether an equity market is under-, fairly, or over-valued using a relative equity valuation model. (page 149)

The topical coverage corresponds with the following CFA Institute assigned reading:

20. Dreaming with BRICs: The Path to 2050

The candidate should be able to:

a. <u>compare</u> the economic potential of emerging markets such as Brazil, Russia, India, and China (BRICs) to that of developed markets, in terms of economic size and growth, demographics and per capita income, growth in global spending, and trends in real exchange rates. (page 167)

b. <u>explain</u> why certain developing economies may have high returns on capital, rising productivity, and appreciating currencies. (page 168)

c. <u>explain</u> the importance of technological progress, employment growth, and growth in capital stock in estimating the economic potential of an emerging market. (page 169)

d. <u>discuss</u> the conditions necessary for sustained economic growth, including the core factors of macroeconomic stability, institutional efficiency, open trade, and worker education. (page 170)

e. <u>evaluate</u> the investment rationale for allocating part of a well-diversified portfolio to emerging markets in countries with above average economic potential. (page 172)

STUDY SESSION 8

The topical coverage corresponds with the following CFA Institute assigned reading:

21. **Asset Allocation**

The candidate should be able to:

a. explain the function of strategic asset allocation in portfolio management and discuss its role in relation to specifying and controlling the investor's exposures to systematic risk. (page 180)

b. compare strategic and tactical asset allocation. (page 180)

c. discuss the importance of asset allocation for portfolio performance. (page 181)

d. contrast the asset-only and asset/liability management (ALM) approaches to asset allocation and discuss the investor circumstances in which they are commonly used. (page 181)

e. explain the advantage of dynamic over static asset allocation and discuss the trade-offs of complexity and cost. (page 182)

f. explain how loss aversion, mental accounting, and fear of regret may influence asset allocation policy. (page 182)

g. evaluate return and risk objectives in relation to strategic asset allocation. (page 183)

h. evaluate whether an asset class or set of asset classes has been appropriately specified. (page 186)

i. select and justify an appropriate set of asset classes for an investor. (page 200)

j. evaluate the theoretical and practical effects of including additional asset classes in an asset allocation. (page 187)

k. explain the major steps involved in establishing an appropriate asset allocation. (page 190)

l. discuss the strengths and limitations of the following approaches to asset allocation: mean–variance, resampled efficient frontier, Black–Litterman, Monte Carlo simulation, ALM, and experience based. (page 191)

m. discuss the structure of the minimum-variance frontier with a constraint against short sales. (page 198)

n. formulate and justify a strategic asset allocation, given an investment policy statement and capital market expectations. (page 200)

o. compare the considerations that affect asset allocation for individual investors versus institutional investors and critique a proposed asset allocation in light of those considerations. (page 207)

p. formulate and justify tactical asset allocation (TAA) adjustments to strategic asset class weights, given a TAA strategy and expectational data. (page 210)

The topical coverage corresponds with the following CFA Institute assigned reading:

22. **The Case for International Diversification**

The candidate should be able to:

a. discuss the implications of international diversification for domestic equity and fixed-income portfolios, based on the traditional assumptions of low correlations across international markets. (page 226)

b. distinguish between the asset return and currency return for an international security. (page 231)

c. evaluate the contribution of currency risk to the volatility of an international security position. (page 232)

    d. <u>discuss</u> the impact of international diversification on the efficient frontier. (page 229)

    e. <u>evaluate</u> the potential performance and risk-reduction benefits of adding bonds to a globally diversified stock portfolio. (page 230)

    f. <u>explain</u> why currency risk should not be a significant barrier to international investment. (page 234)

    g. <u>critique</u> the traditional case against international diversification. (page 234)

    h. <u>discuss</u> the barriers to international investments and their impact on international investors. (page 236)

    i. <u>distinguish</u> between global investing and international diversification and <u>discuss</u> the growing importance of global industry factors as a determinant of risk and performance. (page 238)

    j. <u>discuss</u> the basic case for investing in emerging markets, as well as the risks and restrictions often associated with such investments. (page 239)

The following is a review of the Portfolio Management for Institutional Investors principles designed to address the learning outcome statements set forth by CFA Institute®. This topic is also covered in:

MANAGING INSTITUTIONAL INVESTOR PORTFOLIOS

Study Session 5

EXAM FOCUS

This review addresses issues related to formulating an investment policy statement (IPS) for institutions: pension funds, foundations, endowments, life and nonlife insurance companies, and banks. Focus on the different liability characteristics facing each institution and how they affect investment policies. As always, be sure to consider legal and tax consequences when dealing with institutional investors.

 Professor's Note: Some of the LOS in this topic review are out of order, but every LOS is covered. LOS 15.d, 15.f, and 15.j are in the Concept Checkers.

WARM-UP: PENSION PLANS

General Pension Definitions

- A *pension plan* is created by a plan sponsor to provide deferred compensation in the form of retirement benefits to plan participants.
- The *plan sponsor* is the organization (e.g., a corporation, a government entity, a nonprofit organization) that funds the pension plan.
- *Plan participants* are those receiving a promise of retirement income from the pension plan.

Types of Pension Plans

A **defined-benefit plan** is a pension plan whose retirement promise is framed according to benefits to be paid to participants. Benefits are often calculated by a formula related to years of service, rate of pay over some specified time period, or a combination of both.

A **cash balance plan** is a hybrid defined-benefit plan that maintains individual account records for plan participants showing their current value of accrued benefit. These plans differ slightly from traditional defined-benefit plans in that an account, rather than an actual fund, is maintained for each individual.

A **defined-contribution plan** is a pension plan whose retirement promise is framed according to the contributions made to the plan by the plan sponsor. The liability to the sponsor is only the contribution, not the benefit ultimately received by the participants.

A **profit sharing plan** is a defined-contribution plan whose contributions are established somewhat by the profitability of the plan sponsor.

Pension Plan Funding

- *Funded status* refers to the relationship between the present value of the pension plan's assets and liabilities.
- *Fully funded* means the present value of plan assets is approximately equal to the present value of plan liabilities.
- *Underfunded* means the present value of plan assets is less than the present value of plan liabilities. Underfunded plans may require the plan sponsors to make special contributions in addition to the usual, regular contributions.
- Plan *surplus* is the value by which plan assets exceed plan liabilities. When the plan has a funding surplus, the firm is unlikely to have to make contributions.

Pension Plan Liabilities

- *Accumulated benefit obligation* (ABO) is the total present value of pension liabilities to date, assuming no further accumulation of benefits. In effect, ABO is the pension benefits due to participants if the plan sponsor terminated existence.
- *Projected benefit obligation* (PBO) is the ABO plus projections of future employee compensation increases. The PBO is the pension liability for a going concern and is the liability figure used in calculating funded status.
- *Total future liability* is a measure of pension liability that is the most comprehensive, because it takes into account not only compensation changes, but also changes in the workforce and benefit changes associated with inflation. Total future liability is often used when setting objectives within the investment policy statement (IPS).
- *Retired lives* is the number of plan participants currently receiving benefits (i.e., retirees currently receiving retirement income).
- *Active lives* is the number of plan participants not currently receiving pension benefits (i.e., those working toward retirement).
- *Inactive participants* are individuals no longer employed by the firm or organization who earned retirement benefits from past employment but have not started receiving the benefits.

DEFINED-BENEFIT PLANS AND DEFINED-CONTRIBUTION PLANS

LOS 15.a: <u>Contrast</u> a defined-benefit plan to a defined-contribution plan, from the perspective of the employee and employer and <u>discuss</u> the advantages and disadvantages of each.

CFA® Program Curriculum, Volume 2, page 396

The contrasting features between defined-benefit and defined-contribution plans from the perspective of employee and employer are illustrated in Figure 1.

Figure 1: Features of Defined-Benefit and Defined-Contribution Pension Plans

Plan Type	Employer	Employee
Defined benefit	• Pension benefits are a liability for the employer. • Benefits are determined by stated criteria usually associated with years of service and salary. • The plan sponsor (the firm) is responsible for managing the plan assets to meet pension obligations (i.e., faces the investment risk).	• Receives periodic payments beginning at retirement or other eligibility date according to a formula. • Subject to "early termination" risk if employee is terminated prior to retirement. • Does not bear risk/return consequences of investment portfolio performance.
Defined contribution	• The firm promises to keep all contributions current. • Only financial liability is making contributions to employee's account. • The plan must offer employees a sufficient number of investment vehicles for suitable portfolio construction.	• Owns plan assets and can transport account to other qualified plans. • Must make all investment decisions given available investment vehicles and change the allocation as necessary. • Bears all the investment risk.

Figure 2 summarizes the primary advantages and disadvantages of both types of pension plans from the perspectives of the sponsor (i.e., the firm) and the beneficiary (i.e., the employee). All of these characteristics are discussed in later LOS, but this summary should help you formulate a small list for the exam.

Professor's Note: Defined-contribution (DC) pension plans come in two forms: participant directed and sponsor directed. In a sponsor-directed DC (e.g., profit sharing plan), the sponsor selects the investments. In a participant-directed DC plan, the employees allocate retirement funds (employee and employer contributions) among a list of mutual funds provided by the sponsor. In the United States, a plan is considered qualified if it meets the requirements of federal and state tax laws associated with retirement funds. Figure 2 summarizes the advantages and disadvantages of a participant-directed DC plan.

Figure 2: Advantages and Disadvantages of Defined-Benefit and Defined-Contribution Pension Plans

Plan Type	Advantages		Disadvantages	
	To the Employee	To the Firm	To the Employee	To the Firm
Defined benefit	• No investment risk. • Stable retirement income.	• Possible pension income. • Ability to support stock with some investment in company stock.	• Early termination risk. • Usually a vesting period. • Restricted withdrawal of funds. • Adverse effect on diversification because both job and pension are linked to health of employer.	• Investment risk. • Regular funding (liquidity) obligation. • Early retirement and other options can increase liquidity requirements. • Highly regulated by federal (ERISA in United States) and state governments. • Extra resources needed to fulfill due diligence requirements.

Plan Type	Advantages		Disadvantages	
	To the Employee	To the Firm	To the Employee	To the Firm
Defined contribution	• Legally own all personal contributions. • Once vested, legally own all sponsor contributions. • Assets easily transferred to another plan (i.e., portable). • Can diversify retirement portfolio to suit needs. • Lowers taxable income.	• No financial liability other than matching provisions. • No investment risk. • Lower liquidity requirements. • Less resources required. • Fewer regulations.	• Investment risk. • Must monitor and make necessary reallocation decisions. • Restricted withdrawal of funds.	• Usually legally required to have an IPS that addresses how the plan will help participants meet their objectives and constraints (e.g., types and number of investment alternatives, advice).

For the Exam: Questions on this warm-up (background) material on pension plans, if there are any, will likely not amount to more than a few points either in a morning case or in an afternoon item set. Read and understand it, but place your study emphasis on developing the IPS for both types of plans. Also, note that the Level III curriculum focuses on the characteristics of a participant-directed DC pension plan. You may hear reference to a sponsor-directed DC plan, but you should not see a case or item set devoted to one.

DEFINED-BENEFIT PLAN OBJECTIVES

LOS 15.b: <u>Discuss</u> investment objectives and constraints for defined-benefit plans.

CFA® Program Curriculum, Volume 2, page 398

LOS 15.c: <u>Evaluate</u> pension fund risk tolerance when risk is considered from the perspective of the 1) plan surplus, 2) sponsor financial status and profitability, 3) sponsor and pension fund common risk exposures, 4) plan features, and 5) workforce characteristics.

CFA® Program Curriculum, Volume 2, page 400

Return

The ultimate goal of a pension plan is to have pension assets generate returns sufficient to cover pension liabilities. The specific return requirement will depend on the plan's funded status and contributions dictated by accrued benefits. However, a plan's stated desired return may be higher to reflect concerns relative to the following:

- *Future pension contributions.* Return levels can be calculated to eliminate the need for contributions to plan assets. Minimization of contributions is a more realistic objective.
- *Pension income.* Accounting principles require pension expenses be reflected on sponsors' income statements. Negative expenses, or pension income, can also be recognized.

Plan Surplus

Plan surpluses indicate a cushion provided by plan assets to meet plan liabilities. The greater the surplus, the greater the plan's ability to take risk. Underfunded plans indicate a liability funding shortfall. Although the sponsor may be willing to take greater investment risk to remedy the shortfall, the underfunded status dictates a decreased ability for the plan to take risk.

Sponsor Financial Status and Profitability

- Financial status can be indicated by the sponsor's balance sheet. The debt-to-asset or other leverage ratios often indicate financial condition. Profitability can be represented by the sponsor's current or pro forma financials.
- Lower debt ratios and higher current and expected profitability indicate better capability of meeting pension liabilities and, hence, imply greater ability to tolerate risk.
- Higher debt ratios and lower current or prospective profitability indicate decreased capability of meeting pension liabilities and, hence, may imply a below-average ability to tolerate risk.

Sponsor and Pension Fund Common Risk Exposure

- Common risk exposure is measured by the *correlation* between the firm's operating characteristics and pension asset returns.
- The higher the correlation between a firm's operations and pension asset returns, the lower the risk tolerance.
- The lower the correlation between a firm's operations and pension asset returns, the higher the risk tolerance.

Plan Features

- Some plans offer participants the option of either retiring early or receiving lump-sum payments instead of a retirement annuity.
- Plans that offer early retirement or lump-sum payments essentially decrease the time horizon of the retirement liability and increase the liquidity requirements of the plan. Therefore, the ability to tolerate risk is decreased.

Workforce Characteristics

- These characteristics relate to the age of the workforce and to the ratio of active lives to retired lives.
- In general, the younger the workforce, the greater the ratio of active to retired lives, which indicates an increased ability to tolerate risk when managing pension assets.
- Conversely, an older workforce coupled with a low active-to-retired lives ratio indicates a decreased ability to tolerate risk.

DEFINED-BENEFIT PLAN CONSTRAINTS

Liquidity. The pension plan receives contributions from the plan sponsor and makes payments to beneficiaries. Any net outflow represents a liquidity constraint placed on the plan. Liquidity requirements will be affected by:

- *The number of retired lives.* The greater the number of retirees receiving benefits, the greater the liquidity that must be provided.
- *The amount of sponsor contributions.* The smaller the corporate contributions relative to retirement payments, the greater the liquidity needed.
- *Plan features.* Early retirement or lump-sum payment options increase liquidity requirements.

Time horizon. The time horizon of a defined-benefit plan is mainly determined by two factors:

1. Whether or not the plan is a going concern.
2. The workforce age and the ratio of active to retired lives.

If the plan is expected to terminate, the time horizon will be shortened to the expected termination date. The time horizon for a going concern defined-benefit plan is usually considered long term. Going concern plans can contain multistage time horizons that relate to the active and retired lives portions of plan participants. The active lives portion of the plan will indicate a time horizon associated with expected term to retirement. The retired lives portion will indicate a time horizon as a function of life expectancy for those currently receiving benefits.

For the Exam: On the exam, you will usually define the time horizon for either DB or DC plans as long term. If asked for a DB plan that will terminate, state the years remaining. Average employee age and ratio of active to retired lives are used primarily as measures of liquidity constraints rather than time horizon.

Legal and regulatory factors. In the United States, the Employee Retirement Income Security Act (ERISA) regulates the implementation of defined-benefit plans. As a federal regulation, ERISA *preempts* state and local pension fund law. The overriding standard of care required by ERISA is that pension fund assets must be invested for the sole benefit of plan participants and not those of plan sponsors.

Most countries have applicable laws and regulations governing pension investment activity. The key point to remember is that when formulating an IPS for a pension plan, the adviser must incorporate the regulatory framework existing within the jurisdiction where the plan operates. Consultation with appropriate legal experts is encouraged.

Unique circumstances. There are two main classes of unique circumstances that may constrain investment activity for a defined-benefit plan:

1. ERISA requires plan sponsors to exercise appropriate due diligence when making investment decisions. Smaller firms may not have the requisite human capital to appropriately investigate the investment characteristics of alternative asset classes. Hedge funds, exotic derivatives, and other innovative financial instruments may offer attractive investment opportunities but require substantial due diligence before they can be added to the asset base.

2. Pension plans may impose requirements that prohibit investment in some traditional or alternative asset choices, such as firms in the defense industry, firms that produce alcoholic beverages, or firms that have a reputation for being destructive to the environment.

 Professor's Note: LOS 15.d, 15.f, and 15.j are covered in the Concept Checkers.

INVESTING PENSION PLAN ASSETS

LOS 15.e: Evaluate the risk management considerations in investing pension plan assets.

CFA® Program Curriculum, Volume 2, page 411

This LOS is primarily concerned with the correlation between investment performance of pension assets and the operating performance of the company, as well as how that correlation impacts required contributions to the plan.

If the plan's assets and the firm's operating assets are *highly correlated*:

- When plan assets are generating *high returns*, the firm's operating assets are likely to also be generating high returns. Thus, the firm has the capability of providing a special contribution to the plan at a time when the plan probably doesn't require it.
  - The fund is capable of meeting benefit payments, and the likelihood of drawing down assets or defaulting on pension liabilities is low. This positively impacts firm value due to a lowered or even negative pension expense on the firm's income statement.
- When plan assets are generating *low returns*, the firm's operating assets are likely to also be generating low returns. Low pension asset returns coupled with the firm's inability to provide a special contribution could mean that the fund has to spend out of assets rather than earnings, and its funded status may be reduced.
  - The fund's need for a special contribution can negatively impact firm value, due to the increased pension expense on an already ailing income statement.

The investment policy committee can help avoid this by holding pension plan assets that are highly correlated with plan liabilities but *minimally* correlated with the firm's operating assets. This helps ensure that the plan's assets and liabilities increase and decrease in value simultaneously and makes the plan's funded status uncorrelated with the firm's ability to make special contributions. In the long run, the effect on firm valuation and the firm's constituents is positive due to decreased volatility in the fund surplus.

HYBRID PLANS AND ESOPS

LOS 15.g: <u>Discuss</u> hybrid pension plans (e.g., cash balance plans) and employee stock ownership plans.

CFA® Program Curriculum, Volume 2, page 418

Cash balance plan. A cash balance plan is a type of defined-benefit plan that defines the benefit in terms of an account balance. In a typical cash balance plan, a participant's account is credited each year with a pay credit and an interest credit. The pay credit is usually based upon the beneficiary's age, salary, and/or length of employment, and the interest credit is based upon a benchmark such as U.S. Treasuries. The sponsor bears all the investment risk because increases and decreases in the value of the plan's investments (due to investment decisions, interest rates, etc.) do not affect the benefit amounts promised to participants. At retirement, the beneficiary can usually elect to receive a lump-sum distribution, which can be rolled into another qualified plan, or receive a lifetime annuity upon retirement.

Employee stock ownership plans (ESOPs). An ESOP is a type of defined-contribution benefit plan that allows employees to purchase the company stock, sometimes at a discount from market price. The purchase can be with before- or after-tax dollars, and the final balance in the beneficiary's account reflects the increase in the value of the firm's stock as well as contributions during employment. ESOPs receive varying amounts of regulation in different countries.

Occasionally, an ESOP will purchase a large block of the firm's stock. The block can be purchased through the market or directly from a large stockholder, such as is often the case when a founding proprietor or partner wants to liquidate a holding. The stock is then purchased at regular intervals by plan beneficiaries. It should be noted that just as with any defined-contribution plan, the beneficiary must be aware of the risk of holding too much of the company's stock as a proportion of total retirement assets.

FOUNDATIONS

LOS 15.h: Distinguish among various types of foundations, with respect to their description, purpose, source of funds, and annual spending requirements.

CFA® Program Curriculum, Volume 2, page 421

Figure 3 contains a summary of the characteristics of the four basic types of foundations.[1]

Figure 3: Types of Foundations and Their Important Characteristics

Type of Foundation	Description	Purpose	Source of Funds	Annual Spending Requirement
Independent	Private or family	Grants to charities, educational institutions, social organizations, etc.	Typically an individual or family, but can be a group of interested individuals	5% of assets; expenses cannot be counted in the spending amount
Company sponsored	Closely tied to the sponsoring corporation	Same as independent; grants can be used to further the corporate sponsor's business interests	Corporate sponsor	Same as independent foundations
Operating	Established for the sole purpose of funding an organization (e.g., a museum, zoo, public library) or some ongoing research/medical initiative	Same as independent	Must spend at least 85% of dividend and interest income for its own operations; may also be subject to spending 3.33% of assets
Community	Publicly sponsored grant-awarding organization	Fund social, educational, religious, etc. purposes	General public, including large donors	None

---

1. Based upon Exhibit 2, "Managing Institutional Investor Portfolios," by R. Charles Tschampion, CFA, Laurence B. Siegel, Dean J. Takahashi, and John L. Maginn, CFA, from *Managing Investment Portfolios: A Dynamic Process*, 3rd edition, 2007 (CFA Institute, 2012 Level III Curriculum, Reading 15, Vol. 2, p. 421).

LOS 15.i: <u>Compare</u> the investment objectives and constraints of foundations, endowments, insurance companies, and banks.

CFA® Program Curriculum, Volume 2, page 421

Foundation Objectives

Return. Foundations vary widely in purpose, and it is difficult to state a general return objective for all foundations. One major determining factor is that the return objective depends on the time horizon stated for the foundation. If the foundation was created to provide perpetual support, the preservation of real purchasing power is a goal. One useful guideline is to set a minimum return equal to the required payout plus expected inflation and fund expenses.

Risk. Because there are no contractually defined liability requirements, foundations are usually more aggressive than pensions on the risk tolerance scale. The main driver for risk tolerance is the time horizon of the foundation. The spending level could also have an effect.

Foundation Constraints

Time horizon. Except for special foundations required to spend down their portfolio within a set time frame, most foundations have infinite time horizons. Hence, they can usually tolerate above-average risk and choose securities that tend to offer high returns as well as preservation of purchasing power.

Liquidity. A foundation's anticipated spending requirement is termed its *spending rate*. Other than the minimum spending rate set for private foundations (5% in the United States), most foundations can determine any spending rate desired. A foundation's spending rate will affect its ability to tolerate risk. Most foundations are prudent in their spending stance.

Tax considerations. Except for the fact that investment income of private foundations is currently taxed at 1% in the United States, foundations are not taxable entities. One potential concern relates to *unrelated business income*, which is taxable at the regular corporate rate. On average, tax considerations are not a major concern for foundations.

Legal and regulatory. In the United States, most states have adopted the Uniform Management Institutional Funds Act (UMIFA) as the prevailing regulatory framework. Most other regulations concern the tax-exempt status of the foundation. Otherwise, foundations can choose to invest in what investment activity or instrument they see fit. However, the prudent investor rule generally applies, which means that all investments must be evaluated from a portfolio perspective.

WARM-UP: ENDOWMENTS

Endowments are legal entities that have been funded for the expressed purpose of *permanently* funding the endowment's institutional sponsor (i.e., beneficiary). The intent is to preserve asset principal value in perpetuity and to use the income generated for budgetary support of specific activities. Universities, hospitals, museums, and charitable organizations often receive a substantial portion of their funding from endowments. Spending from endowments is usually earmarked for specific purposes and spending fluctuations can create disruptions in the institutional recipient's operating budget.

Many endowments use spending rules. There are three specific spending rules designed to better manage spending:

- **Simple spending rule.**

  The most straightforward spending rule is the simple spending rule, which calls for spending to equal the specified spending rate multiplied by the beginning period market value of endowment assets:

  $$spending_t = S(market\ value_{t-1})$$

  where:
  S = the specified spending rate

- **Rolling 3-year average spending rule.**

  This modification to the simple spending rule generates a spending amount that equals the spending rate multiplied by an average of the three previous years' market value of endowment assets. The idea here is to dampen volatility that can impact the endowment's portfolio value and the sponsor's operating budget:

  $$spending_t = (spending\ rate)\left(\frac{market\ value_{t-1} + market\ value_{t-2} + market\ value_{t-3}}{3}\right)$$

- **Geometric spending rule.**

  This spending rule addresses one of the criticisms of the rolling average spending rule in that extraordinary changes in portfolio value may cause dramatic shifts in spending. The geometric spending rule weights the prior year's spending level adjusted for inflation by a smoothing rate, which is usually between 0.6 and 0.8, as well as the previous year's beginning-of-period portfolio value. The effect allows previous years' spending to smoothly impact current spending:

  $$spending_t = (R)(spending_{t-1})(1 + I_{t-1}) + (1 - R)(S)(market\ value_{t-1})$$

  where:
  R = smoothing rate
  I = rate of inflation
  S = spending rate

Endowment Objectives

Return. As previously indicated, one of the goals of creating an endowment is to provide a permanent asset base for funding specific activities. Attention to preserving the real purchasing power of the asset base is paramount. The following are two implications from this requirement:

- Balancing the need for current funding with long-term protection of principal.
- Ensuring purchasing power is not affected by the ravages of inflation.

One way to meet the return requirement is to implement a total return approach when choosing investment securities. Under the **total return approach**, endowments may spend not only current income but may also rely on liquidating a portion of the fund's capital gains. Simulation studies indicate low-return, low-volatility investments increase the probability of not meeting endowment objectives. Implementation of the prudent investor rule (i.e., portfolio perspective) allows endowments to invest in higher-return, higher-risk investments with low correlations with the fund's other assets. This increases the fund's expected return while not violating the fund's risk objective.

Finally, stating a long-term spending rate below the long-term expected portfolio return level is crucial to meeting fund objectives. Spending rates above 5% typically lead to an erosion of principal and should be discouraged. To maintain purchasing power, the fund's total return should equal a comfortable maximum spending rate plus an adjustment for expected inflation.

Risk. Risk tolerance for an endowment is determined primarily by the extent to which the sponsor (i.e., the institutional beneficiary) depends on funding from the endowment to meet its annual operating budget. Generally, if the endowment provides a significant portion of the budget, ~10% or more, its ability to tolerate risk is diminished.

Because the time horizon for endowments is usually infinite, the risk tolerance of most endowments is relatively high. Endowments typically have the ability to weather short-term portfolio fluctuations to achieve long-term spending objectives.

Endowment Constraints

Time horizon. Because the purpose of most endowment funds is to provide a permanent source of funding, the time horizon for endowment funds is typically infinite.

Liquidity requirements. The liquidity requirements of an endowment are usually low. Only emergency needs and current spending require liquidity. However, large outlays (e.g., capital improvements) may require higher levels of liquidity.

Tax considerations. Endowment income is tax-exempt, so *tax-exempt bonds are not appropriate investment vehicles.* Keep this in mind if you are asked to choose between asset allocations on the exam. Some assets donated to the endowment, however, may generate unrelated business income. In that case, Unrelated Business Income Tax (UBIT) may have to be paid.

Regulatory and legal considerations. Except for issues related to 501(c)(3) tax regulations, which specify that earnings from tax-exempt entities do not accrue to private individuals, there are very few federal regulations governing the administration of endowments. (Keep in mind that this discussion is written from the perspective of a U.S.-based manager.) Most states have adopted the Uniform Management Institutional Fund Act (UMIFA) of 1972 as the governing regulation for endowments. If no specific legal considerations are stated in the case you see on the exam, be prepared to write, "Prudent investor rules apply."

Unique circumstances. Due to their diversity, endowment funds have many unique circumstances. Social issues (e.g., defense policies and racial biases) are typically taken into consideration when deciding upon individual investments.

WARM-UP: LIFE INSURANCE COMPANIES

Life insurance companies sell insurance policies that provide a death benefit to those designated on the policy when the covered individual dies. Two traditional life insurance policies are *whole life* and *term life* policies:

- *Whole life* insurance policies provide a level death benefit for the "whole" of the insured's life. The policy provides death benefit and cash value components where the death benefit portion remains constant but the cash value portion increases with the *credited rate* (i.e., the interest rate credited to the policyholder).
- *Term life* insurance policies provide a level death benefit for a stated "term" of the policyholder's life. Most term life policies have no cash value, but their premiums are much lower than whole life policies.

Due to increased competition in the financial marketplace, life insurance companies have been required to expand their policy offerings to maintain and attract customers who are convinced it is "best to buy term policies and invest the rest yourself." Two broad new policy forms, *universal life* and *variable life* policies, have been created in response to the competitive environment and represent the industry-wide trend of separating the death benefit from the investment return offered to policyholders:

- *Universal life* policies are composed of a life insurance policy paying an adjustable death benefit and an attached savings account offering competitive current market returns. Income on the savings component accumulates tax deferred.
- *Variable life* products link the death benefit and the cash value components to returns generated by a broad range of investment vehicles chosen by the policyholder.

Life Insurance Company Objectives

Return. Traditional whole life policies have built-in minimum required rates of return (i.e., credited rates). Portfolio returns above the minimum rate generate a *net interest spread* for the insurance company. However, competition has caused life insurance companies to offer higher and higher rates of return, which has reduced this spread and caused them to segment investment portfolios along major product lines. Hence, multiple return objectives are often found in a life insurance company's IPS.

The return objectives for life insurance companies can be segmented along the following lines:

- **Minimum return.** This rate of return is a statutory rate usually set by actuarial assumptions related to the amount of funding required for reserves to meet mortality predictions. Assets are usually chosen by duration-matching strategies to meet liability requirements (e.g., the death benefit payments).
- **Enhanced margin.** These rates are associated with efforts to earn competitive returns on assets that fund well-defined liabilities. "Spread management" techniques are employed to maximize the return earned on investments and the return credited to policy or annuity holders.
- **Surplus return.** In addition to the immunization portfolio (i.e., the portfolio used to meet the insurance company's liabilities), insurance companies manage a surplus portfolio. The primary objective for the surplus portfolio is to achieve higher returns through portfolio growth. Surplus growth is important to the expansion of insurance volume. Equity-oriented investments, including venture capital, are typically used to achieve this purpose.

Risk. Public policy views insurance company investment portfolios as *quasi-trust funds*. Having the ability to pay death benefits when due is a critical concern. The National Association of Insurance Commissioners (NAIC) directs life insurance companies to maintain an asset valuation reserve (AVR) as a cushion against substantial losses of portfolio value or investment income.

Some of the specific factors determining the risk objectives of a life insurance company relate to the following:

- **Valuation concerns.** Market volatility adversely impacts asset valuation. Sizeable declines in asset values may require write-offs that reduce surplus. Valuation concerns limit the risk exposure an insurance company can tolerate.
- **Cash flow volatility.** Life insurance companies have a low tolerance for any loss of income or delays in collecting income from investment activities. Reinvesting interest on interest is a major component of immunization as well as surplus growth. Most companies seek investments that offer minimum cash flow volatility.
- **Reinvestment risk.** An unexpected decline in interest rates can adversely affect the profitability of most annuity and guaranteed investment contracts with fixed credited rates. Controlling interest rate risk through duration management impacts the level of risk that can be tolerated.
- **Credit risk.** Credit quality is associated with the ability of the issuers of debt to pay interest and principal when due. Credit analysis is required to gauge potential losses of investment income and has been one of the industry's strong points. Because immunization portfolios can contain significant amounts of bonds, controlling credit risk is a major concern for life insurance companies and is often managed through a broadly diversified portfolio.

Life Insurance Company Constraints

Liquidity. Volatility and changes in the marketplace have increased the attention life insurance companies now pay to liquidity issues. Life insurance companies need to address three primary concerns when assessing liquidity requirements:

1. **Disintermediation.** Insurance companies have experienced periods of net cash outflows. High interest rate environments accompanied by large numbers of policy loans and surrenders have decreased liability durations dramatically. Industry responses to disintermediation have been a reduction in portfolio durations and provisions for additional liquidity reserves.

    Professor's Note: Surrender *is the term used when a policyholder cancels a life policy and receives its cash value. Rather than paying a future death benefit, the insurance company must meet an immediate cash flow.*

2. **Asset-liability mismatch.** Asset-liability management controls interest rate risk and, subsequently, liquidity needs. To the extent that assets decline at a greater rate than liabilities in an increasing interest rate environment, which also exacerbates disintermediation activities, careful attention must be paid to any duration mismatches between life insurance assets and liabilities.

3. **Asset marketability risk.** Asset liquidity is a direct function of marketability. Investments in low liquidity instruments (e.g., private placements, equity real estate, and venture capital) are now being constrained through maximum allowable positions. Marketability of investments is receiving attention to assure ample liquidity.

Time horizon. Traditionally, life insurance portfolios concentrated on holding periods of 20–40 years. The time horizon for life insurance companies has become progressively *shorter* as the duration of liabilities has decreased due to increased interest rate volatility and competitive market factors. Similar to return objectives being segmented across product offerings, individual segments of the overall portfolio will have their own time horizons. In general terms, time horizons have simply become shorter.

Tax considerations. Life insurance companies are taxable entities. Although a long period of favorable tax treatments has benefited the industry, changes in tax laws have served to increase taxes paid. Taxes are a major consideration in addressing the policy statement. Potential returns should be addressed both on a before- and after-tax basis.

Investment income is divided into two parts for tax purposes:

1. *Policyholder's share (not taxed).* Portion of the investment return used to meet crediting rates.

2. *Funds transferred to the surplus (taxed).* The portion of the investment return that is added to the insurance company's surplus portfolio.

Buildup of cash value in policyholders' accounts is tax deferred and is an attractive feature for the industry, but continual attention to potential changes in tax code is required.

Regulatory and legal constraints. Life insurance companies are heavily regulated, primarily at the state level. These regulations constrain the life insurance company's investment policies and relate to the following:

- **Eligible investments.** Insurance laws dictate eligible investments and asset classes (e.g., a corporate bond issue may have to reach an interest coverage ratio of greater than 1.5 to be considered eligible). Most states limit common stock holdings and foreign investment.
- **Prudent investor rule.** The prudent investor rule has been adopted in many U.S. states and allows companies more flexibility in investment decisions than the traditional "laundry lists" of permissible investments. It specifies that each investment may be analyzed from a portfolio perspective rather than stand-alone basis, so high-risk investments that have low correlations with portfolio assets are acceptable.
- **Valuation methods.** Uniform security valuation methods are administered by the National Association of Insurance Commissioners (NAIC). The NAIC's *Security Valuation Book* is the source for the valuation base for all securities. These values are listed in the firm's annual report of security holdings, Schedule D.

Unique circumstances. Concentration of product offerings, company size, and level of surplus are some of the most common factors impacting the uniqueness of life insurance companies. Unique factors must be taken into account when forming the IPS.

WARM-UP: NONLIFE INSURANCE COMPANIES

 Professor's Note: Nonlife companies include health, property and casualty, and surety companies.

Asset/Liability Management

- Liabilities of a casualty company differ from those of a life insurance company in that the claims reporting, processing, and payment process can take years to complete. This is referred to as the "long-tail" nature of casualty liabilities.
- The liability structure is mainly a function of the product mix that a company sells.
- Liability durations tend to be relatively short.

The underwriting cycle tends to follow *general business cycles.*

- The liquidity needs of a nonlife company are generally dictated by its underwriting cycle.
- The underwriting cycle corresponds to a 3- to 5-year cycle in which underwriting losses are negligible at the outset and become progressively worse, turning into significant losses at the end of the cycle.

Nonlife Insurance Company Objectives

Return. The return objectives for nonlife insurance companies are different from life insurance companies because nonlife firms face greater *uncertainty* due to the possibility of higher claims frequency. However, they are not as interest rate sensitive because their policies do not typically pay periodic returns.

- Primary requirements for nonlife insurance companies:

    1. Maximize the return on their fixed-income portfolio for purposes of meeting (i.e., immunizing) claims.
    2. Use returns from the equity portion of their portfolio to grow the surplus.
    3. Use the surplus portfolio to provide funds for unexpected, large liability claims.

- Nonlife insurance companies hold a greater percentage of equity-type investments in their portfolios than life insurance companies hold.
- Large stock and bond holdings are designed to provide high levels of current income and capital appreciation to build the surplus base.

Factors impacting nonlife insurance company return objectives:

- **Competitive pricing policy.** Today, most nonlife companies recognize that investment income can be used to reduce premiums and, hence, make the firm more competitive. Competition is a major influence in setting premiums.
- **Profitability.** Investment income and total return of the investment portfolio are now primary determinants of profitability. Investment return usually serves to smooth the earnings volatility of the typical underwriting cycle.
- **Growth of surplus.** The investment returns of a nonlife company should be used to increase the company's surplus. Each dollar of additional surplus has the ability to support $2–$3 of new policies. Venture capital, common stocks, and convertibles are the favored investments for surplus growth. Bond portfolios are usually maintained to fund insurance reserve requirements, whereas common stocks are used to provide growth to the surplus.
- **After-tax returns.** Nonlife insurance companies are taxable entities. After-tax returns are extremely important to nonlife companies.
- **Total return.** Active bond portfolio management strategies have been adopted by many large nonlife companies in an attempt to maximize total return. A focus on yield has been shifted to income and capital gain generation. Investment returns vary widely throughout the industry.

Risk. Similar to life companies, nonlife companies also have a quasi-fiduciary requirement. Safety is a major consideration in the company's investment policy. Due to the relatively high uncertainty associated with claims, risk tolerance of nonlife insurance companies must be tempered by their liquidity requirements. Casualty companies generally have limited risk tolerances.

Because most nonlife companies offer replacement cost coverage, inflation risk is also a big concern. There are two important considerations impacting the risk objectives of a nonlife insurance company:

1. The *cash flow characteristics* of nonlife companies are often erratic and unpredictable. Gaps between investment income and maturing securities may arise during the underwriting cycle. Hence, risk tolerance, as it pertains to loss of principal and declining investment income, is quite low.

2. The *common stock-to-surplus ratio* averages between one-half to three-fourths. Many companies have self-imposed ceilings on this ratio that imply even less exposure to equity instruments.

Nonlife Insurance Company Constraints

Liquidity. Due to the high uncertainty of claims, liquidity requirements for nonlife insurance companies are relatively high. Liquidity requirements are quite important, especially towards the end (i.e., trough) of an underwriting cycle. The high requirement for liquidity forces nonlife companies to pay specific attention to the marketability and maturity characteristics of portfolio assets. High liquidity requirements are often met through holding a portfolio of short-term securities, highly marketable U.S. government debt, and by maintaining a laddered maturity schedule of investable assets.

Time horizon. Due to the shorter duration of their liabilities, nonlife insurance companies have shorter time horizons than life insurance companies. Strangely, the average maturity of a nonlife company's bond portfolio is longer than that of a life company because of the predominance of long-term tax-exempt bonds held to maximize after-tax returns.

Equities are held to grow a nonlife company's surplus portfolio. The equities held tend to have growth characteristics and, on average, are held for long time periods. Attention to actively managing the surplus portfolio, however, has introduced a greater level of portfolio turnover, reducing the holding period.

Tax considerations. Nonlife insurance companies are taxable entities. Hence, tax considerations play an important role in formulating the IPS. Tax issues are complex, so frequent discussions with appropriate tax counsel are advised.

Regulatory and legal constraints. Regulatory considerations are slightly less onerous for nonlife insurance companies than for life insurance companies. An asset valuation reserve (AVR) is not required, but risk-based capital (RBC) requirements have been established. Otherwise, nonlife companies are given considerable leeway in choosing investments.

Unique circumstances. The current financial status of nonlife insurance companies, coupled with managing investment risk and liquidity requirements, will influence the preparation of IPS.

WARM-UP: BANKS

> **For the Exam:** None of this warm-up is directly applicable to the LOS. To understand the development of a bank IPS, however, it is important to understand banks' security portfolios and the primary risks that banks face.

Before we can discuss the objectives and constraints associated with a bank IPS, we need to discuss the securities banks hold as part of their assets. We know that banks are in business to take deposits (liabilities) and make loans (assets). A potential problem exists in the relationship between a bank's assets and liabilities, however. Liabilities are mostly in the form of short-term deposits, while assets (loans) can be fairly long term in nature. This leads to a significant mismatch in asset-liability durations and, hence, interest rate sensitivities.

WARM-UP (CONT.)

Bank Security Portfolios

The bank's security portfolio is usually a residual use of funds (i.e., excess funds that have not been loaned out). Banks are required to classify these securities into three distinct categories: hold to maturity, available for sale, and trading. Securities classified as **hold to maturity** are purchased with the intent of holding them until they mature (long-term debt investments) or for long-term capital gains. Banks recognize the annual dividend and interest income on their income statements, but capital gains are only recognized at maturity when the securities are redeemed. Under certain circumstances, the bank can reclassify and sell a hold-to-maturity security.

Securities classified as **available for sale** are purchased with the intent of selling them prior to maturity (short- or long-term investments). Unrealized gains and losses are recorded annually as adjustments to equity, and income is reported in the income statement. Because changes in their values affect the bank's capital, these securities need to be very liquid, and they usually have a fairly short duration/maturity.

The third classification is **trading securities**. These are securities perceived as mispriced that are purchased for short-term gains. Changes in value are reported on the income statement.

Duration, Credit Risk, Income, and Liquidity

Based upon the characteristics of the classifications, it can be seen that each can have significantly different durations, and the manner in which funds are allocated to the three classifications will determine the overall duration of the securities portfolio. In this way, managers can adjust the bank's **asset duration** to keep it in the desired relationship to its **liability duration**. If managers forecast increasing interest rates, for example, they can decrease the duration of the assets by decreasing the duration of the securities portfolio. If interest rates are expected to decrease, they will increase the duration of the assets.

In addition to duration management, a bank can use its security portfolio to manage the **credit risk** and **diversification** of its assets. For example, a bank's loans can become geographically concentrated. To offset the associated credit risk and lack of diversification, management can minimize the credit risk of the securities portfolio, as well as use the securities portfolio as a diversification mechanism.

Bank securities portfolios can generate significant **income** for the bank, sometimes accounting for 20–30% of the bank's total income. Also, because all loans cannot be readily sold, banks typically use the securities portfolio as a source of **liquidity** for needed cash.

WARM-UP (CONT.)

 Professor's Note: The previous paragraph describes uses of securities that are also common for the typical non-financial corporation. Whenever corporations find themselves with temporary excess cash, they purchase short-term marketable securities to generate a little extra income, and because the securities are highly liquid, they can be turned back into cash quickly.

Bank Risk Measures

Because the predominance of both their assets and liabilities are sensitive to changing interest rates, banks must continually monitor their interest rate risk. One risk measure banks use is value at risk (VAR), which can be described as either the minimum or maximum expected loss (see Study Session 14 for an in-depth discussion on VAR). **Leverage-adjusted duration gap** (LADG), more directly applicable to financial institutions, is also used as a measure of interest rate sensitivity.

Leverage-adjusted duration gap, which is actually a measure of the duration of the bank's *equity*, is defined as the duration of the bank's assets less the *leveraged* duration of the bank's liabilities:

$$LADG = D_{assets} - \left(\frac{L}{A}\right) D_{liabilities}$$

where:
$LADG$ = leverage-adjusted duration gap
D_{assets} = duration of the bank's assets
$D_{liabilities}$ = duration of the bank's liabilities
$\frac{L}{A}$ = leverage measure (market value of liabilities over market value of assets)

For an *increase* in interest rates:

If LADG < 0, market value of equity ↑
If LADG > 0, market value of equity ↓
If LADG = 0, market value of equity unchanged (immunized)

For a *decrease* in interest rates:

If LADG < 0, market value of equity ↓
If LADG > 0, market value of equity ↑
If LADG = 0, market value of equity unchanged (immunized)

Now that we have discussed why and how banks hold a portfolio of securities, we can discuss the objectives that are used in developing the IPS for the portfolio.

WARM-UP (CONT.)

For the Exam: The concepts associated with LADG appear in several places in the Level III curriculum. First, as part of asset-liability management (e.g., surplus management), the concept is applied to determining whether the firm has sufficient assets to fund future liabilities as well as estimating changes in the values of liabilities and assets in response to changing interest rates. You will also see the same concept when you adjust the duration of a portfolio using swaps. In both of these cases (i.e., swaps and surplus management), you might have to perform the calculations.

Bank Objectives

Return. The return objective for the bank securities portfolio is to earn a positive interest spread. The interest spread is the difference between the bank's cost of funds and the interest earned on loans and other investments.

Risk. The allocation of the bank security portfolio is determined in an asset-liability framework because the most important objective of the portfolio is meeting the costs and liquidity requirements associated with the bank's liabilities. Therefore, banks usually have a below-average tolerance for risk because they cannot let losses in the security portfolio interfere with their ability to meet their liabilities.

Bank Constraints

Liquidity. A bank's liquidity needs are driven by deposit withdrawals and demand for loans as well as regulation. As mentioned earlier, their securities portfolios typically contain very liquid securities.

Time horizon. Because a bank is an ongoing entity with regular liquidity concerns, the time horizon for the securities portfolio is driven by the average maturity of its liabilities. Because most bank liabilities are short term, the average maturity of securities in the portfolio tends to be short to intermediate term (<10 years).

Taxes. Banks are taxable entities, so taxes must be considered.

Legal and regulatory. Banks in industrialized nations are highly regulated. For example, banks may not be able to hold sub-investment quality securities, and there may be limits on the amount of common equity held. In addition, risk-based capital guidelines require banks to establish capital reserves of 8% against most loan categories. Banks also have to pledge collateral, usually short-term treasuries, against certain uninsured public deposits.

Unique. As with any other institutional investor, unique circumstances vary from bank to bank. As mentioned earlier, loan concentrations and the inability to sell loans are examples of unique circumstances that would impact the objectives and constraints of the securities portfolio IPS.

ASSET/LIABILITY MANAGEMENT FOR INSTITUTIONAL INVESTORS

LOS 15.m: <u>Compare</u> the asset/liability management needs of pension funds, foundations, endowments, insurance companies, and banks.

CFA® Program Curriculum, Volume 2, page 401

Firms with assets and liabilities that are affected by interest rates must actively pursue asset-liability management. Generally, they are concerned with the relative values of their assets and liabilities and their susceptibility to value changes in response to changing interest rates. The return and risk of the asset portfolio are determined by the *asset allocation*. The asset allocation is in turn driven by the nature of the liabilities.

This LOS is addressed throughout the review, but to save time and effort, I have developed Figure 4 for your quick reference.

Figure 4: Asset-Liability Management: Pension Funds, Foundations, Endowments, Insurance Companies, and Banks

Pension funds	Defined benefit	Surplus management is key. There are typically restrictions on short selling and maximum percentage allocations to asset categories or sectors. In addition, there are typically regulatory and liquidity constraints, such as limitations on private debt. Managers usually attempt to match durations of assets and liabilities to minimize the volatility of the surplus. In addition, managers always minimize the risk (standard deviation) of the asset portfolio while meeting return requirements.
	Defined contribution	Once annual contributions are met (the sponsor's only financial obligation), the sponsor's only remaining obligations are monitoring the plan and providing sufficient investment alternatives for participants. Beneficiaries manage their own assets.
Foundations		Foundations generally have to meet all funding requirements (grants and operating expenses) through investment earnings. Because they do not have to grow the foundation's assets (can spend all earnings), they can implement aggressive investment policies. That is, generally low spending requirements imply ability to tolerate risk.
Endowments		The overall goal, typically, is to preserve assets while meeting spending requirements. There is usually some sort of spending rule designed to compensate for low/high earnings years to avoid dramatic yearly fluctuations. The ability to tolerate risk is determined by the level of spending and the importance of the spending to the sponsor's operating budget.
Insurance companies		Insurance companies (life and nonlife) are taxable entities. They segment their general portfolio into sub-portfolios to match assets to various (liability) product lines according to interest rate risk (duration), return, and credit risk. In this fashion, each sub-portfolio will have its own return and liquidity characteristics, which are dictated by its associated liabilities.
Banks		The most important objective of the bank securities portfolio is meeting the bank's liabilities, so the allocation of the bank securities portfolio is determined using an asset-liability framework. The primary objective is earning a positive interest rate spread. As such, the bank could employ an ALM (surplus) efficient frontier as discussed in Study Session 8.

INVESTMENT COMPANIES

LOS 15.k: Contrast investment companies, commodity pools, and hedge funds to other types of institutional investors.

CFA® Program Curriculum, Volume 2, page 465

For the Exam: Whenever you see an LOS asking you to compare or contrast, be ready for statements on the exam made by analysts, portfolio managers, et cetera. You will be asked to indicate whether you agree or disagree with the statement and then explain your answer (if you disagree). In this material, you will see commodity pools mentioned. Due to the lack of testable material, you should not see questions on commodity pools that amount to significant points. For the exam, just remember that investment companies act as intermediaries to financial markets. That is, instead of investing their own funds like pensions plans, banks, insurance companies, endowments, or foundations, they pool and invest investor funds.

The institutional investors we have discussed thus far (pension plans, insurance companies, endowments, foundations, and banks) have their own objectives and constraints associated with their respective industries. For example, all foundations will fit a general description of a foundation (although funding sources vary) and are established to provide grants to applicants. The grants are funded primarily through earnings generated by investing the foundation's portfolio of assets. Endowments are established to help fund the operations of some institution, such as a university, and again the funding usually comes from earnings from the endowment's portfolio. Basically, all these institutional investors manage their own portfolios to fund liabilities (pension funds and insurance companies), help control interest rate risk, generate income (banks), or provide funding for organizations or individuals (endowments and foundations).

Investment companies, on the other hand, gather funds from investors and invest the pooled funds based upon advertised objectives and constraints. There are **mutual funds**, for example, to fit just about any equity or fixed-income investment style, from small-cap growth funds to large-cap value funds to funds that invest exclusively in one of a variety of sectors or industries. **Commodity pools** are similar to mutual funds but invest in pools of commodity futures and options contracts.

Hedge funds are also similar to mutual funds, although it is difficult to group all hedge fund types under the same general heading and then understand exactly what each specific fund does. Hedge funds gather funds from institutional and wealthy individual investors and construct various investment strategies aimed at identifying and capitalizing on mispriced securities.

To sum up, the primary difference between investment companies, commodity pools, and hedge funds and the institutional investors we discussed earlier is the source and use of their invested funds. Pension plans, insurance companies, endowments, foundations, and banks all invest their own assets to meet various funding requirements, while the latter group collects funds from investors and then invests the investors' funds to meet their investors' needs.

INVESTMENT POLICIES OF INSTITUTIONAL INVESTORS

LOS 15.l: Discuss the factors that determine investment policy for pension funds, foundations, endowments, life and nonlife insurance companies, and banks.

LOS 15.n: Compare the investment objectives and constraints of institutional investors given relevant data, such as descriptions of their financial circumstances and attitudes toward risk.

CFA® Program Curriculum, Volume 2, page 399

LOS 15.l and 15.n are summarized in Figure 5.

Figure 5: Factors Affecting Investment Policies of Institutional Investors

	IPS Component		Defined-Benefit Plans	Foundations	Endowment Funds	Life Insurance Companies	Nonlife Insurance Companies	Commercial Banks
Objectives	*Return*		Actuarial rate. A capital gains focus when the fund has low liquidity needs and younger workers. An income focus (duration matching) when there are high liquidity needs and older workers.	Private foundations must generate 5% plus management expenses plus inflation. Total return is appropriate.	Total return approach. The return objective must be balanced between a need for high current income and long-term protection of principal.	*Fixed-income segment:* "spread management" and actuarial assumptions. *Surplus segment:* capital gains.	*Fixed income:* maximize the return for meeting claims. *Equity segment:* grow the surplus/ supplement funds for liability claims.	Return is determined by the cost of funds. Primarily concerned with earning a positive interest rate spread.
	Risk Tolerance		Depends on surplus, age of workforce, time horizon, and company balance sheet.	Moderate to high, depending on spending rate and time horizon.	Moderate to high, depending on spending needs.	*Fixed-income segment:* conservative. *Surplus segment:* aggressive.	*Fixed-income segment:* conservative. *Surplus segment:* aggressive.	Banks are primarily concerned with meeting their liabilities and other liquidity needs and cannot suffer losses in the securities portfolio. Tend to have below-average risk tolerance.

Figure 5: Factors Affecting Investment Policies of Institutional Investors (Cont.)

				Institutional Investor Type			
	IPS Component	Defined-Benefit Plans	Foundations	Endowment Funds	Life Insurance Companies	Nonlife Insurance Companies	Commercial Banks
Constraints	Liquidity	Depends on age of workforce and retired lives proportion.	Other than 5% requirement for private foundations, spending rate is foundation specific.	Low, usually only for emergencies and spending. Spending rules are helpful.	*Fixed-income portion:* relatively high. *Surplus segment:* nil.	*Fixed income portion:* relatively high. *Surplus segment:* nil.	Liquidity is also relative to liabilities. Banks need continuing liquidity for liabilities and new loans.
	Time Horizon	Long if going concern. Short if terminating plan.	Long, usually infinite.	Long, usually infinite.	Getting shorter.	Short due to the nature of claims.	Time horizon tends to be short to intermediate because of mostly short-term liabilities.
	Legal Regulatory	ERISA/ prudent expert rule.*	Few. Prudent investor rule applies.	Low. Prudent investor rule typically applies.	High, especially on the state level/prudent investor rule.	Moderate, but increasing/ prudent investor rule.	Must meet regulatory requirements for liquidity, reserves, and pledging. Usually with short-term treasuries.
	Taxes	None	Few	None	High	High	Banks are taxable entities, so taxes must be considered.
	Unique Needs	Surplus, age of workforce, time horizon, and company balance sheet affect policy.	Foundation specific. Moral/ethical concerns may restrict certain securities.	Restrictions on certain securities/ asset classes common due to nature of funds.	Must distinguish between strategies for the fixed-income segment and the surplus segment.	The financial status of the firm; the management of investment risk and liquidity requirements influence IPS.	Varies from bank to bank. May need to use securities portfolio as diversification tool and/or to provide liquidity.

* The *prudent investor rule* requires a fiduciary to "prudently" invest trust assets as if they were his own based on the knowledge the fiduciary has at the time and considering only the needs of the trust's beneficiaries.

The *prudent expert rule* requires that the fiduciary manage the portfolio with the care, skill, prudence, and diligence, under the circumstances then prevailing, that a prudent investor would use. It extends the prudent investor rule beyond prudence by suggesting a higher level of expertise.

KEY CONCEPTS

LOS 15.a

In a defined-benefit plan, the *employer* promises benefits to be paid at retirement, which creates a liability for the employer. Benefits are calculated on some stated criteria usually associated with years of service and salary. Risk/return characteristics of assets used to meet obligations accrue to the plan sponsor. The *employee* receives periodic payments beginning at retirement or the employee's eligibility date as stated in the pension payment formula. The employee does not bear the risk/return consequences of investment portfolio performance.

In a defined-contribution plan, the *employer* promises contributions to be paid currently. The only financial liability is to make current contributions to the employee's account. The plan must offer employees a sufficient number of investment vehicles for suitable portfolio construction. The *employee* owns plan assets and can transport the account to other employment situations. The employee bears the brunt of investment performance risk/return characteristics and must make all investment decisions given available investment vehicles.

Plan Type	Advantages to the Employee	Advantages to the Firm	Disadvantages to the Employee	Disadvantages to the Firm
Defined Benefit	No investment risk. Stable retirement income.	Possible pension income. Ability to support stock with some investment in company stock.	Early termination risk. Usually a vesting period. Restricted withdrawal of funds. Adverse affect on diversification because both job and pension are linked to health of employer.	Investment risk. Regular funding obligation. Early retirement and other options can increase liquidity requirements. Highly regulated by governments. Extra resources needed to fulfill due diligence.
Defined Contribution	Own all personal contributions. Once vested, own all sponsor contributions. Assets easily transferred to another plan. Can diversify portfolio to suit needs. Lowers taxable income.	No financial liability other than matching provisions. No investment risk. Lower liquidity requirements. Less resources required. Fewer regulations.	Investment risk. Must monitor and make necessary reallocation decisions. Restricted withdrawal of funds.	Usually legally required to have an IPS that addresses how the plan will help participants meet their objectives and constraints (e.g., types and number of investment alternatives, advice).

LOS 15.b

There are two objectives and four constraints for defined-benefit plans.

The two objectives are:
- Risk.
- Return.

The four constraints are:
- Time horizon.
- Liquidity.
- Legal and regulatory factors.
- Unique circumstances.

In determining the investment objectives, it is helpful to first determine the plan sponsor's risk tolerance before the determination of the return objective. Pension plans are typically tax-exempt.

LOS 15.c

Plan surpluses indicate a cushion provided by plan assets to meet plan liabilities. Underfunded plans indicate a liability funding shortfall. Although there may be a willingness to take greater investment risk, the underfunded status dictates a decreased ability to take risk.

Sponsor financial status can be indicated by the sponsor's balance sheet. Profitability can be indicated by the sponsor's current or pro forma financials. Lower debt ratios and higher current and expected profitability indicate better capability of meeting pension liabilities and, therefore, imply greater ability to take risk. The opposite is also true.

Common risk exposure is measured by the correlation between the firm's operating characteristics and pension asset returns. The higher the correlation between firm's operations and pension asset returns, the lower the risk tolerance. The opposite is also true.

Plan features offer participants the option of either retiring early or receiving lump-sum payments from their retirement benefits. Plans that offer early retirement or lump-sum payments essentially decrease the time horizon of the retirement liability and increase the liquidity requirements of the plan. Therefore, the ability to assume risk is decreased.

Workforce characteristics relate to the age of the workforce and the ratio of active lives to retired lives. In general, the younger the workforce, the greater the ratio of active to retired lives, which indicates an increased ability to take risk when managing pension assets. The opposite is also true.

LOS 15.e

If the performance of the plan assets and firm operations are *highly correlated*:
- When pension assets are generating *high returns* with high operating profits, the probability of the firm having to make a contribution is low. If a contribution is necessary, the amount will be low. The ability to make contributions is high when the plan is fully or overfunded. Therefore, the fund is better able to meet benefit payments, which positively impacts firm valuation due to a lowered negative pension expense.

- When pension assets are generating *low returns* with low operating profits, the probability of the firm having to make a pension contribution is high. The firm's ability to make contributions is low at the same time that the plan is underfunded. An underfunded status means that there is a decreased ability to meet retirement payments, which negatively impacts firm valuation due to increased pension expense.

LOS 15.g

A cash balance plan is a defined-benefit plan that defines the benefit in terms of an account balance, which the beneficiary can take as an annuity at retirement or as a lump sum to roll into another plan. In a typical cash balance plan, a participant's account is credited each year with a pay credit and an interest credit. The pay credit is typically based upon the beneficiary's age, salary, and/or length of employment, and the interest credit is based upon a benchmark such as U.S. Treasuries. Rather than an actual account with a balance, the cash balance is a paper balance only and represents a future liability for the company.

An employee stock ownership plan (ESOP) is a type of defined-contribution benefit plan that allows employees to purchase the company stock. The purchase can be with before- or after-tax dollars, and the final balance in the beneficiary's account reflects the increase in the value of the firm's stock as well as contributions during employment.

LOS 15.h
Foundations

Type	Description	Purpose	Source of Funds	Annual Spending Requirement
Independent	Private or family	Grants to public groups	Individual or family	5% of assets
Company-sponsored	By a corporation	Public and company grants	Corporate sponsor	5% of assets
Operating	Established to fund an organization (e.g., museum, zoo, or some ongoing research/medical initiative)		Individual or family	At least 85% of dividend and interest income for operations
Community	Publicly sponsored	Grants to public groups	General public	None

LOS 15.d

IPS for Defined-Benefit Plan

Return: Minimum return requirement is determined by actuarial rate. If liquidity needs are low and workers young, use a capital gains focus; for high liquidity needs and older workers, use an income focus (duration matching). Also consider the number of retirees the plan must support.

Risk tolerance: Depends on surplus, age of workforce, time horizon, and company balance sheet. For example, a surplus indicates a higher risk tolerance.

Liquidity: Consider the age of workforce and retired lives population. Income is required to meet payments to retirees, but contributions are available for longer-term investments.

Time horizon: Same as for liquidity. In addition, the horizon is long if the plan is a going concern but short if it is a terminating plan.

Legal/regulatory: ERISA and the prudent expert rule apply. The plan must be managed for the sole benefit of plan participants.

Unique circumstances: Could include insufficient resources to perform due diligence on complex investments, special financial concerns related to the sponsor firm or the fund, socially responsible investing requirements, et cetera.

LOS 15.f

In a defined-contribution plan, the plan employer does not establish the investment goals and constraints; rather, the employee decides her own risk and return objectives. Therefore, the employee bears the risk of the investment results. Consequently, the investment policy statement (IPS) for a defined-contribution plan describes the investment alternatives available to the plan participants. This IPS becomes a document of governing principles instead of an IPS for an individual. Some of the issues addressed in the IPS would be:

- Making a distinction between the responsibilities of the plan participants, the fund managers, and the plan sponsor.
- Providing descriptions of the investment alternatives available to the plan participants.
- Providing criteria for monitoring and evaluation of the performance of the investment choices.
- Providing criteria for selection, termination, and replacement of investment choices.
- Establishing effective communication between the fund managers, plan participants, and the plan sponsor.

LOS 15.i,j,l,n

Defined-Benefit Plans

Return: Actuarial rate.

Risk tolerance: Depends on surplus, age of workforce, time horizon, and balance sheet.

Liquidity: Depends on age of workforce and retired lives proportion.

Time horizon: Long, if going concern. Short, if terminating plan.

Legal/regulatory: ERISA/prudent expert rule.

Tax considerations: None.

Unique circumstances: Surplus, age of workforce, time horizon, and balance sheet.

Foundation IPS

Return: Depends on time horizon stated for the foundation.

Risk tolerance: Moderate to high, depending on spending rate and time horizon. Usually more aggressive than pension funds.

Liquidity: 5% of assets for independent and company-sponsored foundations, 85% of dividend and interest income for operating foundations, which may be subject to spending 3.33% of assets. No spending requirement for community foundations.

Time horizon: Usually infinite.

Tax considerations: Not taxable with the exception on investment income from private foundations in the United States (1%).

Legal/regulatory: Few—many states in the United States have adopted the Uniform Management Institutional Funds Act as the regulatory framework. Prudent investor rule generally applies.

Endowment IPS

Return: Usually funded for the purpose of permanently funding an activity. Preserve asset base and use income generated for budget needs. No specific spending requirement. Balance the need for high current income with long-term protection of principal. Ensure purchasing power is not eroded by inflation. May use total approach or strive to minimize spending level volatility.

Risk tolerance: Linked to relative importance of the fund in the sponsor's overall budget picture. Inversely related to dependence on current income. Exposure to market fluctuation is a major concern. Infinite life means that overall risk tolerance is generally high.

Liquidity: Usually low but may be high if large outlays are expected.

Time horizon: Usually infinite.

Tax considerations: Income is tax-exempt.

Legal/regulatory: Few—many states in the United States have adopted the Uniform Management Institutional Funds Act as the regulatory framework. Prudent investor rule generally applies.

Unique needs: Diverse and endowment specific.

Life Insurance Company IPS

Return: Three components: (1) minimum required rate of return—statutory rate set by actuarial assumptions, (2) enhanced margin rates of return or "spread management," and (3) surplus rates of return, where surplus equals total assets – total liabilities.

Risk tolerance: Specific factors include (1) how market volatility adversely impacts asset valuation, (2) a low tolerance of any loss of income or delays in collecting income, (3) reinvestment risk is a major concern, and (4) that credit quality is associated with timely payment of income and principal.

Liquidity: There are three primary concerns to address: disintermediation, asset-liability mismatches, and asset marketability risk.

Time horizon: Traditionally 20–40 years but progressively shorter as the duration of liabilities has decreased due to increased interest rate volatility and competitive market factors.

Tax considerations: Taxes are a major consideration. Policyholder's share is not taxed; funds transferred to the surplus are taxed.

Legal/regulatory: Heavily regulated at the state level. Regulations relate to eligible investments, prudent person rule, and valuation methods.

Unique needs: Diversity of product offerings, company size, and level of asset surplus.

Nonlife Insurance Company IPS

Return: Greater uncertainty regarding claims, but they're not as interest rate sensitive. Fixed income component should maximize the return for meeting claims. Equity segment should grow the surplus/supplement funds for liability claims. Impacted by competitive pricing policy, profitability, growth of surplus, after-tax returns, and total return.

Risk tolerance: Risk must be tempered by the liquidity requirements. Inflation risk is a big concern because of replacement cost policies. Cash flow characteristics are unpredictable. Many companies have self-imposed ceilings on the common stock to surplus ratio.

Liquidity: Relatively high.

Time horizon: Short, due to nature of claims.

Tax considerations: Taxes play an important role—frequent contact with tax counsel is advised.

Legal/regulatory: Considerable leeway in choosing investments. Regulations less onerous than for life insurance companies.

Unique needs: The financial status of the firm and the management of the investment risk and liquidity requirements influence the IPS.

Bank IPS

Return: The return objective for the bank's securities portfolio is primarily to generate a positive interest rate spread.

Risk: The most important concern is meeting liabilities, and the bank cannot let losses in the securities portfolio interfere with that. Therefore, its tolerance for risk is below average.

Time horizon: Bank liabilities are usually fairly short-term, so securities in the portfolio should be of short to intermediate maturity/duration.

Liquidity: Because banks require regular liquidity to meet liabilities and new loan requests, the securities must be liquid.

Tax: Banks are taxable entities.

Legal/regulatory: Banks are highly regulated and are required to maintain liquidity, reserve requirements, and pledge against certain deposits.

Unique circumstances: Some potential unique circumstances include lack of diversification or lack of liquidity in the loan portfolio.

LOS 15.k

Investment companies gather funds from investors and invest the pooled funds based upon advertised objectives and constraints.

Commodity pools are similar to mutual funds but invest in pools of commodity futures and options contracts.

Hedge funds gather funds from institutional and wealthy individual investors and construct various investment strategies aimed at identifying and capitalizing on mispriced securities.

In summary, the primary difference between investment companies, commodity pools, and hedge funds and the institutional investors is the source and use of their invested funds. Pension plans, insurance companies, endowments, foundations, and banks all invest their own assets to meet various funding requirements, while the latter group collects funds from investors and invests the funds to meet their investors' needs.

LOS 15.m

Pension funds: For a *defined-benefit plan*, surplus management is key. Managers usually attempt to match durations of assets and liabilities to minimize the volatility of the surplus. Managers always minimize the risk of the asset portfolio while meeting return requirements. For a *defined-contribution plan*, once annual contributions are met, the sponsor's only remaining obligations are monitoring the plan and providing sufficient investment alternatives for participants. Beneficiaries manage their own assets.

Foundations: Generally have to meet all funding requirements (grants and operating expenses) through investment earnings.

Endowments: Typically, the overall goal is to preserve assets while meeting spending requirements.

Insurance companies: Life and nonlife are taxable entities. They segment their general portfolio to match assets to liabilities according to interest rate risk (duration), return, and credit risk.

Banks: The bank's primary objective is meeting its liabilities by earning a positive interest rate spread so that the portfolio allocation is determined using an asset-liability framework.

CONCEPT CHECKERS

LOS 15.d: <u>Prepare</u> an investment policy statement for a defined-benefit plan.

CFA® Program Curriculum, Volume 2, page 408

LOS 15.f: <u>Prepare</u> an investment policy statement for a defined-contribution plan.

CFA® Program Curriculum, Volume 2, page 414

1. Alexander Ellington, President of Ellington Foods, has contacted your firm to discuss the company's defined-benefit pension plan. He has provided the following information about the company and its pension plan:
    - Ellington Foods has annual sales of $300 million.
    - The annual payroll is about $100 million.
    - The average age of the work force is 43 years.
    - 30% of the plan participants are now retired.
    - Company profits last year were $10 million and have been growing at 10% annually. The Ellington Foods pension plan has $80 million in assets and is currently overfunded by 10%.
    - The duration of the plan's liabilities is 15 years.
    - The discount rate applied to liabilities is 6%.
    - Fund trustees wish to maintain 5% of plan assets in cash.

    Ellington would like to achieve a rate of return of 7% on its pension fund (which is less than the 9% that the fund has historically achieved). Ellington would like to be able to reduce contributions to the pension fund and possibly increase employee benefits.

    A. **Formulate** and **justify** investment policy objectives for the Ellington Foods pension plan in the following three areas (use the following template):
       i.   Return objective.
       ii. Risk tolerance.
       iii. Time horizon.

Template for Question 1A

Investment Policy Statement Elements for Ellington Foods Pension Plan	
Element	Discussion
i. Return objective	
ii. Risk tolerance	
iii. Time horizon	

B. **State** whether the original allocation to each asset class (as shown in the table) should be lower, the same, or higher for the Ellington Foods pension plan. **Justify** your response with reference to each of the asset classes (use the following template):

Original Allocation
Ellington Foods Pension Plan

Asset Class	Original Allocation (%)	Expected Total Return (%)
T-bills	5	4
U.S. intermediate-term bonds (5-year duration)	30	6
U.S. long-term bonds (20-year duration)	15	7
U.S. equities	50	12
International developed market equities	0	13
Emerging market equities	0	16

Template for Question 1B

Ellington Foods Pension Plan's Asset Allocation			
Asset Class and Original Allocation	Circle the change (lower/same/higher) and justify your response. STATE YOUR ASSUMPTIONS CLEARLY.		
U.S. Treasury bills (5%)	LOWER	SAME	HIGHER
U.S. intermediate-term bonds (5-year duration) (30%)	LOWER	SAME	HIGHER
U.S. long-term bonds (20-year duration) (15%)	LOWER	SAME	HIGHER
U.S. equities (50%)	LOWER	SAME	HIGHER
Developed market equities (0%)	LOWER	SAME	HIGHER
Emerging market equities (0%)	LOWER	SAME	HIGHER

2. Ellington appreciated your advice but decided to handle the situation "in house." The company also decided to stay with the original allocation. Assume ten years have passed and Ellington has returned to you for advice. The average age of the workforce is now 51 years. Sixty percent of the plan participants are now retired. The duration of the plan's liabilities is four years. The fund is currently underfunded by 20%. The discount rate applied to the liabilities is 9%. Company profits have been in decline for the past two years but are expected to turn around in the upcoming year. Given the updated information:

A. **Formulate** and **justify** investment policy objectives for the Ellington Foods Pension Plan in the following three areas (use the following template):
   i. Return objective.
   ii. Risk tolerance.
   iii. Time horizon.

Template for Question 2A

Investment Policy Statement Elements Ellington Foods Pension Plan	
Element	Discussion
i. Return objective	
ii. Risk tolerance	
iii. Time horizon	

3. **Describe** a defined-benefit pension plan. Be sure to **discuss** all aspects of such a plan.

4. **Describe** a defined-contribution pension plan. Be sure to **discuss** all aspects of such a plan.

LOS 15.j: <u>Prepare</u> an investment policy statement for a foundation, an endowment, an insurance company, and a bank.

CFA® Program Curriculum, Volume 2, page 421

5. Aid to the Homeless is a nonprofit organization that provides funding throughout the Washington D.C. area to run shelters for the homeless. The Cassidy Endowment Fund provides a large portion of the Aid to the Homeless's operating budget. The endowment fund was set up by the Cassidy family as a way to leave a legacy to their father. He was a wealthy entrepreneur throughout his lifetime but suffered from dementia in old age and consequently lived out his last days wandering the streets of D.C. as a homeless person. The fund has assets totaling $5 million, and directors of the endowment anticipate a spending rate of 6%. Inflation is expected to be 3% annually.

    A. **Formulate** and **justify** investment policy objectives for the Cassidy Endowment Fund in the following three areas (use the following template):
        i.   Return objective.
        ii. Risk tolerance.
        iii. Time horizon.

    Template for Question 5A

Investment Policy Statement Elements Cassidy Endowment Fund	
Element	Discussion
i. Return objective	
ii. Risk tolerance	
iii. Time horizon	

B. From the following asset allocations, **select** the one allocation that best serves the needs of the Endowment Fund and **justify** its selection by maximizing the following three criteria simultaneously (use the following template):

i. Return objective.
ii. Diversification.
iii. Efficiency.

Asset Classes	Expected Total Return	Cash Flow Yield	Portfolios			
			A	B	C	D
U.S. stocks	12%	2.0%	20%	40%	35%	20%
Non-U.S. stocks	15%	1.5%	15%	20%	15%	0%
U.S. corporate bonds	8%	8.0%	20%	0%	25%	40%
U.S. Treasury bonds	7%	7.0%	5%	0%	20%	35%
Real estate	10%	4.0%	10%	20%	0%	0%
U.S. Treasury bills	4%	4.0%	30%	20%	5%	5%
Expected total return			8.8%	10.6%	10.1%	8.3%
Expected yield (cash flow)			4.2%	2.7%	4.5%	6.3%
Sharpe measure			0.20	0.21	0.26	0.27

Template for Question 5B

Selected Portfolio	Discussion
	Return objectives:
	Diversification:
	Efficiency:

6. Liles Insurance Company has recently decided to segment its portfolio into those assets used to meet liabilities and those assets considered surplus. George Baxter, CFO, has drafted his proposal for the asset allocation for the surplus portfolio, which appears below. He has contacted your firm to establish an IPS and to review the proposed asset allocation for their surplus portfolio. The surplus portfolio contains $200 million of the firm's $800 million in total assets.

Proposed Allocation—Liles Life Insurance Surplus Portfolio

Asset Class	Proposed Allocation (%)	Expected Return (%)
Cash	10	4
U.S. intermediate bonds (5-year duration)	5	6
U.S. long-term bonds (20-year duration)	45	7
U.S. equities	25	12
Developed market equities	15	13
Equity REITs	0	14
Venture capital	0	22

A. **Formulate** and **justify** investment policy objectives and constraints for Liles Insurance Company Surplus Portfolio in the following three areas (use the template for Question 6A):
    i.   Return objective.
    ii. Risk tolerance.
    iii. Liquidity requirements.

Template for Question 6A

Investment Policy Statement Elements Liles Insurance Company Surplus Portfolio	
Element	**Discussion**
i. Return objective	
ii. Risk tolerance	
iii. Liquidity requirements	

B. **State** whether the current allocation to each asset class as shown in the previous table should be lower, the same, or higher for the Surplus Portfolio of Liles Insurance Company. **Justify** your response with reference to each of the asset classes (use the template for Question 6B):

Template for Question 6B

Liles Insurance Company Surplus Portfolio Asset Allocation			
Asset Class and Original Allocation	**Circle the change (lower/same/higher) and justify your response. STATE YOUR ASSUMPTIONS CLEARLY.**		
Cash (10%)	LOWER	SAME	HIGHER
U.S. intermediate-term bonds (5-year duration) (5%)	LOWER	SAME	HIGHER
U.S. long-term bonds (20-year duration) (45%)	LOWER	SAME	HIGHER
U.S. equities (25%)	LOWER	SAME	HIGHER
Developed market equities (15%)	LOWER	SAME	HIGHER
Equity REITS (0%)	LOWER	SAME	HIGHER
Venture capital (0%)	LOWER	SAME	HIGHER

7. The asset-liability management committee (ALCO) for First Southern Piedmont Bank (FSPB) will implement an IPS and oversee its securities portfolios. Based in Southern North Carolina, nearly 80% of FSPB's loans are in or around the Winston-Salem area. There has been an influx of deposits lately and a reduction in the demand for new loans, and managers are finding themselves with a considerable amount of excess cash. From the information provided, **construct** an appropriate IPS, including *two* objectives and *five* constraints for FSPB's securities portfolio.

ANSWERS – CONCEPT CHECKERS

1. A. Investment policy statement elements, Ellington Foods pension fund.

    i. *Return objective.* The return requirement must at least equal the actuarial assumption of 6%. A desired return level of 7% has been expressed and is less than the fund's average return of 9%. The fund is currently overfunded by 10%, which allows the company to reduce its contributions. As the firm continues to earn more than the actuarially determined required return, the ability of the fund to tolerate risk will also rise.

    ii. *Risk tolerance.* The fund has above-average ability to tolerate risk for at least three reasons. First, the average employee age of 43 is probably relatively young. Next, 30% retired lives gives a ratio of better than two active lives for each retired life. Third, the plan is overfunded by 10%.

    iii. *Time horizon.* The plan's time horizon is long term. Assuming a retirement age of 65 and an average age of 43, the average employee will work another 22 years. Unless stated otherwise, we assume a perpetual life for the plan.

    > *Professor's Note: Visualize passage of each of the next 20 years. As each year passes, some employees retire, but it will take over 20 years for half of the currently active employees to do so. This means that, even with no growth in active employment numbers, the relatively low percentage of retired lives combined with the relatively low average age translates into a long time horizon before the ratio of active to retired lives falls to 1.0.*

    For the Exam: Average can be a relative term. In this case, it implies a comparison to pension plans of firms in comparable industries. When you see an overfunded pension plan, it is generally fair to assume the fund has above-average ability to tolerate risk. Using average work force age to determine ability to tolerate risk, however, depends upon the average age for comparable pension plans. On the Level III exam, candidates have customarily been given the average employee age and funded status of a pension plan and the industry and have been asked to determine what the data suggest. For example, if Ellington's average age is 43 and the industry average age is 45, this would not (by itself) indicate the plan has above-average ability to tolerate risk.

    As time passes, the average age of active employees will change; some employees leave, new employees are hired, and some employees retire. Average employee age is, therefore, a snapshot in time that indicates the plan's time horizon and liquidity needs at that point in time. In general, the lower the average age, the longer the investment time horizon (this usually translates into a greater use of equities) and the lower the liquidity needs. As employees age and the ratio of active to retired lives falls, the plan's liquidity needs increase and the ability to tolerate risk falls. Note, however, that as active employees age and retire, retired employees also age. It is the rate of active employee retirements relative to retired employee deaths combined with the growth of the firm (i.e., new active employees contributing to the plan) that determines how quickly the ratio of active to retired lives falls.

B. Ellington Foods pension fund's asset allocation.

U.S. T-bills/cash (5%); SAME. Comply with trustees' wishes for 5% cash.

U.S. intermediate-term bonds (5-year duration) (30%); LOWER. Intermediate-term bonds tend to be less volatile than longer-term bonds and should represent a substantial portion of the pension fund allocation. However, with a younger workforce producing a longer-term liability stream, a shift away from assets with a shorter duration is warranted.

U.S. long-term bonds (20-year duration) (15%); HIGHER. With a younger workforce producing a longer-term liability stream, a higher allocation is recommended for assets with a longer duration.

U.S. equities (50%); LOWER. Although a substantial portion of the portfolio should contain equities in order to achieve the goals of reducing company contributions and possibly enhancing employee benefits, the equity portion of the portfolio should be distributed across categories within the equity asset class in order to achieve maximum diversification and possibly to enhance returns.

Developed market equities (0%); HIGHER. Developed market equities offer the opportunity for enhanced returns coupled with further diversification potential and should be represented in the pension portfolio.

Emerging market equities (0%); HIGHER. Emerging market equities are expected to return 16% and should be included in the portfolio. Emerging markets usually have a low correlation with developed markets, which helps to provide enhanced diversification benefits.

2. A. Investment policy statement elements for Ellington Foods pension fund.

  i. *Return objective.* To maintain at least its current funded status, the fund needs to generate at least the actuarially determined rate of 9%. The fact that the fund is currently underfunded by 20% would ordinarily call for enhanced returns. However, the workforce is advanced in age, and a majority of the plan participants are now retired. In addition, company profits have been in decline for the past two years, which may indicate an inability for the company to increase contributions. The company must make every attempt to increase current contributions and will have to increase contributions in upcoming years.

  ii. *Risk tolerance.* The risk tolerance (i.e., ability) of the plan has decreased dramatically over the past ten years. A surplus has been replaced with a deficit while the average age of the workforce has increased, a larger proportion of the workforce is now retired, and the duration of the plan's liabilities has decreased significantly. Thus, at exactly the time they need higher returns, the fund has below-average ability to tolerate risk.

  iii. *Time horizon.* The time horizon has decreased due to the shortening of the duration of the plan's liabilities (i.e., the aging of the workforce). The plan remains a going concern, which requires a focus on the longer term while addressing the shorter-term needs, which are currently a major concern for the pension plan.

3. A defined-benefit plan pays pension benefits to employees based on specific formulas that take into account the particular employee's length of service and level of earnings. For example, an employee's annual retirement benefit may be calculated as 60% of his average salary over the past five years.

Plan sponsors bear all investment risk because they have promised a given level of benefits. Any investment return in excess of what is needed to pay employee benefits reverts back to the firm.

Plan assets must be managed in the sole interest of plan participants according to ERISA.

4.   Employers make regular contributions to the plan on behalf of qualified employees. Employees are sometimes required to match a certain percentage of the employer's contribution. For example, the employer may contribute 5% of the employee's gross annual salary to the plan as long as the employees contribute 2.5% of their gross annual salary. The 2.5% contribution is typically handled as a pretax payroll deduction.

Employers like defined-contribution plans because all investment risk is shifted to the employees. Plan participants typically make their own portfolio decisions. They are offered a "menu" of investment options from which they can create their portfolios.

In a participant-directed defined-contribution plan (DCP), the firm:

i.   Must offer sufficient choices to facilitate diversification.

ii. Must provide the ability for participants to switch funds across choices.

iii. Must keep contributions of company stock at a level that will not overweight the participant portfolios and reduce the benefits of diversification.

Because in a DCP the firm (sponsor) is not associated with the investments, per se, the IPS is more of a set of guidelines. The plan sponsor, rather than charged with meeting benefits, must oversee and help employees/participants in their retirement planning. Objectives and constraints for the DCP are determined by plan participants. The sponsor will typically establish a board or committee to oversee the retirement plan. This board will:

i.   See that participants have sufficient educational opportunities to facilitate investment decisions.

ii. Provide descriptions of all investment opportunities.

iii. Select and periodically evaluate fund managers.

iv. Generally oversee the plan and its participants.

5.   A.   Investment policy statement elements, Cassidy Endowment Fund.

i.   *Return objective.* The fund's return objective should focus on a total return approach. Return should equal the maximum spending rate plus an adjustment for expected inflation. In this situation, the return requirement would be 9% in order to achieve a 6% spending rate and protect the corpus against the 3% inflation forecast.

Alternatively: $(1.06)(1.03) - 1 = 9.18\%$. To incorporate management fees (if present in the question), include them in the compounded rate:
$(1 + \text{spending rate})(1 + \text{inflation})(1 + \% \text{ fees}) - 1$.

ii. *Risk tolerance.* The fund's risk tolerance is below average. In general, endowments have a high tolerance for risk based on their long time horizon. In the case of the

Cassidy Endowment Fund, the Aid to the Homeless organization relies heavily on contributions from the endowment to fund a large portion of its operating budget. Therefore, the endowment cannot tolerate much fluctuation in its investments without adversely affecting the funding to the Aid to the Homeless organization. Thus, the endowment has a below-average risk tolerance.

    iii.   *Time horizon.* The time horizon for the Cassidy Endowment Fund is very long (infinite). Most endowment funds are established to perpetually support the budget of the sponsored organization. The case indicates that Cassidy's endowment fund will continue indefinitely.

B.   Selected Portfolio—C.

Return objectives. In order to achieve the total return objective, Portfolio C is expected to generate sufficient return to meet both the spending rate and inflation. Portfolios A and D fail to meet the 9% return requirement. Portfolio B achieves the return target but is poorly diversified.

Diversification. Portfolio C best achieves the required diversification goal. Allocations to both domestic and nondomestic stocks as well as corporate and treasury bonds are present. Portfolios A and D also show promise from a diversification standpoint, although D excludes a vital asset class, international equity. Portfolio B does not contain any debt securities, which is the most efficient way to produce income.

Efficiency. Efficiency is measured through the use of the Sharpe measure, which measures excess return to total risk. From an efficiency standpoint, Portfolio C has the second highest Sharpe measure, only slightly surpassed by Portfolio D. Portfolios A and B have efficiency measures considerably lower than C and D.

6.   A.   Investment policy statement elements for Liles Insurance Company surplus portfolio.

    i.   *Return objective.* The return objective for Liles Insurance Company surplus portfolio is to achieve growth. The primary requirement for the surplus portfolio is to achieve higher returns through portfolio growth. Equity-oriented investments, including venture capital, are typically used to achieve this objective.

    ii.   *Risk tolerance.* The risk tolerance for Liles Insurance Company is relatively high. Because these funds are not supporting a specific liability, the risk tolerance for the surplus portfolio is relatively high. This higher risk tolerance, if rewarded with higher returns, allows life insurance companies to expand insurance volume.

    iii.   *Liquidity requirements.* The liquidity requirements for the surplus portion of the life insurance company are very low. The purpose of the surplus portfolio is to generate growth. Liquidity needs are typically met through the segment of the portfolio used to meet liabilities.

B.   Liles Insurance Company surplus portfolio asset allocation.

Cash (10%); LOWER. The need for cash in the *surplus* segment of a life insurance company is very low. The goal of the surplus segment is to earn competitive returns, which is not typically accomplished by holding cash.

U.S. intermediate-term bonds (5-year duration) (5%); SAME. Having a small presence of fixed-income securities would be wise in the surplus segment for diversification purposes. The current level seems reasonable.

U.S. long-term bonds (20-year duration) (45%); LOWER. Longer-term bonds provide higher returns than intermediate-term bonds over the long term. However, the lower proportion is recommended given that the main objective of the surplus portfolio is to grow the principal.

U.S. equities (25%); HIGHER. The surplus portfolio should be geared toward equity-type investments. The proportion of domestic equities should be increased in order to generate additional growth in principal.

Developed market equities (15%); SAME. The developed market equities are expected to produce slightly higher returns than the U.S. equities and may provide diversification benefits. An allocation of 15% seems reasonable for achieving the objectives of the surplus portfolio. The company may want to consider currency hedging should it decide to retain or increase this allocation.

Equity REITS (0%); HIGHER. Equity REITS provide diversification benefits and an opportunity for enhanced return. The asset class is currently not included in the current asset allocation and should be added.

Venture capital (0%); HIGHER. Venture capital is an appropriate part of a surplus segment investment strategy. The current allocation does not include venture capital. Given its high expected return, the company should consider venture capital as a part of the surplus segment portfolio.

7. From the information provided, we have no reason to assume FSPB has any remarkable characteristics that would distinguish it from other banks.

Objectives:

Return. The return objective for the portfolio is to generate a positive interest rate spread.

Risk. Because the liabilities are certain, the securities must be low risk. FSPB has a below-average risk tolerance.

Constraints:

Time horizon. Liabilities are short term, so securities in the portfolio should be of short-to-intermediate maturity/duration.

Taxes. FSPB is a taxable entity, so tax consequences must be considered in selecting securities.

Liquidity. FSPB requires liquidity to meet depositor withdrawals and new loan requests, so the securities must be liquid.

Legal and regulatory. Through bank regulations, FSPB is required to maintain liquidity, meet reserve requirements, and meet pledging requirements.

Unique. Due to their high concentration of loans in the Winston-Salem area (i.e., high geographic and possibly even industry concentration), FSPB should utilize its securities portfolio to provide diversification.

The following is a review of the Portfolio Management for Institutional Investors principles designed to address the learning outcome statements set forth by CFA Institute®. This topic is also covered in:

LINKING PENSION LIABILITIES TO ASSETS

Study Session 5

EXAM FOCUS

This topic review discusses two approaches to pension fund asset allocation. In the asset-only approach, the focus is on investments with a low correlation to the firm's assets. In a liability-relative approach, investments are chosen for their high correlation to the pension liability. Understand accrued benefits and future benefits and how they impact portfolio construction when mimicking the pension liability. Finally, know the disadvantages to implementing a liability-relative (i.e., mimicking) approach.

ASSET-ONLY AND LIABILITY-RELATIVE ASSET ALLOCATION

LOS 16.a: Contrast the assumptions concerning pension liability risk in asset-only and liability-relative approaches to asset allocation.

CFA® Program Curriculum, Volume 2, page 494

Under an **asset-only approach**, a pension fund focuses on selecting efficient portfolios. It does not attempt to explicitly hedge the risk of the liabilities. This approach ignores the fact that a future liability is subject to market-related risk. Market risk arises from interest rate risk, inflation risk, or from an exposure to economic growth. For example, if a firm does extraordinarily well due to the economy, its wages paid may grow and the firm's future pension liabilities will increase. A failure to recognize the risk in the liabilities could lead to a portfolio that does not adequately satisfy the liabilities.

A more appropriate asset allocation approach would recognize *economic liability*. This approach recognizes the various exposures and components of the pension liability, as will be discussed later. In this **liability-relative approach**, the portfolio is chosen for its ability to mimic the liability (i.e., the portfolio will have a high correlation with the liability). In the asset-only approach, the focus is instead on low-risk investments with a low correlation to firm assets.

In the asset-only approach, the risk-free investment is the return on cash. In a liability-relative approach, the risk-free investment is a portfolio that mimics the liability in performance. Such a portfolio, that has a correlation of one with the liabilities, however, does not exist. The pension fund manager must construct this portfolio by decomposing the liability into its various exposures. This approach can also be applied to non-pension obligations, such as meeting insurance liabilities and retirement planning.

PENSION LIABILITY EXPOSURES

LOS 16.b: Discuss the fundamental and economic exposures of pension liabilities and identify asset types that mimic these liability exposures.

CFA® Program Curriculum, Volume 2, page 494

Many pension managers measure their pension liability through duration management. This approach focuses on short-term changes in the liability relative to changes in interest rates. This approach is valid, however, only when pension risk is short-term, as in the case of firms near bankruptcy.

The future pension obligation, for most corporations, is largely unrelated to short-term changes in long-term interest rates, as most corporate pension plans have a long life. The appropriate liability modeling captures the risk of the fund not satisfying short-term obligations as well as the risk of not satisfying the longer-term liabilities. A better understanding of pension liabilities requires a decomposition of the liabilities' risk exposures. This will help the portfolio manager determine the appropriate discount rate for pension liabilities.

 Professor's Note: In the following discussion of pension plan exposures, you will notice that when the benefits are not indexed to inflation, they will be hedged with nominal bonds (i.e., bonds that are not indexed to inflation). When the benefits are indexed to inflation, they will be hedged with real return bonds (i.e., inflation-indexed bonds, like U.S. Treasury Inflation Protected Securities).

Market Exposures Due to Accrued Benefits

To decompose the liability's exposures, the pension obligation should first be separated into that due to *inactive* and that due to *active participants*. Inactive participants consist of retirees and those no longer employed by the firm who are owed a future benefit (the deferreds). The future benefits for this group are fixed unless the benefits are indexed to inflation. If there is no indexing, the relevant benchmark is a portfolio of bonds paying a nominal amount equal to the promised payments. If the future payments are entirely indexed, the relevant benchmark is a portfolio of inflation-indexed bonds.

Active participants are those currently working for the firm. The obligations to these employees can be separated into that owed for past service and that owed for future service. The obligations for past service are similar to that for the retirees and are again fixed unless there is inflation indexing. The retirement payments owed to inactive participants and the payments for past service to active participants constitute *accrued benefits*.

Market Exposures Due to Future Benefits

In the case where a pension plan is frozen, no future benefits will be paid and the plan's only liability is that which has accrued. In this case, the liability-mimicking portfolio is one consisting of nominal and inflation-indexed bonds. Most pensions, however, are ongoing and have obligations for future benefits.

Future benefits are those from wages to be earned in the future, by existing employees as well as new entrants into the plan. Although future benefits are long-term in nature and do not affect the plan's short-term risk, their effect on the plan's funded status and the ability to hedge these liabilities must be considered.

The first component of future benefits is wages to be earned in the future. Given a known growth rate in wages, one can calculate the expected amount of future benefits. The present value of this amount is referred to as the *future wage liability*, which along with the accrued benefits represents the projected benefit obligation under U.S. Financial Accounting Standards.

The growth in future wages can be decomposed into from inflation and from real growth. In the former case, wages will grow with inflation. Many plans, however, do not index benefits for inflation after the employee retires. Therefore, the liability-mimicking portfolio is a portfolio of inflation-indexed and nominal bonds. The closer the workforce is to retirement, the larger the proportion of nominal bonds in the portfolio.

Wage growth arising from real growth is due to increases in labor productivity. This productivity will be reflected in GDP, which is strongly correlated with the stock market. Again, most pension benefits are not inflation-indexed after retirement, so the liability-mimicking portfolio is a portfolio of nominal bonds and stocks.

The second component of future benefits is from future service rendered. These benefits are those that have not yet been earned but will be credited to employees at some point in the future. As in the case of future retirement payments, future service benefits are linked to wage growth. This amount, however, is uncertain and not usually funded, so it is not modeled in the investment benchmark.

The third component of future benefits, from new entrants into the plan, is also excluded from the benchmark portfolio, as it is the most uncertain of plan benefits.

Non-Market Exposures

The exposures discussed so far are market exposures as they are related to inflation, interest rates, and economic growth. Pensions are also subject to non-market exposures referred to as *liability noise*. These exposures can be divided into two parts: that due to plan demographics and that due to model uncertainty. The former exposure is affected primarily by the number of participants and can be estimated using statistical models. It is more predictable when the number of participants is larger. The latter exposure is less predictable and is different for inactive versus active participants.

Recall that inactive participants can be divided into retirees (i.e., currently receiving benefits) and deferreds (i.e., not working for the company but not yet eligible for benefits). The source of liability noise arising from retirees is the mortality assumption. If the mortality assumption is incorrect, the pension plan will be responsible for the retirees' benefits for a different period of time than that modeled. Unfortunately, there are no financial products that can hedge this risk, although some are being developed. For deferreds, there is risk from the mortality risk (longevity risk) as well as uncertainty arising from when retirement occurs. The sooner the deferreds retire, the smaller the benefit paid for a longer period of time. Thus, for deferreds, there is uncertainty in the timing and amount of liability as well as longevity risk. For these reasons, the liability noise associated with deferreds is larger and less easily hedged than that for retirees.

The liability noise arising from active participants is even greater than that from deferreds. These participants are often many years from retirement and there is much uncertainty regarding the plan's future obligation.

In Figure 1, we summarize the exposures of a pension plan and the assets needed to satisfy them. We assume that the accrued benefits are not indexed to inflation. If they are indexed to inflation, then real return bonds would be used. Recall that term structure risk is the interest rate risk of parallel and nonparallel shifts in the yield curve.

For the Exam: Focus on the first three plan segments (indicated with *) because they are the pension's primary emphasis in the liability-relative portfolio.

Figure 1: Pension Liability Exposures

Pension Plan Segment	Market or Non-Market Exposure	Risk Exposure	Liability Mimicking Assets
*Inactive-accrued	Market	Term structure	Nominal bonds
*Active-accrued	Market	Term structure	Nominal bonds
*Active-future wage growth	Market	Term structure	Nominal bonds
	Market	Inflation	Real return bonds
	Market	Economic growth	Equities
Active-future service rendered	Market	Similar to wage growth but more uncertain	Not typically funded
Active-future participants	Market	Very uncertain	Not typically funded
Liability noise-demographics	Non-market	Plan demographics	Not easily hedged
Liability noise-inactive	Non-market	Model uncertainty & longevity risk	Not easily hedged or modeled
Liability noise-active	Non-market	Model uncertainty & longevity risk	Not easily hedged or modeled

THE LIABILITY-RELATIVE APPROACH IN PRACTICE

LOS 16.c: <u>Compare</u> pension portfolios built from a traditional asset-only perspective to portfolios designed relative to liabilities and <u>discuss</u> why corporations may choose not to implement fully the liability mimicking portfolio.

CFA® Program Curriculum, Volume 2, page 494

In terms of satisfying their future liability over time, the best portfolio for a pension plan will be a liability-mimicking portfolio consisting of nominal bonds, real return bonds, and stocks. The weights in these assets will be determined by the proportion of future obligations relative to accrued, inflation indexing of the benefits, and the plan status (e.g., whether it is frozen or growing). If the workforce is younger, more will be allocated to equities. If there is a significant amount of benefits that is indexed to inflation, inflation-indexed bonds are used more than nominal bonds. If the plan is frozen, there are no future obligations and nominal bonds would dominate the portfolio.

The liability-mimicking, low-risk portfolio, however, will be costly and, by construction, will not provide a return (i.e., accrue value) in excess of the liabilities. Recall that the liability from future service rendered and future participants is uncertain and is not modeled or funded. An investment in the low-risk portfolio, therefore, requires future cash payments by the sponsor to satisfy these obligations.

For pension plans, the best use of the low-risk portfolio is as a benchmark. Outperforming the benchmark will ensure that the majority of the pension's obligations are met. The optimum for pensions is to outperform the benchmark, while minimizing the risk of not being able to meet their obligations.

In the traditional asset-only approach, the portfolio is usually composed of 60–70% equities with the rest in short- and medium-duration nominal bonds. In a liability-relative approach, derivatives can be used to hedge the market-related exposure of the pension. For example, term structure risk is typically the largest plan exposure and can be hedged with bond futures contracts. Derivatives are relatively inexpensive and free up capital for use in a higher expected return portfolio component. Thus, the liability-mimicking portfolio is typically composed of derivatives, long duration bonds, inflation-indexed bonds, and equities, as well as other components dedicated to generating an efficient return.

KEY CONCEPTS

LOS 16.a

Under an asset-only approach, a pension fund focuses on selecting efficient portfolios. It does not attempt to explicitly hedge the risk of the liabilities. This approach ignores the fact that a future liability is subject to market-related risk. Market risk arises from interest rate risk, inflation risk, or from exposure to economic growth.

In the liability-relative approach, the portfolio is chosen for its ability to mimic the liability (i.e., the portfolio will have a high correlation with the liability) and if pension exposures are accounted for.

LOS 16.b

A pension fund is exposed to market and non-market related risks. If the benefits paid are not indexed to inflation, the appropriate liability-mimicking assets are nominal bonds. If the benefits paid are indexed to inflation, the appropriate liability-mimicking assets are inflation-indexed bonds. If the benefits correspond with growth in the firm and economy, the appropriate liability-mimicking assets are equities.

The retirement payments to inactive participants and the payments to active participants for past service constitute accrued benefits. If the benefits are not indexed to inflation, they will be hedged with nominal bonds.

A pension's future obligations are those arising due to wages to be earned in the future and new entrants into the plan. The first component is typically hedged with equities, nominal bonds, and real bonds, while the latter component is uncertain and not easily modeled or funded.

Non-market exposures (liability noise) can be divided into two parts: those that are due to plan demographics and those that are due to model uncertainty. These exposures are not easily hedged.

LOS 16.c

The traditional asset-only portfolio is usually predominantly equities with the remainder in short- and medium-duration nominal bonds. The liability-mimicking portfolio is typically composed of derivatives, long duration bonds, inflation-indexed bonds, and equities, as well as other components dedicated to generating an efficient return.

The liability-mimicking, low-risk portfolio is costly and does not provide a return in excess of the liabilities.

CONCEPT CHECKERS

1.   Correlations are important in both the asset-only approach and the liability-relative approach to investing, but they are used differently in each approach. **Discuss** the differences.

2.   Suppose a pension fund decides to begin indexing the benefits to inflation. What changes would one expect to see in her portfolio, if it is a liability-mimicking portfolio?

3.   When comparing an asset-only approach portfolio and a liability-relative approach portfolio, which portfolio would be *more likely* to contain derivative contracts?

ANSWERS – CONCEPT CHECKERS

1. In an asset-only approach, investments are chosen to have a low correlation with firm assets. In a liability-relative approach, the focus is on hedging the pension liabilities, so investments are chosen to have a high correlation with the liabilities.

2. The pension fund would shift its assets from nominal bonds into inflation-indexed (real return) bonds in order to hedge the inflation-indexed benefits.

3. The liability-relative approach portfolio would be more likely invested in derivatives. This approach focuses on hedging the pension liabilities and might use derivatives to hedge the pension's market-related risks. This would free up capital to pursue higher expected returns.

    The asset-only approach does not explicitly hedge the pension liabilities and would be more likely invested in traditional assets.

The following is a review of the Portfolio Management for Institutional Investors principles designed to address the learning outcome statements set forth by CFA Institute®. This topic is also covered in:

ALLOCATING SHAREHOLDER CAPITAL TO PENSION PLANS

EXAM FOCUS

Focus on the implications of including versus not including the pension plan's assets and liabilities when estimating a firm's weighted average cost of capital. Be able to explain the implications for the firm's asset and equity betas and actions management can take to maintain a desired equity beta. Be sure you can perform any of the calculations in this topic review.

This topic review focuses on calculating the firm's weighted average cost of capital (WACC) used to determine the profitability of potential projects. In calculating the firm's WACC, the analyst traditionally uses the costs and weights of equity and debt on the firm's balance sheet. An alternative method uses the weighted average of the betas of the firm's balance sheet equity and debt to arrive at the asset beta, which is then used in the capital asset pricing model (CAPM). These traditional measures of WACC consider only the operating (i.e., balance sheet) assets and liabilities, not those of the pension fund, while the "true" firm is all its assets and liabilities. Even when assets (e.g., debt and equity securities) are placed in a pension plan account, because the firm is ultimately responsible for the plan's liabilities, those assets are still owned by and are therefore a part of the firm.

A more realistic measure of the firm's WACC, then, would consider these assets. As you approach this material, think in terms of the firm's asset beta, which is a weighted average of its equity and debt betas. We take a simplifying step and assume the debt beta is zero, so the asset beta is really just the equity beta multiplied by the weight of equity in the capital structure. The author contends that a firm's true capital structure considers all the firm's assets (i.e., combination of the operating and plan assets and liabilities), and the asset beta is a weighted average of the firm's operating asset beta and the asset beta of the pension plan. If pension plan assets are composed mostly of equity securities, the pension plan asset beta may be higher than the beta of the firm's operating assets. If pension plan assets are composed mostly of debt securities, however, the pension plan asset beta will likely be lower than the firm's operating asset beta. Remember, the final asset beta for the firm is a weighted average of the two asset betas, so the size of pension assets combined with the composition of those assets can have a significant impact on the firm's overall asset beta and weighted average cost of capital.

FUNDING SHORTFALL AND ASSET/LIABILITY MISMATCH

LOS 17.a: <u>Compare</u> funding shortfall and asset/liability mismatch as sources of risk faced by pension plan sponsors.

CFA® Program Curriculum, Volume 2, page 509

Funding shortfall occurs when the market value of the pension plan's assets is less than the market value of its liabilities (i.e., pension obligations). The risk to the participant is that the fund may have insufficient assets to meet pension obligations. The risk to the firm (i.e., plan sponsor) is that the plan is deemed underfunded. If this happens, the sponsor may be required by regulators to increase annual contributions to the plan or even make one or more special contributions to improve the plan's funded status.

Asset/liability mismatch occurs when the pension plan's assets and liabilities are exposed to different risk factors or are affected differently by the same risk factors. For example, assume the plan's assets are invested in equities. Because the plan's liabilities behave like fixed-income securities, they can react differently to economic conditions. During a recession with accompanying falling interest rates, for example, the value of the plan's assets (i.e., equities) will fall at the same time the present value of the plan's liabilities rises. The double whammy effect of falling asset values combined with rising liability values will significantly reduce the plan's surplus or even push it into an underfunded status.

Asset/liability risk is thought to be a bigger risk than funding shortfall for two reasons: (1) the balance sheet doesn't show the types of securities the pension assets are invested in and, therefore, there is no measure of risk, and (2) as of the end of 2001, the top 20% of U.S. companies ranked by the size of the ratio of pension assets to market capitalization of equity showed the median ratio was two. In other words, those companies' pension assets were twice the size of the company's overall market capitalization. Because roughly 60–70% of pension assets are normally invested in equities, this means that at least 20% of the firms in this sample had pension assets invested in a larger percentage of equities than the firms' overall market capitalizations.

PENSION RISK AND WEIGHTED AVERAGE COST OF CAPITAL

LOS 17.b: <u>Explain</u> how the weighted average cost of capital for a corporation can be adjusted to incorporate pension risk and <u>discuss</u> the potential consequences of not making this adjustment.

CFA® Program Curriculum, Volume 2, page 514

From our studies of corporate finance, we know that weighted average cost of capital (WACC) is a well-accepted benchmark for determining the acceptability of capital projects. Management determines the expected return on the potential project (e.g., its internal rate of return) and compares it to the WACC, the cost of funds that will be used to finance the project. A project with an internal rate of return (IRR) greater than the firm's WACC has a positive expected net present value (NPV), and taking the project should increase the firm's stock price.[1]

The traditional method for calculating WACC finds the weighted average of the firm's after-tax cost of debt and its cost of equity. When we combine the component costs with their respective weights, we see the familiar equation:

$$WACC = W_e(k_e) + W_d(k_d)(1 - t)$$

where:

W_e and W_d = market value weights of equity and debt in the firm's capital structure
k_e and k_d = firm's marginal costs of equity and debt
t = firm's marginal tax rate

The firm's WACC can also be estimated using a variation of the capital asset pricing model (CAPM) with the firm's operating asset beta. First, recall that the familiar CAPM equation estimates the firm's cost of (required return on) equity by adding a risk premium, $\beta_e(R_M - R_F)$, to the risk-free rate:

$$k_e = R_F + \beta_e(R_M - R_F)$$

This form of the CAPM measures the firm's required return on equity based on its systematic risk as measured by its equity beta, β_e. The required return on equity from the CAPM is the component cost of equity that would be inserted into the traditional WACC equation.

If instead of using the firm's equity beta in the CAPM we use the firm's *operating asset beta*, we can calculate the firm's WACC directly. Just as the equity beta captures the systematic risk of the firm's equity, the operating asset beta captures the systematic risk of the firm's operating assets, including the effects of the mix of debt and equity in the firm's capital structure on the firm's systematic risk:

$$WACC = R_F + \beta_{a,o}(R_M - R_F)$$

where:

$\beta_{a,o}$ = firm's operating asset beta

In the discussion that follows, we assume the firm has a defined benefit pension plan in place. We start the discussion by assuming management ignores the pension plan and uses only the balance sheet (operating) assets and liabilities in estimating the firm's WACC.[2] We then calculate the firm's WACC after properly including the pension assets and liabilities in the firm's balance sheet. This will demonstrate that using only the operating assets and liabilities overstates the firm's WACC.

---

1. As with any investment, the expected return on a capital project should be compared to its required return (based on its risk), which could be greater than, equal to, or less than the firm's WACC. Using WACC to evaluate a project implicitly assumes the project has the same risk as the firm's current operating assets; the project could be classified as an expansion project.

2. Most accounting regimes do not require firms to include pension plan assets and liabilities (and any resulting surplus or deficit) in the firm's balance sheet.

Ignoring Pension Plan Assets and Liabilities

The easiest way to demonstrate the relationship is by using a simple numerical example. The balance sheet in Figure 1 contains only the market values (without currency units) of the firm's operating assets, liabilities, and owners' equity.

Figure 1: Balance Sheet With Only Operating Assets and Liabilities

Assets		Beta	Liabilities and Owners' Equity		Beta
Operating	500	0.80	Liabilities	300	0.00
			Owners' Equity	200	2.00
Total	500	0.80	Total	500	0.80

Using the data in Figure 1, we estimate the firm's total asset beta as the weighted average of its liability and equity betas. The weights of liabilities and owners' equity are their market values divided by total assets. The equity beta of 2.0 is the beta of the firm's stock that is observable in the market, and we assume the liability (debt) beta is 0.0.

Referring to Figure 1, we see that the firm's total asset beta is 0.8:

total asset beta, $\beta_{a,t}$ = weighted average of equity and liability (debt) betas

$$\beta_{a,t} = w_e \beta_e + w_d \beta_d$$

$$\beta_{a,t} = \frac{200}{500}(2.0) + \frac{300}{500}(0.0) = \frac{200}{500}(2.0) = 0.80$$

Because in this case the balance sheet contains only operating assets and liabilities, the operating asset beta and total asset beta are equal:

$$\beta_{a,o} = \beta_{a,t} = 0.80$$

Assuming R_F = 3% and the equity market risk premium is 5%, the firm's WACC is 7%:

$$\text{WACC} = R_F + \beta_{a,o}(\text{MRP}) = 3\% + 0.80(5\%) = 7\%$$

For the Exam: The firm's *total asset beta* is equal to the weight of owners' equity in the balance sheet multiplied by the firm's equity beta. This general relationship holds whether or not we include pension assets and liabilities in the balance sheet:

$$\beta_{a,t} = w_e \beta_e$$

Professor's Note: The firm's equity beta captures the total volatility of its stock returns as well as their correlation with the market, so it measures the firm's total, combined systematic risk: the risk of its operating assets, the effects of its capital structure, and the risk of the assets in its pension plan. Thus, the equity beta estimated by regressing the firm's stock returns on market returns captures the risk of the firm's pension assets.

Including Pension Plan Assets and Liabilities

To this point, we have ignored the pension plan's assets and liabilities and their inherent risk when constructing the balance sheet and calculating the WACC. We now extend the example by assuming the plan is just fully funded (surplus = 0) with total assets of 250. We further assume that the plan's assets are 50% allocated to stocks, with an average beta of 1.0, and 50% to bonds.

The asset beta for the *pension plan* is the weighted average of the betas of the stocks and bonds it holds as assets. Because the plan's assets are equally weighted in bonds and stocks, the weights for each are 0.50. Also, we assume bond betas are zero, so the asset beta for the plan, $\beta_{a,p}$, is the proportion (weight) of stocks multiplied by their average beta or 0.50:

$$\text{pension plan asset beta, } \beta_{a,p} = w_{s,p}\overline{\beta}_{s,p} + w_{b,p}\overline{\beta}_{b,p}$$

where:

$w_{s,p}$ and $w_{b,p}$ = weights (allocations) of stocks and bonds in the plan's asset portfolio $\left(\text{assume } w_{s,p} \text{ and } w_{b,p} = 0.5\right)$

$\overline{\beta}_{s,p}$ = average beta of stocks held by the pension plan = 1.0

$\overline{\beta}_{b,p}$ = average beta of bonds held by the pension plan = 0.0

Since $\overline{\beta}_{b,p}$ = 0

$\beta_{a,p}$ = $w_{s,p}\overline{\beta}_{s,p} = 0.5(1.0) = 0.50$

The plan is just fully funded, so its assets and liabilities are equal; assets and liabilities equal 250. When we incorporate the plan assets and liabilities into the firm's balance sheet in Figure 2, we see the downward effects on the weight of owners' equity in the balance sheet and the firm's total asset beta:

Figure 2: Balance Sheet With Pension Plan Assets and Liabilities Included

Assets		Beta	Liabilities and Owners' Equity		Beta
Operating	500	0.54	Operating Liabilities	300	0.00
Pension	250	0.50	Plan Liabilities	250	0.00
			Owners' Equity	200	2.00
Total	750	0.53	Total	750	0.53

- In Figure 1, when plan assets and liabilities are not considered, the weight of owners' equity is 200 / 500 = 0.40, and the firm's total asset beta is 0.80.
- In Figure 2, when we include the plan's assets and liabilities, the weight of owners' equity drops to 200 / 750 = 0.2667, and the total asset beta drops to 0.2667 × 2.0 = 0.5334.

For the Exam: Remember the important relationship from above—the total asset beta is always equal to the weight of owners' equity in the balance sheet multiplied by the equity beta. We now see that when pension plan assets and liabilities are included in the balance sheet, the weight of owners' equity falls and the total asset beta falls.

The Firm's Operating Beta and WACC

The firm's total asset beta, $\beta_{a,t}$, is the weighted average of its operating and pension asset betas:

$$\beta_{a,t} = w_{a,o}\beta_{a,o} + w_{a,p}\beta_{a,p}$$

The firm's total asset beta is estimated using the firm's equity beta, so it explicitly considers the risk of both the firm's operating assets and its pension assets. The firm's WACC, however, should be based only on the risk of its operating assets. Thus to accurately estimate the firm's WACC, we need to "back" the operating asset beta out of the total asset beta using the weights of the pension and operating assets and the beta of the firm's pension assets:

$$\beta_{a,t} = w_{a,o}\beta_{a,o} + w_{a,p}\beta_{a,p} \quad \Rightarrow$$

$$\beta_{a,o} = \frac{\beta_{a,t} - w_{a,p}\beta_{a,p}}{w_{a,o}}$$

From Figure 2, we know that the total asset beta is 0.53 and the pension asset beta is 0.50, so the true operating asset beta and WACC are 0.54 and 5.70%, respectively:

$$\beta_{a,o} = \frac{\beta_{a,t} - w_{a,p}\beta_{a,p}}{w_{a,o}}$$

$$w_{a,o} = \frac{500}{750} = 0.67; \; w_{a,p} = \frac{250}{750} = 0.33; \; \beta_{a,t} = 0.53; \; \beta_{a,p} = 0.50$$

$$\beta_{a,o} = \frac{0.53 - 0.33(0.50)}{0.67} = \frac{0.3650}{0.67} = 0.5448$$

$$\text{WACC} = R_F + \beta_{a,o}(\text{MRP}) = 3\% + 0.54(5\%) = 5.70\%$$

Remember that the firm had the pension plan with its assets and liabilities all along. It's just that in the first case (Figure 1) management simply ignored the pension plan when estimating the firm's WACC of 7%. By ignoring the pension plan assets and liabilities, management overestimated the firm's total asset beta, operating asset beta, and WACC.

By properly including the pension plan assets and liabilities in the balance sheet and WACC calculations (Figure 2), we see that the firm's true WACC is 5.7%. *True* because a WACC of 5.7% more accurately reflects the risk of the firm's operating assets.

Consequences

The primary consequence of not considering pension plan assets and liabilities is that the firm's estimated total asset beta, operating asset beta, and WACC are too high, causing management to reject potentially profitable projects. For example, assume management of the firm is analyzing a project with an expected return of 6%.

By ignoring the pension plan assets and liabilities and using the 7% WACC, they reject the project because of its negative NPV (i.e., IRR < WACC). If they correctly considered plan assets and liabilities and use the correct WACC of 5.7%, however, the project has a positive NPV, and they accept it. Taking the project would be expected to increase the firm's stock price. The bottom line is that, if management does not consider pension plan assets and liabilities in their WACC estimations, they could routinely reject profitable projects and fail to maximize stock price in the long run.

Changing Pension Plan Asset Allocations

LOS 17.c: <u>Explain</u>, in an expanded balance sheet framework, the effects of different pension asset allocations on total asset betas, the equity capital needed to maintain equity beta at a desired level, and the debt-to-equity ratio.

CFA® Program Curriculum, Volume 2, page 514

In all of the calculations thus far (fully funded, under-funded, and over-funded), we assumed the firm had the same equity beta of 2.0. In reality, the firm's equity beta will reflect the risk of the firm's operating assets and capital structure as well as the asset allocation of the pension plan. The risk of the plan assets, as measured by the plan's asset allocation and average asset beta, affects the volatility of the firm's publicly traded stock and is thus reflected in the equity beta. All else equal, the riskier the plan's assets, higher average beta and/or greater allocation to equities, the greater the firm's equity beta.

Figure 3 provides an illustration of how varying the allocation to equity securities in the pension assets might impact the firm's equity beta and total asset beta (the equity beta numbers are hypothetical). As in figures 1 and 2, we assume a plan with assets and liabilities of 250 and equity securities held have an average beta of 1.0. The firm's operating assets, liabilities, and owners' equity are 500, 300, and 200, respectively.

Figure 3: The Firm's Equity Beta and Total Asset Beta With Varying Pension Asset Allocations

Plan Allocation to Equity Securities (%)	Plan Asset Beta[1]	Firm's Equity Beta	Firm's Total Asset Beta[2]
0	0	1.00	0.27
25	0.25	1.50	0.40
50[3]	0.50	2.00	0.53
75	0.75	2.50	0.67
100	1.00	3.00	0.80

[1] $\beta_{a,p} = w_e \bar{\beta}_e; \ \bar{\beta}_e = 1.0$

[2] $\beta_{a,t} = w_e \beta_e; \ w_e = 200/750 = 0.2667$

[3] Values used in previous examples.

There are two critically important relationships in Figure 3. With all else equal, the following is true:

1. Increasing the allocation to equity securities in the plan's assets increases the risk of the plan assets, which in turn increases the firm's equity beta.

2. The firm's equity beta and total asset beta are positively related.

Pension Plan Asset Allocation and the Firm's Operating Asset Beta

Let's continue this line of thinking by looking at how varying the plan allocation to equities affects the firm's operating asset beta and its WACC. We start by recalling Figure 2, which shows the original scenario:

Figure 2: Balance Sheet With Pension Plan Assets and Liabilities Included

Assets		Beta	Liabilities and Owners' Equity		Beta
Operating	500	0.54	Operating Liabilities	300	0.00
Pension	250	0.50	Plan Liabilities	250	0.00
			Owners' Equity	200	2.00
Total	750	0.53	Total	750	0.53

When plan assets and liabilities are included, as in Figure 2, the firm's operating asset beta and WACC are 0.54 and 5.7%, respectively. In that case, we assumed the average stock beta in the plan assets was 1.0, and the plan was 50% allocated to stocks. Thus, the plan asset beta was 0.50. Figure 4 shows how the firm's operating asset beta changes when the risk of the plan changes.[3]

---

3. Throughout the discussion, we assume that the risk of the pension plan assets is related positively to the allocation to equity securities as well as their average beta. Thus, an increase in either increases the risk of the plan assets.

Figure 4: The Firm's Operating Asset Beta and WACC With Varying Pension Asset Allocations[1]

Plan Allocation to Equity Securities (%)	Plan Asset Beta	Firm's Total Asset Beta	Firm's Operating Asset Beta[2]	WACC[3]
0	0	0.27	0.40	5.00%
25	0.25	0.40	0.47	5.35%
50	0.50	0.53	0.54	5.70%
75	0.75	0.67	0.63	6.15%
100	1.00	0.80	0.70	6.50%

[1.] The first three columns are from Figure 3.

[2.] $\beta_{a,o} = \dfrac{\beta_{a,t} - w_{a,p}\beta_{a,p}}{w_{a,o}}$; $w_{a,p} = \dfrac{250}{750} = 0.33$; $w_{a,o} = \dfrac{500}{750} = 0.67$

[3.] $\text{WACC} = R_F + \beta_{a,o}(\text{MRP}) = 3\% + \beta_{a,o}(5\%)$

We again recognize critically important relationships in the figure. If management changes the allocation of its pension plan assets, the change will affect the firm's operating asset beta and WACC. With all else equal, the following is true:

1. Increasing (decreasing) the risk of the pension plan assets increases (decreases) the firm's operating asset beta.

2. Increasing (decreasing) the risk of the pension plan assets increases (decreases) the firm's WACC.

> **For the Exam:** Figures 3 and 4 have provided extremely important concepts to remember for the exam. First, as the risk of the pension plan assets is increased, either by increasing the plan's allocation to equity securities or holding equity securities with a higher average beta, the firm's equity beta increases. Then, as the firm's equity beta increases, the firm's operating asset beta increases, and that increases the firm's WACC.

Optimal Capital Structure

To summarize what we have discussed to this point, the value of the firm's equity beta is positively related to the risk of its operating assets and the risk of its pension plan assets. Varying the allocation to equities in the pension plan changes the risk of the plan assets. An increase in the plan's allocation to equity securities, for example, increases the risk of the plan assets which is reflected in an increased equity beta. As long as the firm's capital structure stays the same, the increase in pension plan risk results in an increased equity beta.

Looking at this question from a different perspective, what can management do to maintain the equity beta if they change the risk of the plan assets? In our previous examples, we assumed an equity beta of 2.0. If management wants to maintain the equity beta at that level but also wants to change the plan asset beta, they must change the firm's capital structure.

To facilitate the discussion, we reproduce Figure 3. We see that when increasing the allocation to equities in the plan assets while maintaining the same capital structure, the risk of the plan's assets increases, which in turn causes the firm's equity beta and total asset beta to increase:

Figure 3: The Firm's Equity Beta and Total Asset Beta With Varying Pension Asset Allocations

Plan Allocation to Equity Securities (%)	Plan Asset Beta	Firm's Equity Beta	Firm's Total Asset Beta
0	0	1.00	0.27
25	0.25	1.50	0.40
50	0.50	2.00	0.53
75	0.75	2.50	0.67
100	1.00	3.00	0.80

From Figure 3, we see that if we increase the plan's allocation to equities to 75%, the firm's equity beta increases to 2.50, and its total asset beta increases to 0.67. Let's assume management wants to increase the allocation to equities in the plan to 75%, but they prefer to maintain the firm's equity beta at 2.0. In order to accomplish this, they will have to increase the amount of owners' equity in the balance sheet to 33.5%:

$$\beta_{a,t} = w_e \beta_e$$

$$0.67 = w_e(2.0); \; w_e = \frac{0.67}{2.0} = 33.5\%$$

Figure 5 shows the weights of owners' equity and debt required to maintain the firm's equity beta at 2.0 with varying plan allocations to equities. We see that as the allocation to equity securities in the plan is increased (decreased), management must increase (decrease) the proportion of owners' equity in the balance sheet. To increase the proportion of owners' equity, management would be expected to issue stock and use the proceeds to repurchase outstanding debt. To decrease owners' equity, management would issue bonds and use the proceeds to repurchase outstanding stock. In either case, the value increase in one is equal to the value decrease in the other.

Figure 5: Capital Structure (D/E) That Would Maintain the Firm's Equity Beta at 2.0

Equity Securities in the Plan Assets	Firm's Total Asset Beta	Firm's Equity Beta	Weight of Owners' Equity[1]	Weight of Debt[2]	D/E[3]
0%	0.27	2.00	13.5%	86.5%	6.41
25%	0.40	2.00	20.0%	80.0%	4.00
50%	0.53	2.00	26.5%	73.5%	2.77
75%	0.67	2.00	33.5%	66.5%	1.99
100%	0.80	2.00	40.0%	60.0%	1.50

1. $w_e = \dfrac{\beta_{a,t}}{\beta_e}$

2. weight of debt = 1 – weight of owners' equity

3. D/E = weight of debt / weight of owners' equity

The important concept here is that as the risk of the pension assets increases, total risk on the left-hand side of the balance sheet (total asset beta) increases. The increase in asset risk will increase the firm's equity beta unless management moves to mitigate it by altering the firm's capital structure.

In order to protect stockholders against an increase in the risk of its pension assets, management must reduce the risk on the right-hand side of the balance sheet. To offset the increased risk of the pension plan, they must increase the proportion of owners' equity, thus decreasing the firm's D/E ratio.

For the Exam: Remember that the risk of the pension plan's assets depends on the allocation to equity securities—the equity securities the plan holds as assets. As the proportion of equities in the plan's portfolio increases, the risk of the plan assets increases. Because total risk on the left-hand side of the firm's balance sheet is a weighted average of the risk of the operating and plan assets, the increase in plan risk increases total asset risk, which is reflected in an increased equity beta. The risk on the right-hand side of the firm's balance sheet is determined by the relative weights of debt and owners' equity in its capital structure. As the proportion of owners' equity in the capital structure increases, the firm's overall risk decreases. Thus, to offset an increase in risk on the left-hand side of the balance sheet due to increasing the plan's risk and to return the firm's equity beta to the desired level, management can reduce the risk on the right-hand side of the balance sheet by increasing the proportion of owners' equity and reducing the amount of outstanding debt.

KEY CONCEPTS

LOS 17.a

Funding shortfall occurs when the market value of the pension plan's assets is less than the market value of its liabilities (i.e., pension obligations). The risk to the participant is that the fund may have insufficient assets to meet pension obligations. The risk to the firm (i.e., plan sponsor) is that the plan is deemed underfunded. If this happens, the sponsor may be required by regulators to increase annual contributions to the plan or even make one or more special contributions to return the plan to fully funded status.

Asset/liability mismatch occurs when the pension plan's assets and liabilities are exposed to different risk factors or affected differently by the same risk factors. For example, assume the plan's assets are invested in equities. Because the plan's liabilities behave like fixed-income securities, they can react differently to economic conditions. For example, during a recession with accompanying falling interest rates, the value of the plan's assets (i.e., equities) will fall at the same time the present value of the plan's liabilities rises. The double whammy effect of falling asset values combined with rising liability values will significantly reduce the plan's surplus or even push it into an underfunded status.

LOS 17.b

The firm's WACC should be based on the risk of its operating assets, measured by the firm's operating asset beta. Including pension plan assets and liabilities in the firm's balance sheet will reduce the weight of owners' equity and lower the firm's total asset beta. The firm's total asset beta is the weight of owners' equity multiplied by the equity beta on the right side of the balance sheet and the weighted average of the firm's operating and pension asset betas on the left side. The firm's WACC falls when pension assets and liabilities are considered.

LOS 17.c

Changing the proportion of pension assets invested in equities will change the overall capital structure of the firm (i.e., operating plus pension assets and liabilities). For example, if the firm's pension asset allocation is changed to include a higher proportion of equities, the result is an increased risk in its pension assets with an accompanying increased asset beta. This will cause the firm's total asset beta to increase and the risk of the firm's equity capital to increase. To maintain the firm's equity beta, management needs to decrease the amount of debt in the firm's capital structure. This is accomplished by issuing new equity and using the proceeds to repurchase outstanding debt. The proper decrease in the firm's D/E ratio will return the equity beta to the desired level. If the plan assets are reallocated to a higher proportion of bonds, the firm's equity beta will fall. To return the equity beta to the higher desired level, management can issue debt and use the proceeds to repurchase outstanding shares, thus increasing the D/E ratio.

CONCEPT CHECKERS

1. Which of the following is the *least accurate* description of an asset/liability mismatch?
    A. Even if there is a pension asset surplus, there can still be an asset/liability mismatch.
    B. An asset/liability mismatch occurs when the pension assets are invested primarily in equities.
    C. An asset/liability mismatch occurs when the market value of pension assets is less than the market value of pension liabilities.

2. When the market value of pension assets equals the market value of pension liabilities and the assets are invested in bonds with the same duration as its liabilities, which of the following statements is *least accurate*?
    A. The firm does not have an asset/liability mismatch.
    B. The pension assets will contribute less risk to the firm than if they were invested in equities.
    C. The firm is considered to be in a worse situation than when the pension assets are invested primarily in equities and there is a funding surplus.

3. Management has calculated the firm's weighted average cost of capital using the operating (i.e., balance sheet) asset beta. Mark Cross, CFA, argues that both should be calculated after considering the firm's pension plan assets. Relative to the beta and WACC already calculated, including pension assets will *most likely* have what impact on the asset beta and WACC?

	Asset beta	WACC
A.	Decrease	Decrease
B.	Increase	Decrease
C.	Decrease	Increase

4. Which of the following is *most likely* to occur if the pension assets are not included in the weighted average cost of capital (WACC)?
    A. The debt-to-equity ratio will be understated.
    B. The overall value of the firm is higher.
    C. Increased investment will occur in the firm's operating assets.

Use the following information to answer Questions 5 and 6.

- Firm's equity beta = 1.00.
- Risk-free rate = 5%.
- Market risk premium = 8%.
- Debt = $9 million.
- Equity = $21 million.
- Pension assets beta = 0.60.
- Pension assets = $15 million.

5. The firm's operating assets beta *before* including the pension liabilities into the balance sheet and the operating assets beta *after* incorporating the pension assets into the balance sheet would be *closest* to:

	Before	After
A.	0.47	0.40
B.	0.70	0.40
C.	0.70	0.47

6. After incorporating the risk of the pension assets into the overall capital structure, the weighted average cost of capital (WACC) for capital budgeting purposes is *closest* to:
   A. 10.6.
   B. 8.2.
   C. 8.8.

7. If a company changes its allocation of pension assets to be invested in a higher percentage of equities while maintaining the same equity beta (beta of the firm's stock), what is the likely effect on the firm's:

	total asset beta?	debt/equity ratio?
A.	Increase	Increase
B.	Decrease	Decrease
C.	Increase	Decrease

8. A firm changes the allocation of its pension assets to be invested in a higher percentage of bonds. The amount of equity capital needed to maintain the same equity beta and the resulting debt/equity ratio would:

	Equity capital	Debt/equity
A.	Increase	Increase
B.	Decrease	Decrease
C.	Decrease	Increase

9. To maintain the same equity beta after increasing the percentage of pension assets invested in equities, a firm would need to:
   A. decrease the amount of risk in its capital structure by using less equity capital.
   B. increase the amount of risk in its capital structure by using more debt financing.
   C. decrease the amount of risk in its capital structure by using less debt financing.

ANSWERS – CONCEPT CHECKERS

1. **C** A funding shortfall is when the market value of pension assets is less than the market value of pension liabilities. An asset/liability mismatch is referring to the mismatch in risk that occurs when the pension assets are invested primarily in equities while the pension liabilities have the same interest rate sensitive characteristics as fixed-income securities. When the pension assets are invested in equities, there can still be an asset/liability mismatch even if there is a pension asset surplus because the value of the pension assets invested in equities could decrease while the value of the pension liabilities would increase if interest rates decrease.

2. **C** Even if there is a funding surplus, there may be more risk to the firm if its pension assets are invested in equities because the equities could decrease significantly in value while a decrease in interest rates would cause the pension liabilities to increase in value. Funding shortfall is when the market value of pension assets is less than the market value of pension liabilities. An asset/liability mismatch is referring to the mismatch in risk that occurs when the pension assets are invested primarily in equities while the pension liabilities have the same interest rate sensitive characteristics as fixed-income securities.

3. **A** Although each case should be analyzed, the overall asset beta for a firm with significant pension assets will usually be lower than the operating (i.e., balance sheet) asset beta. This also reduces the firm's WACC.

4. **A** By not including the risk of the pension assets into the overall risk of the firm, debt will be understated because the pension liabilities, which have debt-like characteristics, will not be included in the capital structure. This causes the debt-to-equity ratio to be understated. Also, by not including the pension risk into the overall WACC, the result will be a higher WACC. This will lead to a higher hurdle rate for new projects, causing many projects to be rejected and the overall value of the firm to be lower than it could be.

5. **B** Balance sheet *not* incorporating the pension plan into the WACC:

	Value ($million)	Beta		Value ($million)	Beta
Operating assets	$30	0.70	Liabilities	$9	0.00
Total assets	$30	0.70	Equity	$21	1.00

The operating assets beta before the inclusion of pension assets and liabilities =
$\frac{21}{30} \times 1.00 = 0.70$.

Balance sheet incorporating the pension plan into the WACC:

	Value ($million)	Beta		Value ($million)	Beta
Operating assets	$30	0.40	Liabilities	$9	0.00
Pension assets	$15	0.60	Pension liabilities	$15	0.00
Total assets	$45	0.47	Equity	$21	1.00

Total assets beta = $\dfrac{21}{45} \times 1.00 = 0.47$.

The beta for the total assets = $\dfrac{30}{45}$ (operating assets beta) + $\dfrac{15}{45}$ (0.6) = 0.47.

Solving for the operating assets beta after the inclusion of pension assets and liabilities = 0.40.

6. **B**   After incorporating the pension assets and liabilities into the capital structure, the new operating assets beta becomes 0.40 as shown in the previous answer; thus, for capital budgeting purposes the WACC is 5 + 0.4(8) = 8.2.

7. **C**   As the pension assets are invested more heavily in equities, the pension asset beta will increase; thus, the total assets beta will increase. To maintain the same equity beta, management will have to decrease the proportion of debt in the firm's capital structure.

8. **C**   A higher percentage of pension assets invested in bonds will lower the risk of the pension assets, resulting in a lower total asset beta. To maintain the same equity beta, there must be an increase in debt financing along with a decrease in equity capital; thus, the debt/equity ratio will increase.

9. **C**   Increasing the percentage of pension assets invested in equities will increase the risk of the pension assets increasing the overall total asset beta. To maintain the same equity beta, there must be a decrease in risk in the capital structure of the firm, which would be accomplished by using less debt financing and increasing the amount of equity capital.

Use the following information for Questions 1 through 6.

Rob Baker, an investment manager at Welker Auto Parts, is responsible for managing his company's defined-benefit pension plan. The plan has been underfunded for several months and Baker is meeting today with Gary Thompson, the company's CFO, to discuss possible ways to erase this liability funding shortfall. Baker is also planning on discussing the firm's weighted average cost of capital (WACC) with Thompson because it currently does not incorporate pension assets and liabilities.

During the meeting, Baker proposes that the plan should increase the value of its pension assets by investing in riskier securities. Currently, the plan invests a majority of its funds in investment grade corporate bonds and large-cap equities. Baker is confident that investments in small-cap equities will help bring the fund back to fully funded status. Thompson, however, is not as confident that investing in riskier securities will guarantee an increase in pension asset values. He points to the company's high debt ratio as an indication of a need to take a more risk-averse stance.

Baker is skeptical of Thompson's risk-averse stance so he notifies Thompson of the high correlation of pension asset returns with the firm's operations. Baker states that the high correlation implies a high tolerance for risk. Thompson disagrees with this statement, suggesting that a firm's high ratio of active to retired lives does not grant the ability to take on more risk.

After discussing the plan's risk tolerance, Baker and Thompson evaluate the firm's WACC and exercise the possibility of adjusting this discount rate to incorporate pension risk. Baker provides Thompson with the following information:

	Value ($million)		Value ($million)	Beta
Operating Assets	50	Liabilities	30	0.0
		Equity	20	1.5

Baker points out that if the WACC calculation does not include pension assets and liabilities, then the WACC is likely overstated and may be causing the firm to reject profitable projects. Thompson agrees with this statement and adds that ignoring pension assets and liabilities will also understate the firm's leverage ratio.

Baker is still convinced that the percentage of pension assets in equities needs to increase to improve the funded status of the plan. He notes that giving more weight to equities will increase the risk of pension assets; in order to keep the equity beta at 1.5, the firm must change its capital structure by decreasing the amount of debt it holds. Thompson concludes that increasing the proportion of pension assets invested in equities while maintaining the same equity beta will actually increase the debt-to-equity ratio.

1. Regarding Baker's view on investing more funds in small-cap equities and Thompson's view on implementing a risk-averse stance:

	Baker	Thompson
A.	Inappropriate	Appropriate
B.	Appropriate	Inappropriate
C.	Inappropriate	Inappropriate

2. Regarding Baker's statement about the correlation between pension assets and firm operations and Thompson's statement about the ratio of active to retired lives:

	Baker	Thompson
A.	Incorrect	Correct
B.	Correct	Incorrect
C.	Incorrect	Incorrect

3. Without consideration of pension assets and liabilities, the asset beta of Welker Auto Parts is *closest* to:
    A. 0.6.
    B. 0.9.
    C. 1.0.

4. Without consideration of pension assets and liabilities, if the risk-free rate is 3% and the return on the market portfolio is 9%, Welker Auto Parts's WACC is *closest* to:
    A. 3.6%.
    B. 6.6%.
    C. 8.4%.

5. Regarding Baker's analysis of the WACC being overstated and Thompson's analysis of the firm's leverage ratio being understated:

	Baker	Thompson
A.	Correct	Correct
B.	Incorrect	Correct
C.	Correct	Incorrect

6. Regarding Baker's thoughts concerning changing the capital structure and Thompson's conclusions on the debt-to-equity ratio:

	Baker	Thompson
A.	Correct	Correct
B.	Incorrect	Correct
C.	Correct	Incorrect

SELF-TEST ANSWERS: PORTFOLIO MANAGEMENT FOR INSTITUTIONAL INVESTORS

1. **A** Baker's views are inappropriate. Despite the willingness to take greater risk by investing in small-cap equities, the plan's underfunded status has decreased the ability to take risk. Therefore, taking greater risk is inappropriate. Thompson's views are appropriate. A higher debt ratio would indicate a decreased capability of meeting the plan's liabilities and, thus, would suggest a more risk-averse stance.

2. **C** Baker's statement is incorrect. A high correlation of pension asset returns with a firm's operations indicates a low risk tolerance. For example, the ability of the firm to make contributions will be low at the same time that the plan is underfunded. Thompson's statement is also incorrect. A high ratio of active to retired lives usually indicates an increased ability to take risk.

3. **A** operating assets beta = (debt weight)(debt beta) + (equity weight)(equity beta)

   operating assets beta = $(0.6)(0.0) + (0.4)(1.5) = 0.6$

4. **B** We know from the previous answer that the firm's operating assets beta is equal to 0.6. We also know from the question that the market risk premium is equal to 6% (= 9% − 3%).

   The WACC is calculated as follows:

   $$WACC = R_F + \beta_i(MRP)$$

   $$WACC = 3\% + 0.6(6\%) = 6.6\%$$

5. **A** Baker's analysis is correct. A consequence of not incorporating the pension assets and liabilities into the WACC is that the WACC will be overstated, causing a hurdle rate too high for future projects. Thompson's analysis is correct. By not incorporating the pension liabilities into the WACC, the level of the firm's debt is understated and the leverage ratio is also understated.

6. **C** Baker is correct. Increases in the percentage of pension assets in equities while maintaining the same equity beta will require the firm to decrease the amount of debt in its capital structure. Thompson is incorrect. The decrease in debt lowers the risk to equity holders and creditors with an associated decrease in the firm's debt-to-equity ratio.

CAPITAL MARKET EXPECTATIONS

Study Session 6

EXAM FOCUS

For years, the CFA Level III curriculum has prescribed determining optimal long-term (policy) as well as short-term (tactical) asset allocations using current and expected capital market conditions in combination with the manager's expectations for industries, sectors, and individual securities. The question of how to develop or interpret market conditions was not described, but this topic review finally gets to that question. Because important concepts and procedures are so numerous in this review, rather than list them in this exam focus, I have made notes directly in the document. Although I recommend focusing on the points I have indicated, this entire review is quite important, so do not skip anything.

FORMULATING CAPITAL MARKET EXPECTATIONS

LOS 18.a: <u>Discuss</u> the role of, and a framework for, capital market expectations in the portfolio management process.

CFA® Program Curriculum, Volume 3, page 7

Capital market expectations can be referred to as **macro expectations** (expectations regarding classes of assets) or **micro expectations** (expectations regarding individual assets).

Using a disciplined approach leads to more effective asset allocations and risk management. Formulating capital market expectations is referred to as **beta research** because it is related to systematic risk. It can be used in the valuation of both equities and fixed-income securities. **Alpha research**, on the other hand, is concerned with earning excess returns through the use of specific strategies within specific asset groups.

To formulate capital market expectations, the analyst should use the following 7-step process.

Step 1: Determine the specific capital market expectations needed according to the investor's tax status, allowable asset classes, and time horizon. Time horizon is particularly important in determining the set of capital market expectations that are needed.

Step 2: Investigate assets' historical performance as well as the determinants of (i.e., factor affecting) their performance. Although future returns may diverge from the past, the analyst can get a feel for the possible ranges of asset performance. This may be approached using a multi-step process. For example, to project the performance of consumer durable small-cap value stocks in the United States, analysts might start by projecting returns for U.S. stocks, then consumer durables, and then for small-cap value stocks. Any projections that diverge sharply from past performance should be substantiated through further scrutiny.

Step 3: Identify the valuation model used and its requirements. For example, a comparables-based, relative value approach used in the United States may be difficult to apply in an emerging market analysis.

Step 4: Collect the best data possible. The use of faulty data will lead to faulty conclusions. The following issues should be considered when evaluating data for possible use:
- Calculation methodologies.
- Data collection techniques.
- Data definitions.
- Error rates.
- Investability and correction for free float.
- Turnover in index components.
- Potential biases.

Step 5: Use experience and judgment to interpret current investment conditions. In reality, the conclusions drawn from data will sometimes be conflicting. The analyst must therefore use judgment to determine the most realistic outcome. The analyst should also be careful to employ a consistent set of assumptions when interpreting data and drawing conclusions.

Step 6: Formulate capital market expectations. Any assumptions and rationales used in the analysis should be explicitly mentioned. Top-down analysis usually involves more economic analysis than bottom-up analysis. An analyst may justify his forecasts using any number of methods (e.g., discounted cash flow analysis, historical performance with adjustments, Black-Litterman model, etc.).

 Professor's Note: The Black-Litterman model is discussed in Study Session 8, Topic Review 21.

Step 7: Monitor performance and use it to refine the process. If actual performance varies significantly from forecasts, the process and model should obviously be refined. High-quality forecasts are consistent, unbiased, objective, well supported, and have a minimum amount of forecast error. As an example, the interest rate projections used to value stocks should be well supported and have the same values as those used to determine future bond returns.

PROBLEMS IN FORECASTING

LOS 18.b: <u>Discuss</u>, in relation to capital market expectations, the limitations of economic data, data measurement errors and biases, the limitations of historical estimates, *ex post* risk as a biased measure of *ex ante* risk, biases in analysts' methods, the failure to account for conditioning information, the misinterpretation of correlations, psychological traps, and model uncertainty.

CFA® Program Curriculum, Volume 3, page 13

For the Exam: CFA Institute has historically treated economics with respect and given it coverage on the Level III exam. You probably noticed that economics is given a topic weight of zero, but there is an entire study session devoted to Economic Concepts for Asset Valuation. When questioned about this seeming contradiction, CFA Institute responded that economics at Level III is tested as part of Portfolio Management.

This signals to me that you would be wise to be able to recognize and discuss the following problems associated with forecasts when you see them in a statement by an analyst or portfolio manager. Even though economics is given a topic weight of zero, I would not be surprised if you see it receive considerable coverage in a morning essay question or even as an entire item set in the afternoon. In either situation, I would be surprised if questions on Study Session 6 do not comprise at least 5% of the exam (18 points).

As mentioned earlier, poor forecasts can result in inappropriate asset allocations. The analyst should be aware of the potential problems in data, models, and the resulting capital market expectations. Nine problems encountered in producing forecasts are (1) limitations to using economic data, (2) data measurement error and bias, (3) limitations of historical estimates, (4) the use of ex post risk and return measures, (5) non-repeating data patterns, (6) failing to account for conditioning information, (7) misinterpretation of correlations, (8) psychological traps, and (9) model and input uncertainty.

1. There are several **limitations to using economic data.** First, the time lag between collection and distribution is often quite long. The International Monetary Fund, for example, reports data with a lag of as much as two years. Second, data are often revised and the revisions are not made at the same time as the publication. Third, data definitions and methodology change over time. For example, the basket of goods in the Consumer Price Index changes over time. Last, data indices are often rebased over time (i.e., the base upon which they are calculated is changed). Although a rebasing is not a substantial change in the data itself, the unaware analyst could calculate changes in the value of the indices incorrectly if she does not make an appropriate adjustment.

2. The formation of capital market expectations can also be adversely affected by several forms of **data measurement errors and biases.** The first problem is *transcription errors*, which will be more problematic if they are biased in a certain direction. A second problem arises from *survivorship bias.* As an example, a return

series based on a stock index will be biased upwards if the return calculation does not include firms that have been dropped from the index due to delistings. Third, the use of *appraisal* (smoothed) *data*, instead of actual returns, results in correlations and standard deviations that are biased downwards. The reason is that actual price fluctuations are masked by the use of appraised data. One potential solution is to rescale the data so that the mean return is unaffected, but the variance is increased based on the underlying economic fundamentals.

3. The **limitations of historical estimates** can also hamper the formation of capital market expectations. The values from historical data must often be adjusted going forward as economic, political, regulatory, and technological environments change. This is particularly true for volatile assets such as equity. These changes are known as *regime changes* and result in *nonstationary* data. For example, the bursting of the technology bubble in 2000 resulted in returns data that were markedly different than that from the previous five years.

    When basing forecasts on historical data, there is a tradeoff between using a time span of data that is too short and one that is too long. Statistical measures require data of sufficient length. Longer time spans of data should also result in mean returns, standard deviations, and correlations that are less sensitive to the time span chosen. Furthermore, a longer time span of data increases the precision of population parameter estimates.

    On the other hand, using too long a time span of data may include data that is no longer relevant, if there have been regime changes. A longer time span of data may also not be available. Some researchers use more frequent data (e.g., using daily instead of monthly returns) in order to increase the length of the data (i.e., number of observations). This, however, increases the likelihood of asynchronous data. Asynchronous data results when, for example, the return for a real estate asset is not available on a given day. The researcher then replaces it with the previous day's return. When measured against equity returns with readily available daily data, the real estate asset standard deviation and correlation with equity are artificially low.

     Professor's Note: In order to produce accurate measures, such as correlation, you need the sets of data to be as synchronous *as possible. For example, to calculate the correlation of two assets using daily returns, you should have corresponding returns for both assets for every day in the sample. If some of the daily returns are missing, we say the returns data for the two assets are* asynchronous.

    As a test of whether a long time series of data should be used, the researcher should determine if there is any reason to believe that the data is nonstationary, and if so, whether the regime change can be detected statistically. There are several statistical tests that can be used to determine if a change has taken place. If both these questions are answered in the affirmative, then a shorter time series of data should be used.

4. Using **ex post data** (after the fact) to determine **ex ante** (before the fact) risk and return can be problematic. For example, suppose that several years ago investors were fearful that the Federal Reserve was going to have to raise interest rates to combat

inflation. This situation would cause depressed stock prices. If inflation abated without the Fed's intervention, then stock returns would increase once the inflation scenario passes. Looking back on this situation, the researcher would conclude that stock returns were high while being blind to the prior risk that investors had faced. The analyst would then conclude that future (ex ante) returns for stocks will be high. In sum, the analyst would underestimate the risks that equity investors face and overestimate their potential returns.

5. Using historical data, analysts can also "uncover" **patterns** in security returns that are unlikely to occur in the future and can produce biases in the data. One such bias is *data mining*. Just by random chance, some variables will appear to have a relationship with security returns, when in fact, these relationships are unlikely to persist. For example, if the analyst uses a 5% significance level and examines the relationship between stock returns and 40 randomly selected variables, two (5%) of the variables are expected to show a statistically significant relationship with stock returns just by random chance. Another potential bias results from the time span of data chosen (*time period bias*). For example, small-cap U.S. stocks are widely thought to outperform large-cap stocks, but their advantage disappears when data from the 1970s and 1980s is excluded.

 Professor's Note: You can think of data mining as "beating the data into submission." That is, using different models, the analyst tests the data until some relationship (even a spurious relationship) is discovered.

To avoid these biases, the analyst should first ask himself if there is any economic basis for the variables found to be related to stock returns. Second, he should scrutinize the modeling process for susceptibility to bias. Third, the analyst should test the discovered relationship with out-of-sample data to determine if the relationship is persistent. This would be done by estimating the relationship with one portion of the historical data and then reexamining it with another portion.

6. Analysts' forecasts may also fail to account for **conditioning information**. The relationship between security returns and economic variables is not constant over time. Historical data reflects performance over many different business cycles and economic conditions. Thus, analysts should account for current conditions in their forecasts. As an example, suppose a firm's beta is estimated at 1.2 using historical data. If, however, the original data are separated into two ranges by economic expansion or recession, the beta might be 1.0 in expansions and 1.4 in recessions. Going forward, the analyst's estimate of the firm's beta should reflect whether an expansion is expected (i.e., the expected beta is 1.0) or a recession is expected (i.e., the expected beta is 1.4). That is, the value used is based on expected market conditions.

7. Another problem in forming capital market expectations is the **misinterpretation of correlations** (i.e., causality). Suppose the analyst finds that corn prices were correlated with rainfall in the Midwestern United States during the previous quarter. It would be reasonable to conclude that rainfall influences corn prices. It would not be reasonable to conclude that corn prices influence rainfall, although the correlation statistic would not tell us that. Rainfall is an exogenous variable (i.e., it arises outside the model), whereas the price of corn is an endogenous variable (i.e., it arises within the model).

It is also possible that a third variable influences both variables. Or it is possible that there is a nonlinear relationship between the two variables that is missed by the correlation statistic, which measures linear relationships.

These scenarios illustrate the problem with the simple correlation statistic. An alternative to correlation for uncovering predictive relationships is a multiple regression. In a multiple regression, lagged terms, control variables, and nonlinear terms can all be included as independent variables to better specify the relationship. Controlling for other effects, the regression coefficient on the variable of interest is referred to as the *partial correlation* and would be used for the desired analysis.

8. Analysts are also susceptible to **psychological traps**. We discuss six possible traps in the following: (1) the anchoring trap, (2) the status quo trap, (3) the confirming evidence trap, (4) the overconfidence trap, (5) the prudence trap, and (6) the recallability trap.

If an analyst is susceptible to the **anchoring trap**, he puts too much weight on the first set of information received. For example, if during a debate on the future of the economy, the first economist to speak states that there will be a recession while the second economist states that there will be an expansion, the analyst may use the recession scenario as an anchor and put less credence on the expansion scenario.

In the **status quo trap**, the analyst's predictions are highly influenced by the recent past. If inflation is currently 4%, for example, it is easier for the analyst to forecast a value close to 4% rather than risk a forecast that differs much from past values.

Professor's Note: I like to think of the status quo trap in terms of inertia. "A body at rest tends to stay at rest..."

The **confirming evidence trap** is when analysts give too much credence to evidence that supports their existing or favored beliefs. This trap may also cause analysts to look for information that supports their perspective and ignores other information. To counter these tendencies, analysts should give all evidence equal scrutiny, seek out opposing opinions, and be forthcoming in their motives.

In the fourth trap, the **overconfidence trap**, analysts sometimes ignore their past mistakes. This leads analysts to believe that others share their views and to forecast too narrow a range of possibilities. To prevent this from influencing their forecasts, analysts should enlarge their spread of potential future values.

In the **prudence trap**, analysts tend to be overly conservative in their forecasts because they want to avoid the *regret* from making extreme forecasts that could end up being incorrect. To counter this fifth trap, the analyst should again widen the range of his forecasted values.

Professor's Note: The prudence trap is similar to herding behavior in that the analyst tries not to stray too far from "the crowd." In this case, however, the analyst does not want to be seen as extreme and risk his job on a far-out forecast.

Lastly, analysts fall into the **recallability trap** when they let past disasters or dramatic events weigh too heavily in their forecasts. Many believe that the U.S. stock market crash of 1929 may have depressed equity values in the subsequent 30 years. To limit the influence of this trap, the analyst should be careful to base predictions on objective data rather than emotions or recollections of the past.

> **For the Exam:** You have no doubt recognized most of these traps as behavioral characteristics discussed in Study Session 3. If you see questions related to these traps/behavioral characteristics on the exam, using either the Study Session 3 terminology or the Study Session 6 terminology should receive full credit. That is, CFA Institute has never framed a question according to a specific study session. For example, the prudence trap mentioned here could certainly be explained in terms of fear of regret (i.e., regret minimizing action). The exam question will probably present some action or statement made by a portfolio manager or analyst, and you will have to identify the trait/trap from among those in the list (i.e., multiple-choice question in an item set) or actually write the name of the trait or trap and explain it (i.e., constructed response essay). In an item set, you will not see two selections that mean the same thing, and in an essay question, the grader will accept either term as long as they are effectively the same thing.

9. Our last problem regarding forecasts of capital market expectations is **model and input uncertainty**. When forecasting, an analyst cannot be sure that his predictive model is the correct one to use or whether his data are correct. As an example of the former, the analyst may be unsure whether to use a discounted cash flow (DCF) model or a relative value approach to valuing stocks. As an example of the latter, even if the analyst knew that the DCF model was appropriate, the correct growth and discount rates cannot be ascertained with certainty.

Tests of market efficiency usually depend on the use of a model. For example, many researchers use the market model, which uses a single independent variable (returns on the market) and beta as the relevant measure of risk. If beta is not the correct measure of risk, then the conclusions regarding market efficiency will be invalid. Some believe that market anomalies, which have been explained by behavioral finance, are in fact due to the actions of investors who are rational but use different valuation models.

FORECASTING TOOLS

LOS 18.c: <u>Demonstrate</u> the application of formal tools for setting capital market expectations, including statistical tools, discounted cash flow models, the risk premium approach, and financial equilibrium models.

CFA® Program Curriculum, Volume 3, page 25

> **For the Exam:** On the exam, be able to explain the forecasting tools discussed, as well as perform any related calculations. Neither time series analysis nor multifactor models is in the Level III curriculum anymore, so you will not be asked questions about them, their assumptions, or corrections of violations. It is possible, however, that a model could be given in a question, and you would be required to *use it* to obtain the answer for the question. Therefore, I recommend that you attain a working familiarity with any calculations presented in this section.

The use of formal tools helps the analyst set capital market expectations. Formal tools are those that are accepted within the investment community. When applied to reputable data, formal tools provide forecasts replicable by other analysts. The formal tools we examine are statistical tools, discounted cash flow models, the risk premium approach, and financial equilibrium models.

Statistical Tools

The various statistical tools for setting capital market expectations include projecting historical data, shrinkage estimators, time series analysis, and multifactor models. **Projecting historical data** is the most straightforward statistical tool. Here, the analyst projects the historical mean return, standard deviation, and correlations for a data set into the future. The arithmetic mean is the best when projecting for a single year, whereas the geometric mean is best for projecting over several years. The geometric mean is always smaller than the arithmetic mean when the variance of returns is non-zero. The difference between the two measures increases as the variance of returns increases. Some analysts prefer to use the historical equity risk premium for setting capital market expectations, whereas others subtract the current risk-free rate from the historical return on equities.

Shrinkage estimators are weighted averages of historical data and some other estimate, where the weights and other estimates are defined by the analyst. Shrinkage estimators reduce (shrink) the influence of historical outliers through the weighting process. The mean return and covariance are the parameters most often adjusted with shrinkage estimators. This tool is most useful when the data set is so small that historical values are not reliable estimates of future parameters.

For example, suppose the historical covariance between two assets is 180. Perhaps the analyst has modeled the covariance matrix between several assets using a factor model that indicates the covariance matrix (a.k.a. the **target covariance matrix**) values will increase in the future. If the estimated covariance is 220 and the analyst weights the historical covariance by 60% and the target by 40%, the shrinkage estimate would be 196 (180 × 0.60 + 220 × 0.40). It has been shown that shrinkage estimate covariances are more accurate forecasts of covariance, especially when the chosen target covariance and weights are appropriate.

Mean returns can also be forecasted with shrinkage estimators. One method weights the historical return of the subject asset the highest with the rest of the weight coming from the returns for other historical assets. For example, if the historical return for equity was 10% and the average return for all other assets was 8%, the analyst might use an 80/20 weighting and project a return of 9.6% (10% × 0.80 + 8% × 0.20) for equities.

Time series analysis (now in the Level II curriculum) forecasts a variable using previous values of itself and sometimes previous values of other variables. These models can be used to forecast means as well as variances. In the latter case, assets such as foreign exchange, stocks, and futures, have been shown to exhibit **volatility clustering**. This is when high volatility tends to be followed by high volatility, or when low volatility persists. A model developed by JP Morgan states that volatility in the current period, σ_t^2, is a weighted average of the previous period volatility, σ_{t-1}^2, and a random error, ε_t^2:

$$\sigma_t^2 = \theta\sigma_{t-1}^2 + (1-\theta)\varepsilon_t^2$$

The term θ measures the relationship, or rate of decay, between volatility in one period to the next. The higher θ is, the greater the persistence of volatility and the greater the tendency for volatility clustering. For example, suppose θ is 0.80 and the standard deviation in returns is 15% in period $t - 1$. If the random error is 0.04, then the forecasted variance for period t is:

$$\sigma_t^2 = 0.80(0.15^2) + 0.20(0.04^2) = 0.01832$$
$$\sigma_t = \sqrt{0.01832} = 0.1354 = 13.54\%$$

The forecasted standard deviation of 13.54% is close to the historical standard deviation of 15% because the historical standard deviation is weighted so heavily.

Multifactor models (also at Level II now) are used to forecast returns. They can also be used to forecast covariances. The advantage of using them to forecast covariances is that the model can simplify the forecasting procedure by reducing the forecast to a common set of factors. This modeling also eliminates the noise present in a sample of data and ensures consistent forecasts given a consistent covariance matrix.

For example, suppose there are two factors driving the returns for all assets—a global equity factor and a global bond factor. If the variance for the global equity factor is 0.0211, the variance for the global bond factor is 0.0019, and the covariance between them is 0.0015, then the *factor covariance matrix* is (note that the covariance of an asset with itself is its variance):

Figure 1: Factor Covariance Matrix for Global Assets

	Global Equity Factor	*Global Bond Factor*
Global equity factor	0.0211	0.0015
Global bond factor	0.0015	0.0019

Using this factor covariance matrix, a covariance matrix for markets can be derived if we know the sensitivities (the factor sensitivities or factor loadings) of the markets to these driving factors.

A 2-factor multifactor model is specified as:

$$R_i = \alpha_i + \beta_{i,1}F_1 + \beta_{i,2}F_2 + \varepsilon_i$$

In this 2-factor model, returns for an asset i, R_i, are a function of factor sensitivities, β, and factors, F. A random error, ε_i, has a mean of zero and is uncorrelated with the factors.

Using the factor model, we can formulate the variance of Market i, σ_i^2, given the covariance, $Cov(F_1, F_2)$, of factor returns:

$$\sigma_i^2 = \beta_{i,1}^2\sigma_{F_1}^2 + \beta_{i,2}^2\sigma_{F_2}^2 + 2\beta_{i,1}\beta_{i,2}Cov(F_1,F_2) + \sigma_{\varepsilon,i}^2$$

The covariance between Markets i and j, $Cov(i,j)$, can be calculated using:

$$Cov(i,j) = \beta_{i,1}\beta_{j,1}\sigma_{F_1}^2 + \beta_{i,2}\beta_{j,2}\sigma_{F_2}^2 + (\beta_{i,1}\beta_{j,2} + \beta_{i,2}\beta_{j,1})Cov(F_1,F_2)$$

For the Exam: The odds of this particular calculation showing up on the exam are quite low. I would not place it on the high priority list, so don't take time away from more important topics to memorize it.

For example, suppose the factor sensitivity to the global equity factor for Market i is 0.90 and 0.80 for Market j. If the sensitivities for both markets to the global bond market are zero, then we can deduce that these two markets are equity markets. Note that this does not mean the pairwise correlation between each market and the global bond market is zero. It means that, once the effect of the equity market is controlled for, the *partial correlation* of each market and the global bond factor is zero.

The covariance in this example would be:

$$Cov(i,j) = (0.90)(0.80)(0.0211) + (0)(0)(0.0019) + [(0.90)(0) + (0)(0.80)]0.0015 = 0.0152$$

The advantage of this approach is that the consistency of the global factor covariance matrix in Figure 1 is readily established because it only has four elements. Given its consistency, the variance and covariance estimates for the markets will then be consistent.

In this example, a 2-layered approach was used; that is, the driving factors were one level and the market parameters were another. In other markets, there may be many layers of factors. For example, perhaps the equity markets in Southeast Asia are highly correlated with each other but less correlated with the rest of the world. The first layer would be the individual markets (China, Hong Kong, Indonesia, Malaysia, Philippines, Singapore, South Korea, Taiwan, and Thailand), and the second layer would be the Southeast Asian equity market as a whole. Other layers would be composed of other markets that are correlated with the Southeast Asian equity market.

Discounted Cash Flow Models

A second tool for setting capital market expectations is **discounted cash flow models.** These models say that the intrinsic value of an asset is the present value of future cash flows. The advantage of these models is their correct emphasis on the future cash flows of an asset and the ability to back out a required return. Their disadvantage is that they do not account for current market conditions such as supply and demand, so these models are viewed as being more suitable for long-term valuation.

Study Session 6
Cross-Reference to CFA Institute Assigned Reading #18 – Capital Market Expectations

Applied to equity markets, the most common application of discounted cash flow models is the Gordon growth model or constant growth model. It is most commonly used to back out the expected return on equity, resulting in the following:

$$P_0 = \frac{Div_1}{\hat{R}_i - g} \Rightarrow \hat{R}_i = \frac{Div_1}{P_0} + g$$

where:

$\hat{R}_i$ = expected return on stock i

Div_1 = dividend next period

P_0 = current stock price

g = growth rate in dividends and long-term earnings

This formulation can be applied to entire markets as well. In this case, the growth rate is proxied by the nominal growth in GDP, which is the sum of the real growth rate in GDP plus the rate of inflation. The growth rate can be adjusted for any differences between the economy's growth rate and that of the equity index. This adjustment is referred to as the *excess corporate growth rate*. For example, the analyst may project the U.S. real growth in GDP at 2%. If the analyst thinks that the constituents of the Wilshire 5000 index will grow at a rate 1% faster than the economy as a whole, the projected growth for the Wilshire 5000 would be 3%.

Grinold and Kroner (2002)[1] take this model one step further by including a variable that adjusts for stock repurchases and changes in market valuations as represented by the price-earnings (P/E) ratio. The model states that the expected return on a stock is its dividend yield plus the inflation rate plus the real earnings growth rate minus the change in stock outstanding plus changes in the P/E ratio:

$$\hat{R}_i = \frac{D_1}{P_0} + i + g - \Delta S + \Delta\left(\frac{P}{E}\right)$$

where:

$\hat{R}_i$ = expected return on stock i; referred to as *compound annual growth rate* on a Level III exam

$\dfrac{D_1}{P_0}$ = expected dividend yield

i = expected inflation

g = real growth rate

ΔS = percentage change in shares outstanding (positive or negative)

$\Delta\left(\dfrac{P}{E}\right)$ = percentage change in the P/E ratio (repricing term)

---

1. Richard Grinold and Kenneth Kroner, "The Equity Risk Premium," *Investment Insights* (Barclay's Global Investors, July 2002).

©2011 Kaplan, Inc.
Page 91

The variables of the Grinold-Kroner model can be grouped into three components: the expected income return, the expected nominal growth in earnings, and the expected repricing return.

1. The **expected income return** is the current yield in percent that stockholders can expect to receive from the stock:

$$\text{expected income return (current yield)} = \left(\frac{D_1}{P_0} - \Delta S \right)$$

D_1 / P_0 is the traditional current yield as seen in the constant growth dividend discount model. It is the expected dividend expressed as a percentage of the current price. The Grinold-Kroner model goes a step further in expressing the expected current yield by considering any repurchases or new issues of stock.

ΔS is the percentage change in the number of outstanding shares. If shares are repurchased, ΔS is negative; the number of outstanding shares decreases. If new shares are sold, ΔS is positive; the number of outstanding shares increases. You should think of $-\Delta S$ (ΔS and the negative sign) as the **repurchase yield**. To help understand the relationship between ΔS and the repurchase yield, consider the following:

*   If the firm repurchases shares from its stockholders, it pays cash to the stockholders for shares they currently hold. This increases the amount of cash they receive from the firm, so they have experienced a *positive repurchase yield* (i.e., they have experienced a cash inflow).
*   When the firm issues new shares, it collects cash from its stockholders. This effectively decreases the amount of cash stockholders receive from the firm, so they have experienced a *negative repurchase yield* (i.e., they have experienced a cash outflow).

For the Exam: In an exam question, you could be provided with either the percentage change in the number of shares outstanding, ΔS, or the repurchase yield. If you are given the percentage change in shares outstanding, remember to multiply it by -1 to arrive at the repurchase yield. For example, if outstanding shares have been increased by 2%, $\Delta S = +2\%$, and the repurchase yield is -2%. If shares have been reduced by 2%, $\Delta S = -2\%$, and the repurchase yield is $+2\%$.

If you are given the repurchase yield in the question (e.g., you are told the repurchase yield is 2%), you know the change in outstanding shares is -2%. In either case, you add the repurchase yield to the dividend yield to estimate the current yield (expected income return).

2. The **expected nominal earnings growth** is the real growth in the stock price plus expected inflation (think of a nominal interest rate that includes the real rate plus inflation):

$$\text{expected nominal earnings growth} = (i + g)$$

©2011 Kaplan, Inc.

3. The **repricing return** is captured by the expected change in the P/E ratio:

$$\text{expected repricing return} = \Delta\left(P\!\!\!\Big/\!E\right)$$

Rearranging the Grinold-Kroner model to group the factors into the three components, the expected return on a stock or stock index can be specified as the sum of the expected income return, the expected nominal growth, and the expected repricing return.

$$\hat{R}_i = \exp(\text{income return}) + \exp(\text{nominal earnings growth}) + \exp(\text{repricing return})$$

$$\hat{R}_i = \left(\frac{D_1}{P_0} - \Delta S\right) + (i + g) + \left(\Delta P\!\!\!\Big/\!E\right)$$

In turn, the re-pricing component plus the nominal growth is the **expected capital gains yield**:

$$\text{expected nominal growth} = (i + g)$$

$$\text{expected repricing} = \Delta\left(\frac{P}{E}\right)$$

$$\text{expected capital gains yield} = (i + g) + \Delta\left(\frac{P}{E}\right)$$

Thus, using the Grinold-Kroner model, the expected equity return can be expressed as the sum of the current yield and the capital gains yield:

$$\hat{R}_i = \text{expected current yield} + \text{expected capital gains yield}$$

$$= \left(\frac{D_1}{P_0} - \Delta S\right) + \left(i + g + \Delta\frac{P}{E}\right)$$

Note that when the change in stock outstanding is negative (i.e., stock is repurchased), this is to the investor's benefit, and the *repurchase yield* is positive. Changes in the P/E ratio also affect the expected return. If investors think, for example, that stocks will be less risky in the future, the P/E ratio will increase, and the expected return on stocks increases. This P/E *repricing* component has been volatile throughout the course of U.S. capital market history.

Suppose an analyst estimates a 2.1% dividend yield, real earnings growth of 4.0%, long-term inflation of 3.1%, a repurchase yield of –0.5%, and P/E re-pricing of 0.3%:

expected *current yield* (income return)   = dividend yield + repurchase yield

$$= 2.1\% - 0.5\% = 1.6\%$$

expected *capital gains yield* = real growth + inflation + re-pricing

$$= 4.0\% + 3.1\% + 0.3\% = 7.4\%$$

The total expected return on the stock market is 1.6% + 7.4% = 9.0%.

One offshoot of this discounted cash flow analysis is the **Fed model**. Under the Fed model, the earnings yield is compared to the yield on 10-year Treasury bonds (T-bonds). If the earnings yield is lower than that of bonds, the investor would shift her money into the less risky T-bonds.

> **For the Exam:** The Fed model is discussed in detail in the next topic review.

Discounted cash flow analysis is also applied to bond markets, where the yield to maturity on the reference bond in a segment is used as the expected return for that segment. The drawback to this approach is that the yield to maturity assumes intermediate cash flows are reinvested at the yield to maturity, which may be implausible if the yield to maturity is quite high. As a zero coupon bond has no intermediate cash flows prior to maturity, its yield to maturity would be preferable to the use of a coupon bond.

Risk Premium Approach

A third method to setting capital market expectations is the risk premium approach, sometimes referred to as the *build-up approach*. To determine the expected return for equities, the analyst would start with the yield to maturity on a long-term government bond and add an equity risk premium. This approach is referred to as the *bond yield plus risk premium* approach.

To determine the expected return for bonds, $\hat{R}_B$, using this approach, the analyst uses the real risk-free rate and risk premiums as follows:

$$\hat{R}_B = \text{real risk-free rate} + \text{inflation risk premium} + \text{default risk premium} + \text{liquidity risk premium} + \text{maturity risk premium} + \text{tax premium}$$

The inflation premium compensates the bond investor for a loss in purchasing power over time. It can be measured by comparing the yields for inflation-indexed government bonds to non-inflation-indexed bonds of the same maturity.

The default risk premium compensates the investor for the likelihood of non-payment and can be estimated by examining the yields for bonds of differing credit risk.

The liquidity premium compensates the investor for holding illiquid bonds. The maturity risk premium reflects the yield differences of bonds of different maturities. Likewise, the tax premium accounts for different tax treatments of bonds.

Financial Equilibrium Models

The financial equilibrium approach assumes that supply and demand in global asset markets are in balance. In turn, financial models will value securities correctly. One such model is the International Capital Asset Pricing Model (ICAPM). Singer and Terhaar

$(1997)^2$ extend the ICAPM by considering the effect of market imperfections such as illiquidity.

The Singer and Terhaar equation for the ICAPM is:

$$\hat{R}_i = R_F + \beta_i\left(\hat{R}_M - R_F\right)$$

where:

$\hat{R}_i$ = expected return on asset i
R_F = risk-free rate of return
β_i = sensitivity (systematic risk) of asset i returns to the global investable market
$\hat{R}_M$ = expected return on the *global* investable market

Think of the global investable market as consisting of all investable assets, traditional and alternative.

We can manipulate this formula to solve for the risk premium on a debt or equity security using the following steps:

Step 1: The relationship between the covariance and correlation is:

$$\rho_{i,M} = \frac{\text{Cov}(i,m)}{\sigma_i \sigma_M} \Rightarrow \text{Cov}(i,m) = \rho_{i,M}\sigma_i\sigma_M$$

where:

$\rho_{i,M}$ = correlation between the returns on asset i and the global market portfolio
σ_i = standard deviation of the returns on asset i
σ_M = standard deviation of the returns on the global market portfolio

Step 2: Recall that:

$$\beta_i = \frac{\text{Cov}(i,m)}{\sigma_M^2}$$

where:

$\text{Cov}(i,m)$ = covariance of asset i with the global market portfolio
σ_M^2 = variance of the returns on the global market portfolio

Step 3: Combining the two previous equations and simplifying:

$$\beta_i = \frac{\rho_{i,M}\sigma_i\sigma_M}{\sigma_M^2} = \frac{\rho_{i,M}\sigma_i}{\sigma_M}$$

---

2. Brian D. Singer and Kevin Terhaar, *Economic Foundations of Capital Market Returns* (Research Foundation of The Institute of Chartered Financial Analysts, September 1, 1997).

Step 4: Rearranging the ICAPM, we arrive at the expression for the risk premium for asset i, RP_i:

$$\hat{R}_i = R_F + \beta_i\left(\hat{R}_M - R_F\right)$$

$$\hat{R}_i - R_F = \beta_i\left(\hat{R}_M - R_F\right)$$

denoting $\hat{R}_i - R_F$ as RP_i

$$RP_i = \beta_i\left(\hat{R}_M - R_F\right); \text{ and since } \beta_i = \rho_{i,M}\frac{\sigma_i}{\sigma_M}$$

$$RP_i = \rho_{i,M}\frac{\sigma_i}{\sigma_M}\left(\hat{R}_M - R_F\right), \text{ or}$$

$$RP_i = \rho_{i,M}\sigma_i\left(\frac{\hat{R}_M - R_F}{\sigma_M}\right)$$

Note that $\left(\dfrac{\hat{R}_M - R_F}{\sigma_M}\right) = $ market Sharpe ratio

The final expression states that the risk premium for an asset is equal to its correlation with the global market portfolio multiplied by the standard deviation of the asset multiplied by the Sharpe ratio for the global portfolio (in parentheses). From this formula, we forecast the risk premium and expected return for a market. The Sharpe ratio for the global portfolio has been estimated at ranges from 0.28 to 0.30 but will change over time. We will use a value of 0.29 in our examples.

Example: Calculating an equity risk premium and a debt risk premium

Given the following data, **calculate** the equity and debt risk premiums for Country X:

	Expected Standard Deviation	Correlation With Global Investable Market
Country X bonds	10%	0.40
Country X equities	15%	0.70
Market Sharpe ratio = 0.35		

RP_{bonds} = 10% × 0.40 × 0.35 = 1.40%

$RP_{equities}$ = 15% × 0.70 × 0.35 = 3.68%

The Singer and Terhaar analysis adjusts the ICAPM for market imperfections, such as illiquidity and segmentation. The more illiquid an asset is, the greater the liquidity risk premium should be. Liquidity is not typically a concern for developed world capital markets, but it can be a concern for assets such as direct real estate and private equity funds. In the case of private equity, an investment is usually subject to a lock-up period.

To estimate the size of the liquidity risk premium, one could estimate the *multi-period Sharpe ratio* for the investment over the time until it is liquid and compare it to the estimated multi-period Sharpe ratio for the market. The Sharpe ratio for the illiquid asset must be at least as high as that for the market. For example, suppose a venture capital investment has a lock-up period of five years and its multi-period Sharpe ratio is below that of the market's. If its expected return from the ICAPM is 16%, and the return necessary to equate its Sharpe ratio to that of the market's was 25%, then the liquidity premium would be 9%.

When markets are segmented, capital does not flow freely across borders. The opposite of segmented markets is integrated markets, where capital flows freely. Government restrictions on investing are a frequent cause of market segmentation. If markets are segmented, two assets with the same risk can have different expected returns because capital cannot flow to the higher return asset. The presence of investment barriers increases the risk premium for securities in segmented markets.

In reality, most markets are not fully segmented or integrated. For example, investors have a preference for their own country's equity markets (the *home country bias*). This prevents them from fully exploiting investment opportunities overseas. Developed world equity markets have been estimated as 80% integrated, whereas emerging market equities have been estimated as 65% integrated. In the example to follow, we will adjust for partial market segmentation by estimating an equity risk premium assuming full integration and an equity risk premium assuming full segmentation, and then taking a weighted average of the two. Under the full segmentation assumption, the relevant global portfolio is the individual market so that the correlation between the market and the global portfolio in the formula is 1. In that case, the equation for the market's risk premium reduces to:

$$\text{if } \rho_{i,M} = 1 \Rightarrow \text{ERP}_i = \sigma_i \left(\frac{\text{ERP}_M}{\sigma_M} \right)$$

In the following example, we will calculate the equity risk premium for the two markets, their expected returns, and the covariance between them. Before we start, recall from our discussion of factor models that the covariance between two markets given two factors is:

$$\text{Cov}(i,j) = \beta_{i,1}\beta_{j,1}\sigma_{F_1}^2 + \beta_{i,2}\beta_{j,2}\sigma_{F_2}^2 + \left(\beta_{i,1}\beta_{j,2} + \beta_{i,2}\beta_{j,1}\right)\text{Cov}\left(F_1, F_2\right)$$

If there is only one factor driving returns (i.e., the global portfolio), then the equation reduces to:

$$\text{Cov}(i,j) = \beta_i \beta_j \sigma_M^2$$

Example: Using market risk premiums to calculate expected returns, betas, and covariances

Suppose an analyst is valuing two equity markets. Market A is a developed market, and Market B is an emerging market. The investor's time horizon is five years. The other pertinent facts are:

Sharpe ratio of the global investable portfolio	0.29
Standard deviation of the global investable portfolio	9%
Risk-free rate of return	5%
Degree of market integration for Market A	80%
Degree of market integration for Market B	65%
Standard deviation of Market A	17%
Standard deviation of Market B	28%
Correlation of Market A with global investable portfolio	0.82
Correlation of Market B with global investable portfolio	0.63
Estimated illiquidity premium for A	0.0%
Estimated illiquidity premium for B	2.3%

Calculate the assets' expected returns, betas, and covariance.

Answer:

First, we calculate the equity risk premium for both markets assuming full integration. Note that for the emerging market, the illiquidity risk premium is included:

$$\text{ERP}_i = \rho_{i,M}\sigma_i\left(\text{market Sharpe ratio}\right)$$
$$\text{ERP}_A = (0.82)(0.17)(0.29) = 4.04\%$$
$$\text{ERP}_B = (0.63)(0.28)(0.29) + 0.0230 = 7.42\%$$

Next, we calculate the equity risk premium for both markets assuming full segmentation:

$$\text{ERP}_i = \sigma_i\left(\text{market Sharpe ratio}\right)$$
$$\text{ERP}_A = (0.17)(0.29) = 4.93\%$$
$$\text{ERP}_B = (0.28)(0.29) + 0.0230 = 10.42\%$$

Note that when we calculate the risk premium under full segmentation, we use the local market as the reference market instead of the global market, so the correlation between the local market and itself is 1.0.

We then weight the integrated and segmented risk premiums by the degree of integration and segmentation in each market to arrive at the weighted average equity risk premium:

$$ERP_i = \text{(degree of integration of } i)\text{(ERP assuming full integration)} +$$
$$\text{(degree of segmentation of } i)\text{(ERP assuming full segmentation)}$$

$$ERP_A = (0.80)(0.0404) + (1 - 0.80)(0.0493) = 4.22\%$$
$$ERP_B = (0.65)(0.0742) + (1 - 0.65)(0.1042) = 8.47\%$$

The expected return in each market figures in the risk-free rate:

$$\hat{R}_A = 5\% + 4.22\% = 9.22\%$$
$$\hat{R}_B = 5\% + 8.47\% = 13.47\%$$

The betas in each market, which will be needed for the covariance, are calculated as:

$$\beta_i = \frac{\rho_{i,M}\sigma_i}{\sigma_M}$$

$$\beta_A = \frac{(0.82)(17)}{9} = 1.55$$

$$\beta_B = \frac{(0.63)(28)}{9} = 1.96$$

Lastly, we calculate the covariance of the two equity markets:

$$\text{Cov}(i,j) = \beta_i\,\beta_j\,\sigma_M^2$$
$$\text{Cov}(A,B) = (1.55)(1.96)(9.0)^2 = 246.08$$

THE USE OF SURVEYS AND JUDGMENT FOR CAPITAL MARKET EXPECTATIONS

LOS 18.d: <u>Explain</u> the use of survey and panel methods and judgment in setting capital market expectations.

CFA® Program Curriculum, Volume 3, page 51

Capital market expectations can also be formed using **surveys**. In this method, a poll is taken of market participants, such as economists and analysts, as to what their expectations are regarding the economy or capital market. If the group polled is fairly constant over time, this method is referred to as a **panel method**. For example, the

U.S. Federal Reserve Bank of Philadelphia conducts an ongoing survey regarding the U.S. consumer price index, GDP, and so forth.[3]

Surveys have been taken regarding the equity risk premium, with investors expecting a premium in the range of 2–3.9%.[4] Other studies have found that the expectations of practitioners are consistently more optimistic than that of academics.[5] For the analyst wishing to back out market-wide expectations from analyst forecasts for individual firms, the data are provided by commercial services such as Thomson Financial's I/B/E/S and Zacks.[6]

Judgment can also be applied to project capital market expectations. Although quantitative models provide objective numerical forecasts, there are times when an analyst must adjust those expectations using their experience and insight to improve upon those forecasts.

CYCLICAL ANALYSIS

LOS 18.e: Discuss the inventory and business cycles, the impact of consumer and business spending, and monetary and fiscal policy on the business cycle.

CFA® Program Curriculum, Volume 3, page 54

The Inventory and Business Cycle

Understanding the business cycle can help the analyst identify *inflection points* (i.e., when the economy changes direction), where the risk and the opportunities for higher return may be heightened. To identify inflection points, the analyst should understand what is driving the current economy and what may cause the end of the current economy.

In general, economic growth can be partitioned into two components: (1) cyclical and (2) trend-growth components. The former is more short-term whereas the latter is more relevant for determining long-term return expectations. We will discuss the cyclical component first.

Within cyclical analysis, there are two components: (1) the inventory cycle and (2) the business cycle. The former typically lasts two to four years whereas the latter has a typical duration of nine to eleven years. These cycles vary in duration and are hard to predict because wars and other events can disrupt them.

---

3. Accessible at *www.philadelphiafed.org*; accessed August 2011.
4. Antti Ilmanen et al., "Stocks versus Bonds: Balancing Expectations and Reality" (Schroder Salomon Smith Barney, 2002).
   Jim O'Neill et al., "The Equity Risk Premium From an Economics Perspective" (Goldman Sachs, Global Economics Paper No. 84, 2002).
5. Martin Lally et al., "The Market Risk Premium in New Zealand Survey Evidence." *INFINZ Journal,* (Winter) 5–12.
6. See *www.zacks.com* for further details; accessed August 2011.

Changes in economic activity delineate cyclical activity. The measures of economic activity are GDP, the output gap, and a recession. GDP is usually measured in real terms because true economic growth should be adjusted for inflationary components. The **output gap** is the difference between the current GDP and GDP based on a long-term trend line (i.e., potential GDP). When the trend line is higher than the current GDP, the economy has slowed and inflationary pressures have weakened. When it is lower, economic activity is strong, as are inflationary pressures. This relationship is used by policy makers to form expectations regarding the appropriate level of growth and inflation. The relationship is affected by changes in technology and demographics. The third measure of economic activity, a **recession**, is defined as decreases (i.e., negative growth) in GDP over two consecutive quarters.

The **inventory cycle** is often measured using the inventory to sales ratio. The measure increases when businesses gain confidence in the future of the economy and add to their inventories in anticipation of increasing demand for their output. As a result, employment increases with subsequent increases in economic growth. This continues until some precipitating factor, such as a tightening in the growth of the money supply, intervenes. At this point, inventories decrease, employment declines, and economic growth slows.

When the inventory measure has peaked in an economy, as in the United States in 2000, subsequent periods exhibit slow growth as businesses sell out of their inventory. When it bottoms out, as in 2004, subsequent periods have higher growth as businesses restock their inventory. The long-term trend in this measure has been downward due to more effective inventory management techniques such as just-in-time inventory management.

The longer-term **business cycle** is characterized by five phases: (1) the initial recovery, (2) early expansion, (3) late expansion, (4) slowdown, and (5) recession. We discuss the business cycle in greater detail later when we examine its effect on asset returns.

Inflation

Aggregate inflation is measured most frequently by consumer price indices. Inflation rises in the latter stages of economic expansion and falls during a recession and the initial recovery. When forecasting, the analyst should adjust the inflation figure for long-term changes in inflation. Historically, inflation had been low because monetary growth was limited by the gold standard. Inflation rose in the developed world in the 1970s but has been tamed more recently.

Deflation, or periods of decreasing prices, reduces the ability of the central bank to stimulate the economy. Deflation results in interest rates near zero, so the central bank cannot lower rates any further to stimulate the economy. For this reason, central banks prefer a low level of inflation to the prospect of deflation.

Consumer and Business Spending

As a percentage of GDP, consumer spending is much larger than business spending. Consumer spending is usually gauged through the use of store sales data, retail sales, and consumer consumption data. The data has a seasonal pattern, with sales increasing near holidays. In turn, the primary driver of consumer spending is consumer after-tax income, which in the United States is gauged using non-farm payroll data and new unemployment claims. Employment data is important to markets because it is usually quite timely.

Given that spending is income net of savings, savings data are also important for predicting consumer spending. Saving rates are influenced by consumer confidence and changes in the investment environment. Specifically, consumer confidence increases as the economy begins to recover from a recession, and consumers begin to spend more. At the same time, stock prices start to rise and momentum begins to build. Consumers continue spending until the economy shows definite signs that it has peaked (i.e., top of the business cycle) and reversed. At this point, consumers begin saving more and more until the economy "turns the corner," and the cycle starts over.

Business spending is more volatile than consumer spending. Spending by businesses on inventory and investments is quite volatile over the business cycle. As mentioned before, the peak of inventory spending is often a bearish signal for the economy. It may indicate that businesses have overspent relative to the amount they are selling. This portends a slowdown in business spending and economic growth.

Monetary Policy

Central banks use monetary policy to optimize the economy's performance. Most banks strive to balance price stability against economic growth. The ultimate goal is to keep growth near its long-run sustainable rate, because growth faster than the long-run rate usually results in increased inflation. As discussed previously, the latter stages of an economic expansion are often characterized by increased inflation. As a result, central banks usually resort to restrictive policies towards the latter part of an expansion.

To spur growth, a central bank will cut short-term interest rates. This results in greater consumer spending, greater business spending, higher stock prices, and higher bond prices. Lower interest rates also usually result in a lower value of the domestic currency, which is thought to increase exports. In addition to the direction of a change in interest rates being important, it is also the level of interest rates that is important. If, for example, rates are increased to 4% to combat inflation but this is still low compared to the average of 6% in a country, then this rate may still be low enough to allow growth and inflation to continue. The equilibrium interest rate in a country (the rate at which a balance between growth and inflation is achieved) is referred to as the neutral rate. It is generally thought that the neutral rate is composed of an inflation component and a real growth component. If, for example, inflation is targeted at 3% and the economy is expected to grow by 2%, then the neutral rate would be 5%.

Fiscal Policy

Another tool at the government's disposal for managing the economy is fiscal policy. If the government wants to stimulate the economy, it can decrease taxes and/or increase spending, thereby increasing the budget deficit. If they want to rein in growth, the government does the opposite.

There are two important aspects to fiscal policy. First, it is not the level of the budget deficit that matters—it is the change in the deficit. For example, a deficit by itself does not stimulate the economy, but increases in the deficit are required to stimulate the economy. Second, changes in the deficit that occur naturally over the course of the business cycle are not stimulative or restrictive. In an expanding economy, deficits will decline because tax receipts increase and disbursements to the unemployed decrease. The opposite occurs during a recession. Only changes in the deficit directed by government policy will influence growth.

BUSINESS CYCLES, INFLATION, AND ASSET RETURNS

LOS 18.f: <u>Discuss</u> the impact that the phases of the business cycle have on short-term/longterm capital market returns.

CFA® Program Curriculum, Volume 3, page 56

LOS 18.g: <u>Explain</u> the relationship of inflation to the business cycle and the implications of inflation for cash, bonds, equity, and real estate returns.

CFA® Program Curriculum, Volume 3, page 58

For the Exam: Be able to discuss the inventory and business cycles, as well as their relationship to one another. Do not focus on memorizing the bullet points under Initial Recovery, Early Expansion, et cetera. Instead, have a working knowledge of, and be able to explain, the general relationships between interest rates, inflation, stock and bond prices, inventory levels, et cetera, as you progress over the cycle. For example, approaching the peak of the business cycle, everything is humming along. Confidence and employment are high, but inflation is starting to have an impact on markets. As inflation increases, bond yields increase and both bond and stock prices start to fall.

Be able to write out this type of discussion, but do not overemphasize the various phases of the cycle or their relative lengths. You may see questions aimed directly at this material, but you are more likely to see an analyst who has made forecasts based on where the economy is in the cycle and then have to agree or disagree and state why (if you disagree).

The Business Cycle and Asset Returns

The relationship between the business cycle and assets returns is well documented. Assets with higher returns during business cycle lows (e.g., bonds and defensive stocks) should be favored by investors because the return supplements their income during recessionary periods. These assets should have lower risk premiums. Assets with lower returns during recessions should have higher risk premiums. Understanding the relationship between an asset's return and the business cycle can help the analyst provide better valuations.

As mentioned before, inflation varies over the business cycle, which has five phases: (1) initial recovery, (2) early expansion, (3) late expansion, (4) slowdown, and (5) recession. Inflation rises in the latter stages of an expansion and falls during a recession and the initial recovery. The phases have the following characteristics:

Initial Recovery

- Duration of a few months.
- Business confidence is rising.
- Government stimulation is provided by low interest rates and/or budget deficits.
- Falling inflation.
- Low or falling short-term interest rates.
- Bond yields have bottomed out.
- Rising stock prices.

Early Expansion

- Duration of a year to several years.
- Increasing growth with low inflation.
- Increasing confidence.
- Increasing inventories.
- Rising short-term interest rates.
- Flat or rising bond yields.
- Rising stock prices.

Late Expansion

- Confidence and employment are high.
- Inflation increases.
- Central bank limits the growth of the money supply.
- Rising short-term interest rates.
- Rising bond yields.
- Rising stock prices, but risk increases with investor nervousness.

Slowdown

- Duration of a few months to a year or longer.
- Declining confidence.
- Inflation is still rising.
- Falling inventory levels.
- Short-term interest rates are at a peak.
- Bond yields have peaked and may be falling.
- Falling stock prices.

Recession

- Duration of six months to a year.
- Large declines in inventory.
- Declining confidence and profits.
- Inflation tops out.
- Falling short-term interest rates.
- Falling bond yields, rising prices.
- Stock prices increase during the latter stages anticipating the end of the recession.

Although it is straightforward to describe the characteristics of the various phases of the business cycle, it is not so easy to predict when they will occur. Furthermore, even if the start of a recession could be predicted, the length and severity of a recession is unpredictable.

Inflation and Asset Returns

The link between asset prices and inflation is inextricably tied to the business cycle. As noted previously, inflation increases as the economy expands and declines when the economy slows. Inflation is negative for bonds. Hence, in a strong expansion, bonds tend to decline in price as inflationary expectations and interest rates rise. Bond prices will rise during a recession when inflation and interest rates are declining. This is also true during deflationary times. The exception here is when credit risk for a particular issue or sector increases during a recession.

Low inflation can be positive for equities given that there are prospects for economic growth free of central bank interference. Equities provide an inflation hedge when inflation is moderate and when price increases can be passed along to the consumer. Inflation rates above 3% can be problematic, though, because of increased likelihood that the central bank will restrict economic growth. Declining inflation or deflation is also problematic because this usually results in declining economic growth and asset prices. The firms most affected are those that are highly levered and are thus most sensitive to changing interest rates. They would face declining profits yet would still be obligated to pay back the same amount of interest and principal.

Deflation also reduces the value of real assets financed with debt. In the case of real estate, if the property is levered with debt, declines in the property's value lead to steeper declines in the equity position. As a result, investors flee in an attempt to preserve their equity. Fortunately, with central banks no longer tied to the gold standard, they are free to pursue the measures necessary to avoid deflation, so its occurrences are quite rare. When inflation is at or below expectations, the cash flows for real estate and other real assets rise slowly, and returns are near their long-run average. When inflation is high, the cash flows and returns for real assets are higher. In the case of many properties, rents often increase as inflation increases. Thus, real estate provides a good inflation hedge.

Low inflation does not affect the return on cash instruments. Higher inflation is a positive for cash because the returns on cash instruments increase as inflation increases. Deflation is negative for cash because the return falls to almost zero.

THE TAYLOR RULE

LOS 18.h: <u>Demonstrate</u> the use of the Taylor rule to predict central bank behavior.

CFA® Program Curriculum, Volume 3, page 66

Recall that the neutral interest rate is the short-term interest rate that will balance the risks of inflation and recession. The neutral rate is the rate that most central banks strive to achieve as they attempt to balance the aforementioned risks. If inflation is too high, the central bank should increase short-term interest rates. If economic growth is too low, it should cut interest rates. The **Taylor rule** embodies this concept. It is thus used as a prescriptive tool (i.e., it states what the central bank should do). It also is fairly accurate at predicting central bank action.

For the Exam: Be able to discuss and apply the Taylor rule.

The Taylor rule determines the target interest rate using the neutral rate, expected GDP relative to its long-term trend, and expected inflation relative to its targeted amount. It can be formalized as follows:

$$r_{target} = r_{neutral} + \left[0.5\left(GDP_{expected} - GDP_{trend}\right) + 0.5\left(i_{expected} - i_{target}\right) \right]$$

where:

r_{target} = short-term interest rate target

$r_{neutral}$ = neutral short-term interest rate

$GDP_{expected}$ = expected GDP growth rate

GDP_{trend} = long-term trend in the GDP growth rate

$i_{expected}$ = expected inflation rate

i_{target} = target inflation rate

Example: Calculating the short-term interest rate target

Given the following information, **calculate** the short-term interest rate target.

Neutral rate	4%
Inflation target	3%
Expected inflation	7%
GDP long-term trend	2%
Expected GDP	0%

Answer:

$$r_{target} = 4\% + \left[0.5\left(0\% - 2\%\right) + 0.5\left(7\% - 3\%\right) \right]$$
$$= 4\% + \left(-1\% + 2\%\right) = 5\%$$

In this example, the weak projected economic growth calls for cutting interest rates. If inflation were not a consideration, the target interest rate would be 1% lower than the neutral rate. However, the higher projected inflation overrides the growth concern because projected inflation is 4% greater than the target inflation rate. In net, the target rate is 5% because the concern over high inflation overrides the weak growth concern.

THE YIELD CURVE

LOS 18.i: Evaluate 1) the shape of the yield curve as an economic predictor and 2) the relationship between the yield curve and fiscal and monetary policy.

CFA® Program Curriculum, Volume 3, page 69

The yield curve demonstrates the relationship between interest rates and the maturity of the debt security and is sensitive to actions of the federal government as well as current and expected economic conditions. When both fiscal and monetary policies are expansive, for example, the yield curve is sharply upward sloping (i.e., short-term rates are lower than long-term rates), and the economy is likely to expand in the future. When fiscal and monetary policies are restrictive, the yield curve is downward sloping (i.e., it is *inverted,* as short-term rates are higher than long-term rates), and the economy is likely to contract in the future.

When fiscal and monetary policies are in disagreement, the shape of the yield curve is less definitive. Recall that monetary policy controls primarily short-term interest rates. If monetary policy is expansive while fiscal policy is restrictive, the yield curve will be upward sloping, though it will be less steep than when both policies are expansive. If monetary policy is restrictive while fiscal policy is expansive, the yield curve will be more or less flat.

ECONOMIC GROWTH TRENDS

LOS 18.j: Identify and interpret the components of economic growth trends and demonstrate the application of economic growth trend analysis to the formulation of capital market expectations.

CFA® Program Curriculum, Volume 3, page 69

Economic growth can be partitioned into cyclical and trend components. Economic trends determine long-term economic growth whereas as cyclical components are shorter term. Trends are determined in part by demographics, productivity, and structural changes in governmental policies.

In forecasting a country's long-term economic growth trend, the trend growth rate can be decomposed into two main components: (1) **changes in employment levels** and (2) **changes in productivity**. Essentially, the two together measure how many people are working and what each person's output is. The former component can be further broken down into **population growth** and the **rate of labor force participation**.

For example, employment levels may increase in the United States both due to an influx of immigrants and due to senior citizens staying in the workforce longer. Some developed countries tend to have an older population that limits their growth (e.g., Japan). Government policies that encourage workforce participation increase the labor force participation growth rate.

The productivity component can be broken down into subcomponents as well: **spending on new capital inputs** and **total factor productivity growth**. The latter results from more efficient use of inputs and better technology. The former component accounts for much of the fast growth in Asia, as much has been spent there on new equipment. Note that as an investment grows, the earnings derived from it must grow faster for higher stock prices to result. This may explain why some fast growing, high investment economies have unimpressive stock returns (i.e., their fast growth is not fast enough). Some developed countries have laws that limit increases in productivity. For example, in Germany, labor regulations are fairly rigid and limit increases in worker productivity.

Example: Forecasting the long-term economic growth rate

Assume that the population is expected to grow by 2% and that labor force participation is expected to grow by 0.25%. If spending on new capital inputs is projected to grow at 2.5% and total factor productivity will grow by 0.5%, what is the long-term projected growth rate?

Answer:

The sum of the components equals 2% + 0.25% + 2.5% + 0.5% = 5.25%, so the economy is projected to grow by this amount.

Higher long-term growth rate trends benefit the equity investor through a higher growth rate, usually without excessive inflation. The trend growth rates for developed countries are fairly stable over time, while emerging countries are expected to have higher trending growth rates. Eventually, though, emerging countries grow into developed countries, and their growth slows.

As mentioned before, consumer spending is the largest component of GDP and is fairly stable over the business cycle. The reason is that individuals tend to consume an amount that is fairly constant over time and related to their expected long-run income. This is the essence of Milton Friedman's permanent income hypothesis. As applied to the formulation of capital market expectations, it means that economic slowdowns will not affect consumer consumption much. In a recession, individuals will save less and decrease their consumption by only a small amount. In an expansion, individuals consume more, but less than their income increases. In sum, when events occur that consumers perceive as temporary, their consumption and aggregate consumer spending will not change a great deal.

A more important component of changes in the long-term growth rate in an economy is governmental structural policies, which are policies designed to enhance or regulate growth. The question, however, is the types of policies that enhance growth, and there are four general guidelines.

First, although the government should provide the infrastructure needed for growth (e.g., roads, the internet, educational systems), the government should interfere with the economy as little as possible. It is generally agreed that the private sector provides the most efficient allocation of resources. Although most governments are trending towards privatization of formerly owned government businesses, there is still a good deal of government regulation.

Second, a government should have a responsible *fiscal policy*. Although budget deficits may be used to stimulate the economy, consistently high budget deficits often lead to inflation when the central bank accommodates the deficit with higher growth in the money supply. Budget deficits are also often accompanied by trade deficits, which may result in an eventual devaluation of the home currency. In addition, public borrowing may *crowd out* more productive private borrowing.

Third, a government should have tax policies that are transparent, consistently applied, pulled from a wide base, and not overly burdensome. Although some inefficiency is expected from the redistribution of wealth, tax policies should promote growth as much as possible.

Lastly, the government should promote competition in the marketplace, thereby increasing the efficiency of the economy. Technological advances and openness to foreign competition through the reduction of tariffs are important factors for growth.

In addition to being influenced by governmental policies, trends are still subject to unexpected surprises or shocks that are exogenous to the economy, and many shocks and the degree of their impact on capital markets cannot be forecasted. For example, turmoil in the Middle East may change the long-term trend for oil prices, inflation, and economic growth in the developed world. Shocks may also arise through the banking system. An extreme example is the U.S. banking crisis of the 1930s, when a severe slowdown in bank lending paralyzed the economy.

LOS 18.k: <u>Explain</u> how exogenous shocks may affect economic growth trends.

CFA® Program Curriculum, Volume 3, page 75

Exogenous shocks are unanticipated events that occur outside the normal course of an economy. Since the events are unanticipated, they are not already built into current market prices, whereas normal trends in an economy, which would be considered endogenous, are built into market prices. Exogenous shocks can be caused by different factors, such as natural disasters, political events, or changes in government policies.

Although positive shocks are not unknown, exogenous shocks usually produce a negative impact on an economy and oftentimes spread to other countries in a process referred to as *contagion*. Two common shocks relate to changes in oil supplies and crises in financial markets. Oil shocks have historically involved increasing prices caused by a reduction in oil production. The increased oil prices can lead to increased inflation and a subsequent slowdown of the economy from decreased consumer spending and increased unemployment. Conversely, a decline in oil prices, as was the case in 1986 and 1999, can produce lower inflation, which boosts the economy. A significant decline in oil prices, however, can lead to an overheated economy and increasing inflation.

Financial crises are also not uncommon. Consider the Latin America debt crisis in the early 1980s, the devaluation of the Mexican peso in 1994, the Asian and Russian financial crises of the late 1990s, and most recently, the worldwide decline in property values. Banks are usually vulnerable in a financial crisis, so the central bank steps in to provide financial support by increasing the amount of money in circulation to reduce interest rates. This is difficult to do, however, in an already low inflation, low interest rate environment and especially in a deflationary environment.

LINKS BETWEEN ECONOMIES

LOS 18.l: <u>Identify</u> and <u>interpret</u> macroeconomic, interest rate, and exchange rate linkages between economies.

CFA® Program Curriculum, Volume 3, page 77

Economic links between countries have become increasingly important through time, especially for small countries with undiversified economies. Larger countries with diverse economies, such as the United States, are less affected but are still influenced by globalization.

Macroeconomic links refer to similarities in business cycles across countries. Economies are linked by both international trade and capital flows so that a recession in one country dampens exports and investment in a second country, thereby creating a slowdown in the second country. Note, though, that even among developed countries, economies are not perfectly integrated. For example, the Federal Reserve in the United States and the European Central Bank will respond to local effects in their economies, which creates differences in U.S. and European economic growth.

Another link between economies results from **exchange rates**. As an extreme case, Ecuador has adopted the U.S. dollar as its currency. More commonly, many countries peg their currency to others. For example, until 2005, China pegged their currency to the U.S. dollar. The benefit of a peg is that currency volatility is reduced and inflation can be brought under control. Countries are not always successful in maintaining a peg, however, because the weaker country in the peg usually abandons it, devaluing their currency. For this reason, interest rates between the two countries will often reflect a risk premium, with the weaker country having higher interest rates.

Professor's Note: When a currency is pegged, its value is set at a fixed exchange rate with another currency (or to a basket of currencies or another measure of value, such as gold). As the value of the other currency rises and falls, so does the value of the currency pegged to it. The opposite of a fixed exchange rate is a floating exchange rate, which is often preferred because it allows the currency to respond directly to foreign exchange markets. In addition, pegged exchange rates deprive federal governments the use of monetary policy to help control economic growth.

Interest rate differentials between countries can also reflect differences in economic growth, monetary policy, and fiscal policy. For example, in the early 1980s, the United States had a robust economy, an increasing budget deficit, and high real and nominal interest rates due to a tight monetary policy. It is theorized that real interest rate differentials between countries should not exist, and over time, exchange rates will equalize differences. Countries with high *real interest rates* should see the value of their currency increase.

Professor's Note: Don't be confused with the relationships in Study Session 10, in which the currency of the country with the higher relative nominal interest rate will sell at a forward discount (i.e., is expected to depreciate). In Study Session 10, we assume real rates are equal, so forward discounts or premiums are based upon inflation expectations.

EMERGING MARKET ECONOMIES

LOS 18.m: <u>Discuss</u> the risks faced by investors in emerging-market securities and the country risk analysis techniques used to evaluate emerging market economies.

CFA® Program Curriculum, Volume 3, page 79

Emerging markets offer the investor high returns at the expense of higher risk. Many emerging markets require a heavy investment in physical and human (e.g., education) infrastructure. To finance this infrastructure, many emerging countries are dependent on foreign borrowing, which can later create crisis situations in their economy, currency, and financial markets.

Many emerging countries also have unstable political and social systems. The lack of a middle class in these countries does not provide the constituency for needed structural reforms. These small economies are often heavily dependent on the sale of commodities, and their undiversified nature makes them susceptible to volatile capital flows and economic crises.

The investor must carefully analyze the risk in these countries. For the bond investor, the primary risk is credit risk—does the country have the capacity and willingness to pay back its debt? For equity investors, the focus is on growth prospects and risk. There are six questions potential investors should ask themselves before committing funds to these markets.

1. **Does the country have responsible fiscal and monetary policies?** To gauge fiscal policy, most analysts examine the deficit to GDP ratio. Ratios greater than 4% indicate substantial credit risk. Most emerging counties borrow short term and must refinance on a periodic basis. A buildup of debt increases the likelihood that the country will not be able to make its payments.

2. **What is the expected growth?** To compensate for the higher risk in these countries, investors should expect a growth rate of at least 4%. Growth rates less than that may indicate that the economy is growing slower than the population, which can be problematic in these underdeveloped countries. The structure of an economy and government regulation is important for growth. Tariffs, tax policies, and regulation of foreign investment are all important factors for growth.

3. **Does the country have reasonable currency values and current account deficits?** A volatile currency discourages needed foreign investment, and an overvalued currency may encourage excessive borrowing by the emerging market government. Current

account deficits (roughly speaking, imports are greater than exports) greater than 4% of GDP can be problematic because the deficit must be financed through external borrowing.

4. **Is the country too highly levered?** Although emerging countries are dependent on foreign financing for growth, too much debt can eventually lead to a financial crisis if foreign capital flees the country. These financial crises are accompanied by currency devaluations and declines in emerging market asset values. Foreign debt levels greater than 50% of GDP indicate that the country may be overlevered. Debt levels greater than 200% of the current account receipts also indicate high risk.

5. **What is the level of foreign exchange reserves relative to short-term debt?** Foreign exchange is important because many emerging country loans must be paid back in a foreign currency. The investor should be wary of countries where the foreign exchange reserves are less than the foreign debt that must be paid off within one year.

6. **What is the government's stance regarding structural reform?** If the government is supportive of structural reforms necessary for growth, then the investment environment is more hospitable. When the government is committed to responsible fiscal policies, competition, and the privatization of state-owned businesses, there are better prospects for growth.

ECONOMIC FORECASTING

LOS 18.n: Compare the major approaches to economic forecasting.

CFA® Program Curriculum, Volume 3, page 82

To determine capital market expectations, analysts use a variety of approaches. We examine three of the most common methods: (1) econometrics, (2) economic indicators, and (3) a checklist approach. After a brief introduction to each, we describe each method's advantages and disadvantages.

Econometric analysis utilizes economic theory to formulate the forecasting model. The models can be quite simple to very complex, involving several data items of various time period lags to predict the future. For example, the analyst may want to forecast GDP using current and lagged consumption and investment. The analyst may even input forecasts of consumption and investment to forecast GDP. Ordinary least squares regression is most often used, but other statistical methods are also available.

Advantages:

- Once established, can be reused.
- Can be quite complex and may accurately model real world conditions.
- Can provide precise quantitative forecasts of economic conditions.

Disadvantages:

- May be difficult and time intensive (expensive) to create.
- Proposed model may not be applicable in future time periods.
- Better at forecasting expansions than recessions.
- Requires scrutiny of output to verify validity.

Economic indicators are available from governments, international organizations (e.g., the Organization of Economic Cooperation and Development), and private organizations (e.g., the Conference Board in the United States). They attempt to characterize an economy's phase in the business cycle and are separated into lagging indicators, coincident indicators, and leading indicators. Using their own indicators or those provided by an outside source, analysts prefer leading indicators because they help predict the future path of the economy. The leading indicators can be used individually or as a composite. As an example of the latter, the Conference Board provides ten leading indicators. Some analysts would use these in an index, where if the majority of the indicators predict expansion, the analyst forecasts an economic expansion.

Advantages:

- Available from outside parties.
- Easy to understand and interpret.
- Can be adapted for specific purposes.
- Effectiveness has been verified by academic research.

Disadvantages:

- Not consistently accurate as economic relationships change through time.
- Forecasts from leading indicators can be misleading.

In a **checklist approach**, the analyst checks off a list of questions that should indicate the future growth of the economy. For example, to forecast GDP the analyst may want to ask himself, "What was the latest employment report? What is most likely the central bank's next move, given the latest information released? What is the latest report on business investment?"

Given the answers to these questions, the analyst can then use his judgment to formulate a forecast or derive a more formal model using statistics. In either case, subjective assessments must be made as to what variables are important for the forecasts.

Advantages:

- Simple.
- Allows changes in the model over time.

Disadvantages:

- Requires subjective judgment.
- May be time intensive to create.
- May not be able to model complex relationships.

> **For the Exam:** This forecasting material could easily be put into the framework of two analysts arguing about forecasting techniques, and you would have to critique statements they make.

ECONOMIC CONDITIONS AND ASSET CLASS RETURNS

LOS 18.o: <u>Demonstrate</u> the use of economic information in forecasting asset class returns.

CFA® Program Curriculum, Volume 3, page 90

LOS 18.p: <u>Evaluate</u> how economic and competitive factors affect investment markets, sectors, and specific securities.

CFA® Program Curriculum, Volume 3, page 96

Investors ultimately use capital market expectations to form their beliefs about the attractiveness of different investments. This is one of the primary steps in top-down analysis. We next examine how economic information can be used in forecasting asset class returns. We start with cash.

> **For the Exam:** Now we get to allocating assets according to our capital market expectations and how we expect assets to react to them. I would expect this to show up on the exam in determining a tactical allocation for an active manager.

Cash Instruments

Cash typically refers to short-term debt (e.g., commercial paper) with a maturity of one year or less. Cash managers adjust the maturity and creditworthiness of their cash investments depending on their forecasts for interest rates and the economy. If, for example, a manager thinks interest rates are set to rise, he will shift from 9-month cash instruments down to 3-month cash instruments. If he thinks the economy is going to improve, so that less creditworthy instruments have less chance of default, he will shift more assets into lower-rated cash instruments. Longer maturity and less creditworthy instruments have higher expected return but also more risk.

The interest rate for overnight loans among U.S. banks is the Federal Funds rate and is set by the Federal Reserve through its purchases and sales of government debt. This rate is fairly stable except during periods of unusual market volatility. In the European Union, the European Central Bank targets the repo rate.

The yield for debt securities of various maturities reflects the market's anticipation of yields over future periods. To earn excess returns, the manager must be able to forecast future rates better than other managers, and this in part requires anticipation of what the central bank will do in the future.

Credit Risk-Free Bonds

The most common type of credit risk-free bonds are those issued by governments in developed countries. The yield on these bonds is composed of a real yield and the expected inflation over the investment horizon. If, for example, the investor thinks that inflation will be 2% over the life of the bond and the investor requires a real return of 4%, then the investor would only purchase the bond if its yield were 6% or more. Based on historical data, the real yield on an ex ante basis should be roughly 2–4%.

The investor with a short time horizon will focus on cyclical changes in the economy and changes in short-term interest rates. Higher expected economic growth results in higher yields because of anticipated greater demand for loanable funds and possibly higher inflation. A change in short-term rates, however, has less predictable effects. Usually an increase in short-term rates increases the yields on medium- and long-term bonds. Medium- and long-term bond yields may actually fall, though, if the interest rate increase is gauged sufficient to slow the economy.

Over the past 40 years, the inflation premium embedded in bonds has varied quite a bit in developed countries. In the 1960s, it was quite low but rose in the late 1970s as investors became accustomed to higher inflation. More recently, it has dropped as inflation has been low.

Credit Risky Bonds

The most common type of credit risky bonds are corporate bonds. To estimate the credit risk premium assigned to individual bonds, the analyst could subtract the yield of Treasuries from that of corporate bonds of the same maturity. During a recession, the credit risk premium increases because default becomes more likely. At the same time, the credit offered by banks and the commercial paper market also dries up so that corporations have to offer higher yields to attract investors. More favorable economic conditions result in lower credit risk premiums.

Emerging Market Government Bonds

The key difference between developed country government bonds and emerging market government bonds is that most emerging debt is denominated in a non-domestic currency. Emerging market bonds are usually denominated in a hard currency (e.g., dollars, euros); thus, the emerging market government must obtain the hard currency to pay back the principal and interest. The default risk for emerging market debt is appropriately higher. To assess this risk, analysts use country risk analysis, which focuses on the economic and political environment in a country (as discussed previously for emerging markets).

Inflation-Indexed Bonds

Several governments issue bonds that adjust for inflation so that the investor is protected against it. An example is U.S. Treasury Inflation Protected Securities (TIPS). These bonds are both credit risk and inflation risk free. Their yields still vary, however, as economic conditions change and as the supply and demand for these instruments vary. In fact, if inflation starts rising, the yields for these bonds will actually fall because the demand for them increases as investors seek out their inflation protection.

Common Stock

To understand how economic conditions affect stock values, recall that the value of an asset is the present value of its future cash flows. For stocks, both the cash flows (earnings) and discount rate (risk-adjusted required return) are important. Earnings are commonly used to value the stock market because they should be reflected in both the cash paid out as dividends and as capital gains. Aggregate earnings depend primarily on the trended rate of growth in an economy, which in turn depends on the growth in the labor force, new capital inputs, and total factor productivity growth.

As discussed earlier, when the government promotes competition in the marketplace, this increases the efficiency of the economy and should lead to higher long-term growth in the economy and the stock market. Of course, an investor would prefer an individual stock to have a monopolistic, noncompetitive position in their product market. This, however, would not be healthy for the growth of the overall stock market.

Shorter-term growth is affected by the business cycle. In a recession, sales and earnings decrease. Noncyclical or defensive stocks (e.g., utilities) are less affected by the business cycle and will have lower risk premiums and higher valuations than cyclical stocks (e.g., technology firms). Cyclical stocks are characterized by high business risk (sensitivity to the business cycle) and/or high fixed costs (operating leverage).

Recall that in the early expansion phase of the business cycle, stock prices are generally increasing. This is because sales are increasing, but input costs are fairly stable. For example, labor does not ask for wage increases because unemployment is still high, and idle plant and equipment can be pushed into service at little cost. Furthermore, firms usually emerge from a recession leaner because they have shed their wasteful projects and excessive spending. Later on in the expansion, earnings growth slows because input costs start to increase. As mentioned earlier, interest rates will also increase during late expansion, which is a further negative for stock valuation.

A stock's valuation in the market is reflected in its price-earnings (P/E) ratio. P/E ratios are higher in an early expansion period when interest rates are low and earnings prospects are high. They decline as earnings prospects decline. Note that for cyclical stocks, P/E ratios may be quite high in a recession, if investors are anticipating that the economy will soon recover. P/E ratios are also affected by long-term trends. For example, the 1990s was thought to be a new era of productivity, earnings growth, low inflation, and low interest rates. P/E ratios were abnormally high during this time period. Low inflation results in high P/E ratios because earnings are more *real* and less subject to interpretation.

Emerging Market Stocks

Historical returns for emerging market stocks are higher and more variable than those in the developed world and seem to be positively correlated with business cycles in the developed world. This correlation is due to trade flows and capital flows. In addition, emerging countries share many of the same sectors as those in the developed world. The analyst should thus have a good understanding of country and sector patterns when valuing emerging market stocks.

Real Estate

Real estate assets are affected by interest rates, inflation, the shape of the yield curve, and consumption. Interest rates affect both the supply of, and demand for, properties through mortgage financing rates. They also determine the capitalization rate (i.e., discount rate) used to value cash flows.

FORECASTING EXCHANGE RATES

LOS 18.q: <u>Discuss</u> the relative advantages and limitations of the major approaches to forecasting exchange rates.

CFA® Program Curriculum, Volume 3, page 103

The value of a currency is determined by its supply and demand, which in turn is affected by trade flows and capital flows. For example, if the United States has a trade deficit with Japan (i.e., it imports more from Japan than it exports to Japan), the value of the dollar should decline against the yen. The reason is that to obtain the foreign good, U.S. consumers are essentially selling their dollars to obtain yen.

In regard to capital flows, if U.S. Treasury bonds are in high demand due to their safety and attractive return, foreign investors will sell their currency in order to obtain dollars. The value of the foreign currency will fall while the value of the dollar will rise. Capital will flow into a country when capital restrictions are reduced, when an economy's strong growth attracts new capital, or when interest rates are attractive. Higher interest rates generally attract capital and increase the domestic currency value. At some level, though, higher interest rates will result in lower currency values because the high rates may stifle an economy and make it less attractive to invest there.

The emphasis on international diversification has increased capital flows. Capital flows can be volatile but are less so if the capital is invested in real assets through foreign direct investment. Currency values can also become volatile when a country is forced to abandon a pegged value targeted by its government.

The volatility in currency values makes them difficult to forecast but presents both risks and rewards for portfolio managers. We examine four methods of forecasting exchange rates: (1) relative purchasing power parity, (2) relative economic strength, (3) capital flows, and (4) savings and investment imbalances.

The first method is the relative form of **purchasing power parity** (PPP). PPP states that differences in inflation between two countries will be reflected in changes in the exchange rate between them. Specifically, the country with higher inflation will see its currency value decline. For example, assume Japanese inflation is projected to be a cumulative 8.2% over the next five years, while U.S. inflation is 13.2% over the same period. U.S. inflation is thus projected to be 5% higher. If the current exchange rate is ¥100/$, then the projected exchange rate is approximately ¥100/$ × (1 − 0.05) = ¥95/$ (note that the dollar has depreciated here because it buys five less yen).

PPP does not hold in the short term or medium term but holds approximately in the long term (five years or more). PPP is given attention by governments and forecasters, but its influence on exchange rates may be swamped by other factors, such as trade deficits.

The second method of forecasting currency values is the **relative economic strength approach**. The idea behind this approach is that a favorable investment climate will attract investors, which will increase the demand for the domestic currency, increasing its value. Investors may be attracted by short-term interest rates or by the economic growth in a country. High short-term interest rates will attract investors who bid up the currency value over the short term. Low short-term interest rates will result in borrowing in the currency. After the borrowers take out their loan, they sell the currency for another, thereby putting downward pressure on the low interest rate currency.

The third approach to forecasting exchange rates is the **capital flows approach**. This approach focuses primarily on long-term capital flows, such as those into equity investments or foreign direct investments. For example, the strength of the U.S. dollar in the later 1990s was thought to be due to the strength of the U.S. stock market.

The flow of long-term funds complicates the relationship between short-term rates and currency values as discussed in the relative strength approach. For example, a cut in U.S. short-term rates may actually strengthen the dollar because the cut might promote U.S. growth and the attractiveness of U.S. stocks. This makes the central bank's job more difficult. If the Federal Reserve wanted to boost short-term rates to increase the value of the dollar and tame inflation, their action may actually result in a decline in the value of the dollar as investors find U.S. capital assets less attractive.

The last approach is the **savings-investment imbalances approach**. This approach is not readily implemented for forecasting but explains why currencies may diverge from equilibrium values for extended periods. This approach starts with the concept that an economy must fund investment through savings. If investment is greater than domestic savings, then capital must flow into the country from abroad to finance the investment. A savings deficit can be attributable to both the government and private sector.

In order to attract and keep the capital necessary to compensate for the savings deficit, the domestic currency must increase in value and stay strong (perhaps as a result of high interest rates or economic growth). At the same time, the country will have a current account deficit where exports are less than imports. Although a current account deficit would normally indicate that the currency will weaken, the currency must stay strong to attract foreign capital.

The aforementioned scenario typically occurs during an economic expansion when businesses are optimistic and use their savings to make investments. Eventually, though, the economy slows, investment slows, and domestic savings increase. It is at this point that the currency will decline in value.

In addition to the four approaches described previously, one could also examine government intervention to determine the future path of exchange rates. This approach is not very fruitful, though, because most observers don't think governments can exert much control over exchange rates. The reason is that government trading is too small in volume to affect the massive currency markets. Furthermore, currencies are more influenced by economic fundamentals than by periodic trading by governments.

REALLOCATING A GLOBAL PORTFOLIO

LOS 18.r: <u>Recommend</u> and <u>justify</u> changes in the component weights of a global investment portfolio based on trends and expected changes in macroeconomic factors.

CFA® Program Curriculum, Volume 3, page 96

For the Exam: This LOS asks you to use much of what you have learned here and apply it to portfolio management. Given that the emphasis of the Level III exam is portfolio management, you need to be able to pull all this material together.

Example: Applying capital market expectations

A portfolio manager has a global portfolio invested in several countries and is considering other countries as well. The decisions the manager faces and the economic conditions in the countries are described in the following. In each case, the portfolio manager must reallocate assets based on economic conditions.

Decision #1: Reallocation to Country A

The portfolio manager has noticed that the yield curve is downward sloping in this country. The current portfolio in this country is 60% stocks and 40% bonds. Suggest changes to the portfolio based on this information.

Decision #2: Allocation to Country B

Country B has experienced declining prices and this trend is expected to continue. The manager has no funds invested in this country yet but is considering investments in bonds, equity, and real estate. In which assets should the manager invest?

Decision #3: Allocations to Emerging Country C or Country D

The manager is considering the purchase of government bonds in either emerging Country C or D.

The countries have the following characteristics:

Characteristics of Countries C and D

	Country C	Country D
Foreign exchange/Short-term debt	147%	78%
Debt to GDP	42%	84%

Decision #4: Country, Asset, and Currency Allocations

The manager will make a long-term investment in either Country E or F, based on projections of each economy's trended growth rate. Given that decision, the manager will then decide whether to invest in stocks or bonds. Lastly, the manager will use the savings-investment imbalances approach to gauge the strength of the currencies. The countries have the following characteristics:

Characteristics of Countries E and F

	Country E	Country F
Population growth	2.5%	2.0%
Labor force participation growth	0.2%	0.9%
Growth in spending on new capital inputs	1.5%	2.2%
Growth in total factor productivity	0.4%	0.8%
Expected savings relative to investment	Surplus	Deficit

Answers:

Decision #1: Reallocation to Country A

The downward sloping yield curve indicates that the economy is likely to contract in the future. In recessions, bonds outperform stocks because inflation and interest rates decrease and economic growth is slow. Assuming the accuracy of the yield curve forecast and that interest rates will fall further, the portfolio manager should consider reallocating from stocks into bonds.

Decision #2: Allocation to Country B

The manager should invest in bonds. In periods of declining prices or deflation, bonds perform well because there is no inflation and interest rates are declining. Stocks usually perform poorly during deflationary periods because economic growth is slowing. Real estate also performs poorly during deflationary times, particularly when the investment is financed with debt.

Decision #3: Allocations to Emerging Country C or Country D

The manager should purchase the bonds of Country C. Many emerging market bonds are denominated in a hard currency, so less risky countries have greater foreign currency reserves. Low levels of leverage are also preferred. One measure of leverage is the debt to GDP ratio.

Decision #4: Country, Asset, and Currency Allocations

To forecast the long-term economic growth rate, we sum population growth, labor force participation growth, growth in spending on new capital inputs, and growth in total factor productivity.

In Country E, it is 2.5% + 0.2% + 1.5% + 0.4% = 4.6%.

In Country F, it is 2.0% + 0.9% + 2.2% + 0.8% = 5.9%.

Country F has the higher trended growth rate, so the manager should invest there. The growth rate of 5.9% is quite attractive, and given that the manager is investing for the long term, the investment should be made in equities because equities will benefit the most from this high growth rate. Bond returns are based more on expectations of interest rates and inflation. A high growth economy may experience higher inflation and interest rates at some point that would be negative for bonds.

In the absence of other information, we would surmise from the savings-investment imbalances approach that Country E's currency will depreciate because the country has a savings surplus. Foreign capital will not be needed and, hence, Country E does not require a high currency value. Country F's currency will appreciate because the savings deficit will require a strong currency to attract foreign capital.

For the Exam: In sum, you need to be able to determine the relevant inputs to economic forecasts and what the forecasted economic conditions mean for asset values. Also, be ready to use the forecasting tools discussed earlier and identify problems in forecasting.

KEY CONCEPTS

LOS 18.a

Capital market expectations (macro expectations) help in formulating the strategic asset allocation. They can also assist in detecting short-term asset mispricing exploitable through tactical asset allocation. Formulating capital market expectations is referred to as beta research because it is related to systematic risk.

To formulate capital market expectations, use the following process:
- Determine the relevant capital market expectations given the investor's tax status, allowable asset classes, and time horizon.
- Investigate assets' historical performance as well as the determinants of their performance.
- Identify the valuation model used and its requirements.
- Collect the best data possible.
- Use experience and judgment to interpret current investment conditions.
- Formulate capital market expectations.
- Monitor performance and use it to refine the process.

LOS 18.b

High-quality forecasts are consistent, unbiased, objective, well supported, and have a minimum amount of forecast error.

There are several limitations to using economic data associated with data timeliness, data revisions, changes in index composition, and rebasing of the index.

Forecasts can be adversely affected by transcription errors, survivorship bias, and the use of appraisal (smoothed) data.

The use of historical estimates for forecasts is less relevant if there has been a regime change that results in nonstationary data. The arguments for using a short time span of data are the presence of regime change, the data may not be available, and there may be asynchronous data. The arguments for using a long time span of data are statistics often require it, it increases the precision of population parameter estimates, and the parameter estimates will be less sensitive to the time span chosen.

Using ex post data may cause the analyst to underestimate ex ante risk and overestimate ex ante return if the analyst is unaware of risk faced by investors in the past.

Using historical data, analysts can *uncover* patterns in security returns that are due to data mining and time period bias. To avoid these biases, the analyst should examine the economic basis for the variables, scrutinize their modeling process for susceptibility to these biases, and test the discovered relationship with out-of-sample data.

Analysts' forecasts may also fail to account for conditioning information. Their forecasts should reflect current economic conditions.

The simple correlation statistic may be misleading for evaluating predictive relationships. An alternative to the correlation statistic is a multiple regression.

Analysts are susceptible to the following psychological traps:

- Anchoring trap—an analyst puts too much weight on the first set of information he receives.
- Status quo trap—an analyst bases predictions on the recent past.
- Confirming evidence trap—an analyst gives too much credence to evidence that supports her existing or favored beliefs.
- Overconfidence trap—an analyst ignores his shortcomings and forecasts too narrow a range of possibilities.
- Prudence trap—an analyst tends to be overly conservative in her forecasts.
- Recallability trap—an analyst lets past disasters or dramatic events weigh too heavily in his forecasts.

When forecasting, an analyst cannot be sure that her predictive model is correct and/or whether the data are correct.

LOS 18.c

The statistical tools for setting capital market expectations include projecting historical data, shrinkage estimators, time series analysis, and multifactor models.

When using historical data, the arithmetic mean is the best when projecting for a single year, whereas the geometric mean is best for projecting over several years.

Shrinkage estimators are weighted averages of historical data and another analyst-determined estimate.

Using time series analysis, an analyst can forecast means as well as variances, which is useful when assets exhibit volatility clustering.

Multifactor models can be used to forecast returns, variances, and covariances. Their advantage is that they simplify the forecasting procedure by reducing the forecast to a common set of factors. This modeling also eliminates the noise present in a sample of data and ensures consistent forecasts given a consistent covariance matrix.

Using a modified discounted cash flow analysis for an equity market, the expected return is the dividend yield plus the inflation rate plus the real earnings growth rate minus the change in stock outstanding plus changes in the P/E ratio.

The yield to maturity on a reference bond is used as the expected return for a bond segment. The drawback to this approach is that the yield to maturity assumes that intermediate cash flows are reinvested at the yield to maturity.

A risk premium approach estimates the expected return on equity as a long-term government bond yield plus an equity risk premium. For bonds, the expected return is determined using the real risk-free rate plus an inflation premium, a default risk premium, a liquidity premium, a maturity risk premium, and a tax premium.

Using a financial equilibrium approach, the equity risk premium for a market is equal to its correlation with the global portfolio, multiplied by the standard deviation of the asset, multiplied by the Sharpe ratio for the global portfolio.

LOS 18.d

Capital market expectations can also be formed using surveys. In this method, a poll is taken of market participants (e.g., economists and analysts) to determine what their expectations are regarding the economy or capital market. If the group polled is constant over time, this method is referred to as a panel method.

Surveys have been taken regarding the equity risk premium, with investors expecting a premium in the range of 2% to 3.9%. Other studies have found that the expectations of practitioners are consistently more optimistic than that of academics.

Judgment can also be applied to project capital market expectations. Although quantitative models provide objective numerical forecasts, there are times when an analyst must adjust those expectations using her experience and insight to improve upon those forecasts.

LOS 18.e

Understanding the business cycle can help the analyst identify inflection points where the risk and opportunities for higher return may be heightened. To identify inflection points, the analyst should understand what is driving the current economy and what may cause the end of the current economy.

The inventory cycle is often measured using the inventory to sales ratio. The measure increases when businesses gain confidence in the future of the economy and add to their inventories in anticipation of increasing demand for their output. As a result, employment increases with subsequent increases in economic growth. This continues until some precipitating factor, such as a tightening in the growth of the money supply, intervenes. At this point, inventories decrease, employment declines, and economic growth slows.

LOS 18.f

The relationship between the business cycle and assets returns is well documented. Assets with higher returns during business cycle lows (e.g., bonds and defensive stocks) should be favored by investors because the return supplements their income during recessionary periods—these assets should have lower risk premiums. Assets with lower returns during recessions should have higher risk premiums. Understanding the relationship between an asset's return and the business cycle can help the analyst provide better valuations.

LOS 18.g

Inflation varies over the business cycle, rising in the latter stages of an expansion and falling during a recession and the initial recovery.

Deflation reduces the value of investments financed with debt (e.g., real estate) because leverage magnifies losses.

Bond prices will rise during a recession when inflation and interest rates are declining. In a strong expansion, bonds tend to decline in price as inflationary expectations and interest rates rise.

Equities provide an inflation hedge when inflation is moderate. High inflation can be problematic because slow growth may result from central bank action. Declining inflation or deflation is harmful because this can result in declining economic growth.

Increasing inflation is positive for cash instruments because the returns on cash instruments increase as inflation increases. Deflation is negative for cash because the return falls to zero.

LOS 18.h

The Taylor rule can be formalized as follows:

$$r_{target} = r_{neutral} + \left[0.5\left(GDP_{expected} - GDP_{trend}\right) + 0.5\left(i_{expected} - i_{target}\right)\right]$$

Example:
Given the following information, calculate the short-term interest rate target.

Neutral rate	4%
Inflation target	3%
Expected Inflation	7%
GDP long-term trend	2%
Expected GDP growth	0%

Answer:

$$r_{target} = 4\% + \left[0.5(0\% - 2\%) + 0.5(7\% - 3\%)\right] = 5\%$$

LOS 18.i

The yield curve demonstrates the relationship between interest rates and the maturity of the debt security and is sensitive to actions of the federal government as well as current and expected economic conditions. For example, when both fiscal and monetary policies are expansive, the yield curve is sharply upward sloping, which indicates that the economy is likely to expand in the future. When fiscal and monetary policies are restrictive, the yield curve is downward sloping, indicating that the economy is likely to contract in the future.

When fiscal and monetary policies are in disagreement, the shape of the yield curve is less definitively shaped. Recall that monetary policy controls primarily short-term interest rates. If monetary policy is expansive while fiscal policy is restrictive, the yield curve will be upward sloping, though it will be less steep than when both policies are expansive. If monetary policy is restrictive while fiscal policy is expansive, the yield curve will be more or less flat.

LOS 18.j

In forecasting a country's long-term economic growth trend, the trend growth rate can be decomposed into two main components and their respective subcomponents:

1. Changes in employment levels.
   - Population growth.
   - Rate of labor force participation.

2. Changes in productivity.
   - Spending on new capital inputs.
   - Total factor productivity growth.

Example:

Assume that expected population growth is 2% and expected labor force participation growth is 0.25%. If spending on new capital inputs is projected to grow at 2.5% and total factor productivity will grow by 0.5%, what is the long-term projected growth rate?

Answer:

The sum of the components equals 2% + 0.25% + 2.5% + 0.5% = 5.25%, so the economy is projected to grow by this amount.

LOS 18.k

Exogenous shocks are unanticipated events that occur outside the normal course of an economy and have a negative impact upon it. They can be caused by different factors, such as natural disasters, political events, or changes in government policies. Typically, two types of shocks have occurred, which are oil shocks and financial crises. Oil shocks are usually caused by crises in the Middle East followed by decreased oil production, leading to increasing prices, inflation, reduced consumer spending, higher unemployment, and a slowed economy. The opposite shock would be a decline in oil prices, leading to lower inflation and boosting the economy. Financial crises have occurred when countries can't meet their debt payments, currencies are devalued, and property values have declined. In a financial crisis, banks usually become vulnerable, forcing the central bank to provide stability to the economy by reducing interest rates, which is difficult to do in an already low interest rate environment.

LOS 18.l

Macroeconomic links refer to similarities in business cycles across countries. Economies are linked by both international trade and capital flows so that a recession in one country dampens exports and investment in a second country, thereby creating a slowdown in the second country.

Exchange rate links are found when countries peg their currency to others. The benefit of a peg is that currency volatility is reduced and inflation can be brought under control. Interest rates between the countries will often reflect a risk premium, with the weaker country having higher interest rates.

Interest rate differentials between countries can also reflect differences in economic growth, monetary policy, and fiscal policy. It is theorized that real interest rate differentials between countries should not exist, and over time exchange rates will equalize differences.

LOS 18.m

Emerging market risks stem from unstable political and social systems and heavy infrastructure investments financed by foreign borrowing. Investors should answer six questions before investing in these markets:

1. Does the country have responsible fiscal and monetary policies? This is determined by examining the deficit to GDP ratio.

2. What is the expected growth? Should be at least 4%.

3. Does the country have reasonable currency values and current account deficits? A volatile currency discourages needed foreign investment, and an overvalued currency encourages excessive government borrowing.

4. Is the country too highly levered? Too much debt can lead to a financial crisis if foreign capital flees the country.

5. What is the level of foreign exchange reserves relative to short-term debt? Many emerging country loans must be paid back in a foreign currency.

6. What is the government's stance regarding structural reform? A supportive government makes the investment environment more hospitable.

LOS 18.n

Econometric analysis utilizes economic theory to formulate the forecasting model. The models range from being quite simple to very complex, involving several data items of various time period lags to predict the future.

Economic indicators attempt to characterize an economy's phase in the business cycle and are separated into lagging indicators, coincident indicators, and leading indicators. Analysts prefer leading indicators because they help predict the future path of the economy.

In a checklist approach, the analyst checks off a list of questions that should indicate the future growth of the economy. Given the answers to these questions, the analyst can then use his judgment to formulate a forecast or derive a more formal model using statistics.

LOS 18.o

Investors ultimately use capital market expectations to form their beliefs about the attractiveness of different investments. Following are examples of how specific information can be used to forecast asset class returns.

*   If a cash manager thought that interest rates were set to rise, she would shift to short-term cash instruments.
*   A change in short-term rates has unpredictable effects for the yields on long-term bonds.
*   During a recession, the risk premium on credit risky bonds increases.
*   Most emerging market debt is denominated in a non-domestic currency, which increases its default risk.
*   The yields for inflation-indexed bonds will fall if inflation increases.
*   In the early expansion phase of the business cycle, stock prices are increasing. Later in the expansion, earnings growth and stock returns slow.
*   The returns for emerging market stocks are affected by business cycles in the developed world.
*   Interest rates affect real estate returns through both the supply and demand as well as the capitalization rate used to discount cash flows.

LOS 18.p

When the government promotes competition in the marketplace, the efficiency of the economy increases, likely leading to higher long-term growth in the economy and the stock market.

Shorter-term growth is affected by the business cycle. In a recession, sales and earnings decrease. Non-cyclical or defensive stocks are less affected by the business cycle and thus will have lower risk premiums and higher valuations than cyclical stocks. Cyclical stocks are characterized by high business risk and/or high fixed costs.

LOS 18.q

- The relative form of purchasing power parity (PPP) states that differences in inflation between two countries will be reflected in changes in the exchange rate between them. Specifically, the country with higher inflation will see its currency value decline.
- The relative economic strength approach: The idea behind this approach is that a favorable investment climate will attract investors, which will increase the demand for the domestic currency, therefore increasing its value.
- The capital flows approach focuses primarily on long-term capital flows such as those into equity investments or foreign direct investments.
- The savings-investment imbalances approach starts with the concept that an economy must fund investment through savings. If investment is greater than domestic savings, then capital must flow into the country from abroad to finance the investment.

LOS 18.r

This LOS effectively asks you to apply LOS 18.a through LOS 18.q in determining the optimal reallocation for a global portfolio. For the exam, you should be able to interpret forecasts as well as develop forecasts for market returns using the Grinold-Kroner model. You could be asked to assess the valuation of a stock market using the H-model, Fed model, Yardeni model, Tobin's q, or the equity q. Using the Taylor model, you should be able to determine the proper level of short-term interest rates. You should be able to calculate the risk premium for integrated and segmented markets to determine whether expected returns are appropriate.

Know the effects of stages in the economic business cycle on different types of investments and be able to determine which investments are best given the current stage of the cycle and government fiscal and monetary policies. You should be able to discuss the relative strengths of currencies given current interest rates and investment opportunities. The bottom line is the necessity of using a thorough economic analysis to determine which of several global investments is most appropriate for the investor.

CONCEPT CHECKERS

1. Suppose an analyst values stocks using discount rates based on projected risk-free rate ranges of 3% to 5%. The same analyst uses risk-free rate projections of 4% to 6% to determine the allocation to fixed income. **Discuss** the likely effect on the investor's asset allocation.

2. It is now January 2007. An analyst would like to forecast U.S. equity returns. She is considering using either 15 years of historical annual returns or 50 years of historical annual returns. **Provide** the arguments for and against each selection of data length.

3. An analyst realizes that the variance for an exchange rate tends to persist over a period of time, where high volatility is followed by more high volatility. What statistical tool would the analyst *most likely* use to forecast the variance of the exchange rate?

4. Suppose an analyst is valuing two markets, A and B. What is the equity risk premium for the two markets, their expected returns, and the covariance between them, given the following?

Sharpe ratio of the global portfolio	0.29
Standard deviation of the global portfolio	8.0%
Risk-free rate of return	4.5%
Degree of market integration for Market A	80%
Degree of market integration for Market B	65%
Standard deviation of Market A	18%
Standard deviation of Market B	26%
Correlation of Market A with global portfolio	0.87
Correlation of Market B with global portfolio	0.63
Estimated illiquidity premium for Market A	0.0%
Estimated illiquidity premium for Market B	2.4%

5. Are there any attractive investments during deflationary periods?

6. During an economic expansion, an analyst notices that the budget deficit has been declining. She concludes that the government's fiscal policy has shifted to a more restrictive posture. **Comment** on her conclusion.

7. **Calculate** the short-term interest rate target given the following information.

Neutral rate	5%
Inflation target	3%
Expected Inflation	6%
GDP long-term trend	3%
Expected GDP	5%

8.   A forecaster notes that the yield curve is steeply upwardly sloping. **Comment** on the likely monetary and fiscal policies in effect and the future of the economy.

9.   An analyst would like to project the long-term growth of the economy. Which of the following would you recommend he focus on: changes in consumer spending or potential changes in tax policy due to a new government coming into office?

10.   An analyst is evaluating an emerging market for potential investment. She notices that the country's current account deficit has been growing. Is this a sign of increasing risk? If so, **explain** why.

11.   An analyst is evaluating two countries. Maldavia has a GDP of $60 billion and has an economy that is dominated by the mining industry. Oceania has a GDP of $1.2 trillion and has an economy that sells a variety of items. He is predicting a global economic slowdown. Which country is at greater risk?

12.   An analyst believes that GDP is best forecast using a system of equations that can capture the fact that GDP is a function of many variables, both current and lagged values. Which economic forecasting method is she *most likely* to use?

13.   At a conference, Larry Timmons states that the relationship between short-term interest rates and long-term bond yields is not uniform. He also states that the relationship between a domestic currency value and interest rates is not uniform. **Explain** what Timmons is talking about.

14.   At the beginning of the fiscal year, Tel-Pal, Inc., stock sells for $75 per share. There are 2,000,000 shares outstanding. An analyst predicts that the annual dividend to be paid in one year will be $3 per share. The expected inflation rate is 3.5%. The firm plans to issue 40,000 new shares over the year. The price-to-earnings ratio is expected to stay the same, and nominal earnings will increase by 6.8%. Based upon these figures, what is the expected return on a share of Tel-Pal, Inc., stock in the next year?

15.   An analyst forecasts the historical covariance of the returns between Tel-Pal, Inc., stock and Int-Pal, Inc., stock to be 1,024. A newly forecasted covariance matrix predicts the covariance will be 784. The analyst weights the historical covariance at 30% and the forecast at 70%. **Calculate** the shrinkage estimate of the covariance.

16.   **List** and **explain** three psychological traps that would encourage an analyst to place too much weight on past information and less weight on new information.

©2011 Kaplan, Inc.

17.   An analyst notices that the growth of the national inventory-to-sales ratio has slowed in recent years. **Identify** the traditional interpretation of this in the formation of capital expectations. **Explain** a recent phenomenon that would give another interpretation of this slowing of growth, which may reduce the ratio's significance.

18.   The phase of the business cycle where we *most likely* expect to observe rising short-term interest rates and flat bond yields is:
        A. late expansion.
        B. initial recovery.
        C. early expansion.

19.   **Describe** three characteristics each for an oil shock and a financial crisis.

ANSWERS – CONCEPT CHECKERS

1. It is likely that the investor's asset allocation will be too heavily weighted towards equity, given that the discount rates used to determine the equity allocation will be lower than that used for fixed income. This example illustrates that high-quality forecasts using capital market expectations should be consistent. They also should be objectively formed, unbiased, well supported, and have a minimum amount of forecast error.

2. If the analyst uses 15 years of historical data, then her sample may be unduly influenced by the time span chosen. In this case, the U.S. equity returns for the past 15 years are likely quite high relative to probable future returns. Using 15 years of historical data would also not provide enough data points for statistical calculations if annual returns are used. A longer time span of data would increase the precision of population parameter estimates.

    Using 50 years of data may also be problematic if there has been regime change. For example, changes in Federal Reserve policy may render stock return data from 50 years ago irrelevant. Although data availability and asynchronous data can sometimes be a problem when using long time spans of data, this is unlikely the case for historical U.S. equity data.

3. The analyst would most likely forecast the variance using time series analysis. In time series analysis, forecasts are generated using previous values of a variable and previous values of other variables. If an exchange rate exhibits volatility clustering, then its variance will persist for periods of time and can be forecasted using a time series model.

4. First, we calculate the equity risk premium for both markets assuming full integration. Note that for Market B, the illiquidity risk premium is added in:

$$ERP_i = \rho_{i,M}\sigma_i\left(\frac{ERP_M}{\sigma_M}\right)$$
$$ERP_A = 0.87(0.18)0.29 = 4.54\%$$
$$ERP_B = 0.63(0.26)0.29 + 0.0240 = 7.15\%$$

    The equity risk premium for both markets assuming full segmentation is:

$$ERP_i = \sigma_i\left(\frac{ERP_M}{\sigma_M}\right)$$
$$ERP_A = (0.18)0.29 = 5.22\%$$
$$ERP_B = (0.26)0.29 + 0.0240 = 9.94\%$$

    Weighting the integrated and segmented risk premiums by the degree of integration and segmentation in each market:

$$ERP_A = (0.80 \times 0.0454) + [(1 - 0.80) \times 0.0522] = 4.68\%$$
$$ERP_B = (0.65 \times 0.0715) + [(1 - 0.65) \times 0.0994] = 8.13\%$$

    The expected return in each market is then:

$$\hat{R}_A = 4.5\% + 4.68\% = 9.18\%$$
$$\hat{R}_B = 4.5\% + 8.13\% = 12.63\%$$

The betas in each market are:

$$\beta_i = \rho_{i,M}\sigma_i / \sigma_M$$
$$\beta_A = (0.87)(18)/8 = 1.96$$
$$\beta_B = (0.63)(26)/8 = 2.05$$

The covariance is then:

$$cov_{i,j} = \beta_i \beta_j \sigma_M^2$$
$$cov_{A,B} = (1.96)(2.05)(8.0)^2 = 257.15$$

5. Bonds actually perform well during periods of falling inflation or deflation because interest rates are declining. This holds true as long as credit risk does not increase. Equities do poorly in periods of declining inflation or deflation due to declining economic growth and asset prices. Deflation also reduces the value of investments financed with debt, such as real estate, because leverage magnifies losses. Deflation is negative for cash because the return on cash declines to near zero.

6. Her conclusion may not be warranted. In an economic expansion, the budget deficit will decline naturally because tax receipts increase and disbursements to the unemployed decrease. The changes she is observing may be independent of the government's fiscal policy.

    Note that only government-directed changes in fiscal policy influence the growth of the economy. Changes in the deficit that occur naturally over the course of the business cycle are not stimulative or restrictive.

7. $$r_{target} = 5.0\% + [0.5 \times (5\% - 3\%) + 0.5 \times (6\% - 3\%)]$$
    $$= 5.0\% + [1.0\% + 1.5\%] = 7.5\%$$

    In this example, the higher than targeted growth rate and higher than targeted inflation rate argue for a targeted interest rate of 7.5%. This rate hike is intended to slow down the economy and inflation.

8. If the yield curve is steeply upwardly sloping, then it is likely that both fiscal and monetary policies are expansive. The economy is likely to expand in the future.

9. Although consumer spending is the largest component of GDP, it is fairly stable over the business cycle. The reason is that consumers tend to spend a fairly constant amount over time. Thus, it is likely that the analyst should focus on the potential changes in tax policy. This governmental structural policy has a potentially large impact on the long-run growth rate of an economy.

10. When exports are less than imports, a current account deficit results. This can be problematic because the deficit must be financed through external borrowing. If the emerging country becomes overlevered, it may not be able to pay back its foreign debt. A financial crisis may ensue where foreign investors quickly withdraw their capital. These financial crises are accompanied by currency devaluations and declines in emerging market asset values.

11. A global economic slowdown would affect smaller countries with undiversified economies more because economic links are more important for these types of countries. Larger countries with diverse economies are less affected by events in other countries.

12. Econometric analysis would be the best approach to use. It can model the complexities of reality using both current and lagged values. Ordinary least squares regression is most often used, but other statistical methods are also available.

13. The relationship between short-term interest rates and long-term bond yields is not uniform because although bond yields usually increase when short-term rates increase, this is not always the case. If short-term rates increase enough such that a recession becomes more likely, the yields on bonds will fall as investors anticipate that the demand for loanable funds will fall.

    The relationship between a domestic currency value and interest rates is not uniform because although the currency value will increase as interest rates increase, this is not the case if interest rates increase high enough to slow down the economy. In this case, foreign investors shy away from the country because the country becomes a less attractive place to invest.

14. The equation for expected return on Tel-Pal, Inc., using these inputs is:

$$\hat{R}_T = \frac{Div_1}{P_0} + \text{inflation} + \text{real growth in earnings} - \%\Delta \text{ shares} + \Delta\left(\frac{P}{E}\right)$$

$$\hat{R}_T = \left(\frac{\$3}{\$75} \times 100\right) + 3.5\% + 3.3\% - 2\% + 0$$

$$\hat{R}_T = 8.8\%$$

    The expected return is 8.8%. The expected dividend return is 4%, and the expected percentage increase in the number of shares is 2%. Expected inflation is 3.5%, which should be subtracted from the nominal earnings forecast to get the forecast of real earnings growth.

15. The shrinkage estimate is simply the weighted average of the historical value and the forecasted value. The shrinkage estimate is:

    $856 = 30\% \times 1,024 + 70\% \times 784$

16. *Anchoring Trap*: The analyst places too much weight on the first information received. Once having formed an opinion, the analyst will not want to deviate too far from the first opinion as new information arrives.

    Status Quo Trap: The analyst will not want to deviate too far from the recent past.

    The Prudence Trap: The analyst will tend to ignore information that will lead to extreme forecasts.

    The Recallability Trap: The analyst lets past disasters and dramatic events weigh too heavily in the forecast and ignores newer information.

17. *Traditional Interpretation*: A slowing in the growth of the inventory-to-sales ratio has traditionally indicated increased pessimism by the business community. It slows inventory growth in an anticipation of slower future sales, which should lower the expected earnings and the returns of capital markets.

    Another Interpretation: Increased technology and just-in-time inventory approaches have allowed businesses to reduce the amount of inventory they hold. Thus, a slowing inventory growth may be positive as firms find ways to lower the amount of inventory they must hold for each level of sales. This would be positive for earnings because it would lower costs.

18. C   *Early Expansion*: In this period of the business cycle, we expect to observe rising short-term interest rates and flat or rising bond yields.

The expectations of short-term and long-term yields for the other phases are listed as follows:
Late Expansion: Both short-term and long-term rates increasing.
Initial Recovery: Low or falling short-term rates, and bond yields have bottomed out.

19.   Oil shocks and financial crises are two types of exogenous shocks that have been repeatedly observed over time and tend to spread to other countries. Oil shocks are usually characterized as (1) a reduction in oil production as a result of turmoil in the Middle East, (2) leading to higher oil prices and inflation, (3) reduced consumer spending, (4) increased unemployment, and (5) a slowed economy. (6) An oil shock could also be a reduction in oil prices resulting in the opposite effects.

A financial crisis is usually characterized by (1) a country not being able to meet its debt payment, (2) a currency devaluation, or (3) a significant reduction in asset prices. (4) Banks usually become vulnerable in a financial crisis. To stabilize the economy, the country's central bank intervenes to increase liquidity by reducing or maintaining low interest rates.

EQUITY MARKET VALUATION[1]

Study Session 7

EXAM FOCUS

Be sure you know all the formulas in this topic review so, if necessary, you can calculate any of the measures and discuss the results and implications of the values. Calculations using the change in expected economic output equation, as well as the H-model for equity valuation, are likely. You should expect to see questions about the effects of changing economic factors on the economy's expected rate of growth.

COBB-DOUGLAS PRODUCTION FUNCTION

LOS 19.a: <u>Explain</u> the terms of the Cobb-Douglas production function and <u>demonstrate</u> how the function can be used to model growth in real output under the assumption of constant returns to scale.

CFA® Program Curriculum, Volume 3, page 134

The **Cobb-Douglas production function (CD)** uses the country's labor input and capital stock to estimate the total real economic output. The general form of the function is:

$$Y = AK^{\alpha}L^{\beta}$$

where:
Y = total real economic output
A = total factor productivity (TFP)
K = capital stock
L = labor input
α = output elasticity of K ($0 < \alpha < 1$)
β = output elasticity of L ($\alpha + \beta = 1$)

---

1. Terminology used throughout this topic review is industry convention as presented in Reading 19 of the 2012 CFA Level III exam curriculum.

Applying natural logs, assuming that $\beta = (1 - \alpha)$, and making a few other assumptions, we see the form of the CD that is used to estimate *expected changes* in real economic output. Each of the inputs, as well as the output, is now stated in terms of growth (i.e., percentage change):

$$\frac{\Delta Y}{Y} \cong \frac{\Delta A}{A} + \alpha \frac{\Delta K}{K} + (1-\alpha)\frac{\Delta L}{L}$$

where:

$\dfrac{\Delta Y}{Y} = $ % change in real output $(\%\Delta Y)$

$\dfrac{\Delta A}{A} = $ % change in total factor productivity $(\%\Delta TFP)$

$\dfrac{\Delta K}{K} = $ % change in capital stock $(\%\Delta K)$

$\dfrac{\Delta L}{L} = $ % change in labor $(\%\Delta L)$

Put into words, the equation tells us that the percentage change in economic output is the sum of the percentage changes in factor productivity, capital stock, and labor input. Assuming *constant returns to scale*,[2] if labor and capital increase by a given percentage, economic output will increase by the same percentage, regardless of the value of α. For example, assuming a 10% increase in capital stock and in labor:

$$\%\Delta Y = \alpha(\%\Delta K) + (1-\alpha)\%\Delta L = \alpha(10\%) + (1-\alpha)(10\%) = 10\%$$

Assumes $\%\Delta A = 0$ (constant returns to scale)

Percentage changes in capital and labor can be obtained from national accounts, and α and β, the output elasticities of capital and labor, vary from country to country. The change in TFP (i.e., $\%\Delta A$) is the **Solow residual** and can be determined by rearranging the equation:

$$\text{Solow residual} = \%\Delta TFP = \%\Delta Y - \alpha(\%\Delta K) - (1-\alpha)\%\Delta L$$

An economy's TFP can change over time due to the following:

- Changing technology.
- Changing restrictions on capital flows and labor mobility.
- Changing trade restrictions.
- Changing laws.
- Changing division of labor.
- Depleting/discovering natural resources.

---

2. Constant returns to scale means TFP is constant. That is, productivity (think efficiency) remains constant so that a given percentage change in labor and capital produces the same percentage change in output.

LOS 19.b: Evaluate the relative importance of growth in total factor productivity, in capital stock, and in labor input given relevant historical data.

CFA® Program Curriculum, Volume 3, page 138

Once we have estimated the growth equation, $\%\Delta Y = \%\Delta A + \alpha \%\Delta K + (1 - \alpha) \%\Delta L$, we can use the historical growth of capital and labor, along with the estimates of output elasticities for labor and capital, to decompose the growth of GDP in order to evaluate the relative effects of labor growth, capital accumulation, and increases in factor productivity on economic growth.

> **For the Exam:** Questions on economic growth could take either a qualitative or quantitative format as illustrated in the two following examples.

Example: Effects of changing factors on economic growth

In the template provided, **state** and **explain** the probable effect on total economic output associated with an *increase* in each of the factors, holding the other factors constant:

Factor Increased	Probable Effect on Economic Growth	Explanation
Savings rate	Increase	More capital available at reduced interest rates. Increased investment in capital stock.
Labor force	Increase	Increase in labor force growth rate.
Production efficiency	Increase	Increase in TFP.
Environmental and pollution controls	Decrease	Retooling and other costs; possibly reduced and/or more expensive output.
Children per household	Increase	Increase in labor force growth rate.
Number of two-wage-earner households	Increase	Increase in labor force growth rate.
Retirement age	Increase	Increase in labor force growth rate.
Import taxes/restrictions	Decrease	Increased costs; possibly reduced and/or more expensive output.

For the Exam: When asked to state the effect that changing factors can have on economic output ($\Delta Y/Y$), consider the factors' possible impacts on production efficiency, the labor force, and/or capital stock. Always think in terms of partial derivatives. Consider the impact of each factor individually while holding the others constant. Resist considering the impact that a change in one factor will have on another factor.

Also, some factors might have only a short-term effect on economic output, while others can have longer-lasting effects. For example, one-time costs incurred to meet increased environmental restrictions by replacing outdated equipment will have a short-term dampening effect. Once the retooling is completed, the economy would be expected to return to its long-term average growth rate. Factors, such as import restrictions, however, could have a longer-lasting impact on economic growth, depending on how quickly (and if) domestic replacements can be established.

Example: Estimating the change in economic output

While performing an analysis of three economies, an analyst compiled the growth and elasticity data in the following table.

10-Year Forecast (Growth Figures Are Annual Averages)

Country	% Growth in Total Factor Productivity	% Growth in Capital Stock	% Growth in Labor Input	Output Elasticity of Capital (α)
A	1.0	2.0	1.0	0.5
B	2.0	2.5	4.5	0.3
C	3.0	8.0	2.5	0.7

i.   For each economy, **determine** the expected 10-year average annual GDP growth rate.
ii. **Comment** on the three economies.

Answer:

i.   Expected growth in GDP:

$$\%\Delta Y \cong \%\Delta A + \alpha(\%\Delta K) + (1-\alpha)(\%\Delta L)$$

A: $\%\Delta Y = 1.0 + 0.5(2.0) + 0.5(1.0) = 2.50\%$
B: $\%\Delta Y = 2.0 + 0.3(2.5) + 0.7(4.5) = 5.90\%$
C: $\%\Delta Y = 3.0 + 0.7(8.0) + 0.3(2.5) = 9.35\%$

ii. Over the next ten years, economies A, B, and C are expected to experience average annual GDP growth rates of 2.50%, 5.90%, and 9.35%, respectively. The population of Economy A would appear to be close to equilibrium, as it is expected to grow at an average annual rate of only 1%. Together, the lower growth rates in capital, labor, TFP, and output for Economy A suggest it is a large, developed economy.

The workforce growth rate of 4.5% for Country B is relatively high, and Country B gains significantly from growth in the workforce. Increases in the capital stock, on the other hand, have less of an effect on output. The impressive workforce growth rate combined with a modest expected growth in capital stock could indicate a relatively small economy in the early stages of development.

Growth in the workforce of Economy C has slowed. Capital stock, however, is expected to increase significantly over the next ten years. Relative to Economy B, rapidly growing capital stock combined with an ability to translate capital growth into increased economic output (i.e., $\alpha = 0.7$) indicates an economy that is larger, more developed, and faster growing.

LOS 19.c: <u>Demonstrate</u> the use of the Cobb-Douglas production function in obtaining a discounted dividend model estimate of the intrinsic value of an equity market.

LOS 19.d: <u>Critique</u> the use of discounted dividend models and macroeconomic forecasts to estimate the intrinsic value of an equity market.

CFA® Program Curriculum, Volume 3, page 138

When we use a dividend discount model to estimate the value of an equity market index, we implicitly assume that the growth rate in corporate earnings and dividends is the same as the growth rate in gross domestic product (GDP). Even though these growth rates can differ in the short run, over longer periods, this assumption is reasonably accurate.

If an economy is expected to grow at a relatively high rate currently that will decline to a sustainable rate of growth over a period of years, we can apply a form of the dividend discount model—the **H-model**. The H-model assumes that the current "super-normal" growth rate (g_S) of dividends will decline linearly to the long-term sustainable growth rate (g_L). For a stock index, we can use the annual dividend at time zero (D_0), the number of years to reach the sustainable growth rate (N), and the required rate of return on equity securities (r) to calculate the current index value based on economic fundamentals (V_0) as:

$$P_0 = \frac{D_0}{r - g_L}\left[(1 + g_L) + \frac{N}{2}(g_S - g_L)\right]$$

where:

P_0 = current price (value)

D_0 = current dividend

r = real equity discount rate

g_S = short-term real rate of growth expected to decline linearly over N years to the real, long-term sustainable growth rate, g_L

Compare the H-model to the *constant growth dividend discount model*, which assumes the stock or stock index has already reached the period of long-term, sustainable growth:

$$P_0 = \frac{D_1}{r - \bar{g}} = \frac{D_0(1 + \bar{g})}{r - \bar{g}} \qquad r = \frac{D(1 + \bar{g})}{P_0} + \bar{g}$$

where:

D_0 = current dividend

P_0 = current price (value)

D_1 = next expected dividend

r = real required return on equity

$\bar{g}$ = real, long-term sustainable (constant) growth rate; compare to g_L in the H-model

When we utilize the H-model, we use real (inflation-adjusted) discount rates and growth rates[3], and the discount rate depends on the expected volatility of the market. High volatility in a developing market can be caused by significant structural and regulatory changes as well as behavioral factors. Also, in a developing market, the government can own considerable proportions of the publicly available stocks. The uncertainty (i.e., risk) associated with the ultimate disposition of government-owned equities (e.g., whether the government will exert its ownership interests or divest of the equities) can have a dampening effect on P/E ratios.

Professor's Note: As you saw in Topic Review 18, Capital Market Expectations, and will see in Topic Review 30, Emerging Markets Finance, the degree to which the developing country's economy (GDP) is correlated with the developed world can affect the discount rate applied to its equity. If the developing economy is not highly correlated with the developed world, for example, the diversification benefit from including its equities in a global portfolio can reduce the return required by global investors.

---

3. In valuing an index, we can use either nominal or real rates, but real rates are preferred because they are more stable and easier to predict.

Example: Estimating the intrinsic value and justified P/E ratio of a developing equity market

To estimate the intrinsic value of a developing market index using the H-Model, we need the real required return, r, the current dividend, D_0, the supernormal rate of growth, g_s, the long-term sustainable rate of growth, g_L, and the period of time, N, over which the growth rate will decline linearly.

Answer:

The market's forecasted EPS is 20.30. Assuming a required real return on equity of 10%, a current dividend of 12, current supernormal growth of 10.5%, a long-term sustainable rate of growth of 3.0%, and a 30-year period of linear growth decline, the estimated intrinsic value of the index is 369.43, and with forecasted earnings per share of 20.30, the justified P/E ratio is 18.2:

$$V_0 = \frac{D_0}{r - g_L}\left[(1 + g_L) + \frac{N}{2}(g_S - g_L)\right]$$

$$= \frac{12}{0.10 - 0.03}\left[(1.03) + \frac{30}{2}(0.105 - 0.03)\right] = 369.43$$

$$\frac{P}{E}(\text{justified}) = \frac{369.43}{20.30} = 18.199 = 18.20$$

Problems associated with estimating the intrinsic values of developing markets can be significant. For example, above we mentioned the problems associated with estimating a required return for a developing market. Uncertainty in the required return can be related to significant government equity holdings, as well as significant structural changes. The long-term sustainable rate of growth, including the period of growth decline, can also be difficult to estimate with any certainty, especially in an emerging economy that can be subject to currency fluctuations with periods of uncertain inflation.

Figures 1 through 4 show the sensitivity of intrinsic value to changes in each of the input variables in the H-model.[4] Each input variable is increased and decreased by 10% and 20% from its value in the example while holding the others constant. (The shaded rows in the tables indicate the base values in the example.) The third column in each table shows the resulting intrinsic value, and the last column shows the percentage change in intrinsic value from the base case. The sign and magnitude of the relationship between the input variable and intrinsic value is indicated in the title of each table. For example, in Figure 1, we see that the relationship between intrinsic value and N is positive and less than 1.0. That means the change in intrinsic value is in the same direction as the change in N but is smaller in percentage terms. Required return is the only input variable that exhibits a negative relationship with intrinsic value, and the relationship is greater than –1.0. The change in intrinsic value is opposite the change in required return and is greater in percentage terms.

---

4. Because the goal is showing the sensitivity of calculated intrinsic value to changes in estimates of the inputs, the current dividend, D_0, which is not an estimate, is held constant in each of the tables.

**Figure 1: Sensitivity of Intrinsic Value to Length of Period of Growth Decline, *N*
(Positive Relationship < 1.0)**

Period of Growth Decline (N) in Years	% Change	Intrinsic Value	% Change
24	–20%	330.86	–10.44
27	–10%	350.15	–5.22
30	—	369.43	—
33	+10%	388.72	+5.22
36	+20%	408.00	+10.44

Forecasted EPS 20.30; real return on equity of 10%; current dividend 12; g_s = 10.5%; g_L = 3.0%.

**Figure 2: Sensitivity of Intrinsic Value to Sustainable Growth Rate, g_L
(Positive Relationship < 1.0)**

Sustainable Growth Rate (g_L) in Percent	% Change	Intrinsic Value	% Change
2.4	–20%	353.52	–4.31
2.7	–10%	361.14	–2.24
3.0	—	369.43	—
3.3	+10%	378.44	+2.44
3.6	+20%	388.31	+5.11

Forecasted EPS 20.30; real return on equity of 10%; current dividend 12; g_s = 10.5%;
N = 30 years.

**Figure 3: Sensitivity of Intrinsic Value to Supernormal Growth Rate, g_S
(Positive Relationship < 1.0)**

Supernormal Growth Rate (g_S) in Percent	% Change	Intrinsic Value	% Change
8.40	–20%	315.43	–14.62
9.45	–10%	342.43	–7.31
10.50	—	369.43	—
11.55	+10%	396.43	+7.31
12.60	+20%	423.43	+14.62

Forecasted EPS 20.30; real return on equity of 10%; current dividend 12; g_L = 3.0%;
N = 30 years.

Figure 4: Sensitivity of Intrinsic Value to Required Real Return on Equity
(Negative Relationship > −1.0)

Required Real Return (r) in Percent	% Change	Intrinsic Value	% Change
8.0	−20%	517.20	+40.00
9.0	−10%	431.00	+16.67
10.0	—	369.43	—
11.0	+10%	323.25	−12.50
12.0	+20%	287.33	−22.22

Forecasted EPS 20.30; current dividend 12; g_s = 10.5%; g_L = 3.0%; N = 30 years.

Example: Estimating the sustainable rate of growth, required return, and intrinsic value of a developed equity market

An analyst has gathered the data in the following table for a large, mature developed market index. The current level of the index is 3,250, and the current dividend is $150.

Long-Term Economic Growth Factors

% Growth in Total Factor Productivity	% Growth in Capital Stock	% Growth in Labor Input	Output Elasticity of Capital (α)	Output Elasticity of Labor ($1 - \alpha$)
1.5	1.5	0.5	0.6	0.4

i.   **Determine** the implied sustainable rate of growth in GDP.
ii. Using the growth rate calculated in *i*, **calculate** the required market return.
iii. The analyst believes a required return of 7.0% is appropriate for this market. Based on the analyst's required return, **calculate** the intrinsic value of the index.

Answer:

i.   Based on the expected long-term rates of change in capital, labor, and total factor productivity, the long-term sustainable growth in GDP is estimated at 2.6%:

$$\%\Delta Y \cong \%\Delta A + \alpha(\%\Delta K) + (1-\alpha)(\%\Delta L) = 1.5 + 0.6(1.5) + 0.4(0.5) = 2.6\%$$

ii. Because this is a mature, developed market, we can use the constant growth dividend discount model, rearranged to solve for *r*, to estimate the market required return:

$$P_0 = \frac{D_1}{r - g} = \frac{D_0(1+g)}{r - g} \Rightarrow r = \frac{D_0(1+g)}{P_0} + g$$

$$r = \frac{150(1+0.026)}{3,250} + 0.026 = \frac{153.90}{3,250} + 0.026 = 0.07335 = 7.3\%$$

iii. Using the current dividend of $150, the long-term sustainable rate of growth of 2.6%, and the analyst's required return of 7.0%, the analyst would estimate the intrinsic value of the index at 3,498:

$$P_0 = \frac{D_1}{r-g} \Rightarrow \frac{153.90}{0.07-0.026} \cong 3,498$$

Based on the analyst's estimated required return, the index is undervalued by 3,498 – 3,250 = 248 points.

Professor's Note: The long-term average sustainable rate of growth in GDP is fairly stable for a large, mature economy. Any significant differences between analysts' estimated intrinsic values and the actual values of a mature market index would, therefore, likely be due to disagreement in the market's required return.

Changes in Required Return, *r*

Using data from the previous example, Figure 5 shows the sensitivity of the value of the market to changes in the estimated required return. In each calculation, the assumed long-term growth in GDP is 2.6%, and the current dividend is $150:

Figure 5: Intrinsic Values With Changing Rates of Return

$g_L = 2.6\%$; $D_0 = \$150$	
Market Required Return, *r*	V_0 (or P_0) = $D_1 / (r - g_L)$
6.4%	153.90 / (0.064 – 0.026) = 4,050
6.7%	153.90 / (0.067 – 0.026) = 3,754
7.0%	153.90 / (0.070 – 0.026) = 3,498
7.3%	153.90 / (0.073 – 0.026) = 3,274
7.6%	153.90 / (0.076 – 0.026) = 3,078
7.9%	153.90 / (0.079 – 0.026) = 2,904

LOS 19.e: <u>Contrast</u> top-down and bottom-up approaches to forecasting the earnings per share of an equity market index.

CFA® Program Curriculum, Volume 3, page 149

In a **top-down forecast**, the analyst utilizes macroeconomic factors (e.g., interest rate expectations, expected growth in GDP) to estimate the performance of market-wide indicators, such as the S&P 500. Successive steps include identifying sectors in the market that will perform best, given market expectations.

The analyst could start by comparing the relative values of various market composites to their historical patterns to identify any that appear to be under- or over-priced. Next, the analyst could attempt to identify any momentum in the indices. In the final macro-analysis, the analyst compares the expected performance of the indices to general asset classes, such as equities, bonds, and alternatives to identify which class of assets will be expected to under- or out-perform.

In a **bottom-up forecast**, the analyst first takes a microeconomic perspective by focusing on the fundamentals of individual firms. The analyst starts the bottom-up analysis by looking at an individual firm's product or service development relative to the rest of the industry. The analyst should assess the firm's management and its willingness and ability to adopt the technology necessary to grow or even maintain its standing in the industry. Given the analyst's expectations for the firm, the analyst uses some form of cash flow analysis to determine the firm's investment potential (i.e., expected return).

Which to Use

The method used depends on the analyst's strategy, as well as any portfolio constraints. For example, a manager who focuses on a long-short, market-neutral strategy would probably pursue a purely bottom-up analysis. The manager has little need for aggregating the forecasts for individual securities into industry or market forecasts. Another manager's strategy could focus on allocating among markets or industries. In these cases, there is little need for the top-down manager to go any lower, or the bottom-up manager to go any higher, than the first step.

> **For the Exam:** To determine which approach is better for the manager, you will have to determine the manager's focus. For example, if you encounter a macro hedge fund manager who focuses on optimal allocations of global markets or currencies, a purely top-down approach would be indicated. An active manager who buys and sells individual securities to capture short-term pricing inefficiency should utilize a bottom-up approach.

Estimating Earnings Per Share (EPS)

Analysts are sometimes encouraged to confirm EPS estimates by using both the top-down and bottom-up methods. If the methods yield significantly different estimates, the analyst should analyze both estimates to determine the source(s) of discrepancy. There are two primary reasons why forecasting earnings per share with the two methods can yield different results:

1. *The models used in a top-down analysis.* Econometric models use historical values and variables adjusted to varying degrees by the user, and they suffer from the same weaknesses as all such models. For example, they may be slow in capturing structural changes (i.e., changes in the sensitivities of the individual factors). The model might have worked well in the past, but recent structural changes might have altered the relationships between the independent and dependent variables.

The models can also be specified incorrectly. Variables in the model that explained behavioral and financial relationships in the past might no longer be appropriate, and/or other variables might be more appropriate.

2. *Manager bias.* A bottom-up analysis is usually based, to a degree, on manager expectations. Because most managers expect their firms to out-perform the industry average, aggregating individual manager expectations can lead to significantly over-estimated industry expectations.

   Also, believing they can hold on longer than other firms as the economy sinks into a recession, individual managers tend to be more optimistic than would be warranted by a top-down model. On the other hand, they will tend to be more pessimistic as the market begins to recover. The potential for these biases must be assessed when the economy is entering or leaving a recession. If there is evidence of significant manager bias, the top-down method might be more appropriate.

> **For the Exam:** The bottom line is that both top-down analysis and bottom-up analysis have strengths and weaknesses. Top-down analysis doesn't incorporate the input of individual managers, while individual managers tend to be overly optimistic about their firm's future. Be able to recognize the deficiencies of each method and discuss the implications.

RELATIVE EQUITY MARKET VALUATION

LOS 19.f: Discuss the strengths and limitations of relative valuation models.

LOS 19.g: Judge whether an equity market is under-, fairly, or over-valued using a relative equity valuation model.

CFA® Program Curriculum, Volume 3, page 156

Relative value models use the relative values of assets and markets to identify investment opportunities. In the following material, we will discuss three relative value models: (1) the Fed model, (2) the Yardeni model, and (3) the 10-year Moving Average Price/ Earnings model [P/10-year MA(E)].

The **Fed model** assumes that the expected operating earnings yield on the S&P 500 (i.e., expected aggregate operating earnings divided by the current index level) should be the same as the yield on long-term U.S. Treasuries:

$$\text{Fed model ratio} = \frac{\text{S\&P earnings yield}}{\text{Treasury yield}}$$

If the S&P 500 earnings yield is higher than the treasury yield, the interpretation is that the index value is too low relative to earnings. Equities are undervalued and should increase in value. Likewise, if the earnings yield is lower than the treasury yield, the index is considered too high for the level of earnings. Equities are over-valued and should fall.

There are three basic criticisms of the Fed model, based on implied assumptions regarding risk, growth, and inflation.

The Fed model does the following:

1. *Ignores the equity risk premium.* Assuming the yield on treasuries is the same as the earnings yield on the S&P ignores the inherent risk of equities.

2. *Ignores earnings growth.* Growth expectations affect earnings, but treasury yields have no growth components. By assuming the yield on a treasury should be the same as corporate earnings yield, the model implicitly assumes zero growth in earnings.[5]

3. *Compares a real variable to a nominal variable.* The yield on a treasury is adjusted to incorporate changes in inflation and is thus considered nominal. The earnings yield will not automatically adjust to incorporate changes in inflation and could be considered real.

Although flawed, the Fed model is used by analysts in a type of spread analysis. Rather than assume the two yields should be equal, as in the model, analysts watch the *ratio* of the earnings and treasury yields. When the ratio is above its long-term average, the difference between the earnings yield and treasury yield (the spread) is historically high. Equity prices would be expected to increase, lowering the earnings yield and, thus, the ratio of the two yields (i.e., the yield spread would narrow).

> **For the Exam:** If asked to list criticisms of the Fed model, mention that it:
>
> - Does not consider the equity risk premium.
> - Ignores growth in earnings.
> - Compares a real variable (index level) to a nominal variable (Treasury yield).

The Yardeni Model

The **Yardeni model** for estimating the equilibrium earnings yield (i.e., the fair earnings yield) is based on a variation of the constant growth dividend discount model (CGM), in which investors value total earnings rather than dividends:

$$P_0 = \frac{E_1}{r - g}$$

We can restate the CGM to show that the earnings yield must be the difference between the required return on equity and expected long-term growth. This is logical, because we

---

5. Consider the constant growth dividend discount model rearranged to solve for the expected total return: $k_e = E_1 / P_0 + g$. The earnings yield for the index (E_1 / P_0) is its current yield. The total return also includes a growth factor for the expected capital gain (earnings and price change).

assume the total return on equity, r, must be the sum of the earnings yield, E_1 / P_0, and growth (i.e., capital gains), g:

$$P_0 = \frac{E_1}{r-g} \;\Rightarrow\; r = \frac{E_1}{P_0} + g \;\Rightarrow\; \frac{E_1}{P_0} = r - g$$

Yardeni incorporates risk into his model by using the yield on A-rated corporate bonds, Y_B, as the required return on equity, r. The difference between the yields on A-rated corporates and risk-free treasuries serves as a proxy, although most likely understated, for the equity risk premium. Also, instead of the long-term growth assumed in the CGM, Yardeni uses a 5-year growth forecast, LTEG,[6] for the S&P 500. The model becomes:

$$\frac{E_1}{P_0} = Y_B - d(LTEG)$$

where:

$\dfrac{E_1}{P_0}$ = expected market $(\text{e.g., S\&P})$ earnings yield

Y_B = yield on A-rated corporate bonds

d = weighting factor for the importance of earnings growth; historically around 0.10

$Y_B - d(LTEG)$ = Yardeni earnings yield

 Professor's Note: Yardeni uses the yield on A-rated corporates to approximate the equity risk premium and, then, to account for the fact that the earnings yield on the left-hand side of the equation ignores growth, he subtracts a growth factor.

The earnings yield from the Yardeni model is compared to the market earnings yield. If the market yield is high compared to the Yardeni earnings yield, equities are under-priced. Equities would be expected to rise in value, reducing the market earnings yield.

$$\text{if } \frac{E_1}{P_0} - \left[Y_B - d(LTEG)\right] > 0 \Rightarrow \text{market is under-valued}$$

$$\text{if } \frac{E_1}{P_0} - \left[Y_B - d(LTEG)\right] < 0 \Rightarrow \text{market is over-valued}$$

Like the Fed model, the Yardeni model can be applied as a ratio:

$$\text{if } \frac{E_1}{P_0} - \left[Y_B - d(LTEG)\right] > 0 \Rightarrow \frac{\text{earnings yield}}{Y_B - d(LTEG)} > 1.0 \Rightarrow \text{market is under-valued}$$

$$\text{if } \frac{E_1}{P_0} - \left[Y_B - d(LTEG)\right] < 0 \Rightarrow \frac{\text{earnings yield}}{Y_B - d(LTEG)} < 1.0 \Rightarrow \text{market is over-valued}$$

---

6. LTEG is the 5-year consensus growth forecast provided by Thomson Financial.

The Yardeni model can also be used to estimate a fair value for the equity market. If we rearrange the model to solve for P_0, it starts to look like the traditional CGM with Y_B in place of the required return and $d(LTEG)$ in place of g:

$$\frac{E_1}{P_0} = Y_B - d(LTEG) \Rightarrow P_0 = \frac{E_1}{Y_B - d(LTEG)}$$

Example: Using the Yardeni Model

i. Assume the long-term (5-year) growth forecast is 9.85% and d = 0.10. If A-rated corporate bonds yield 6%, **determine** the fair earnings yield.

ii. If the current earnings yield implied by the equity index and projected forward earnings is 5.5%, **determine** whether equities are over- or undervalued.

iii. Using the Yardeni model, **calculate** a fair value of the market P/E ratio.

Answer:

i. $$\frac{E_1}{P_0} = Y_B - d(LTEG)$$
    $$= 0.06 - 0.10(0.0985) = 0.05015 = 5.015\%$$

ii. The fair earnings yield predicted by the Yardeni model is about 5%. If the current market earnings yield is 5.5%, this would imply that the value of the index is too low compared to projected earnings. According to the Yardeni model the market is *undervalued*.

iii. The Yardeni model calculates the fair earnings ratio, which is the ratio of earnings to price. To convert the earnings ratio to a P/E ratio, we simply invert it:

$$\frac{E_1}{P_0} = 0.05015 \Rightarrow \frac{P_0}{E_1} = \frac{1}{0.05015} = 19.94$$

For the Exam: When answering questions about the Yardeni model, important considerations include the following:

*   It incorporates a proxy for the equity market risk premium (the yield on A-rated corporate debt).
*   The risk premium used is actually a measure of default risk, not a true measure of equity risk.
*   It relies on an estimate of the value investors place on earnings growth (*d*), which is assumed to be constant over time.
*   The growth rate used in the model (LTEG) might not be an accurate estimate of long-term sustainable growth.

10-Year Moving Average Price/Earnings Ratio, P/10-Year MA(E)

The numerator of the **P/10-year MA(E)** is the value of the S&P 500 price index, and the denominator is the average of the previous ten years' reported earnings. Both are adjusted for inflation using the consumer price index. Similar to a trailing P/E ratio, the P/10-year MA(E) compares the inflation adjusted price of the market at a point in time to the market's average real earnings over the previous ten years.

To use the P/10-year MA(E) the analyst compares its current value to its historical average to determine whether the market is over- or underpriced. If the ratio currently stands at 18.0, and the historical average is 16.0, for example, the current price (i.e., level of the index) is high relative to earnings. The index would be considered over-priced and would be expected to revert to its historical mean of 16.

> *Professor's Note: Real simply means restating the price or earnings in today's dollars. For example, you could restate earnings from past years in real terms by multiplying the earnings figure by the ratio of today's CPI to the relevant year CPI. Assume earnings per share for 2008 were $3.00, and you wish to restate them as of June 2010 (i.e., restate them in June 2010 dollars). You would multiply December 2008 EPS by the ratio of 217.965 to 210.228, the CPIs for June 2010 and December 2008, respectively.*[7]

$$restated\ 2008\ earnings = nominal\ 2008\ earnings \times inflation\ adjustment\ factor$$

$$= nominal\ 2008\ earnings \times \left(\frac{CPI_{6/2010}}{CPI_{12/2008}} \right)$$

$$= \$3.00 \times \left(\frac{217.965}{210.228} \right) = \$3.00 \times 1.036803 = \$3.1104$$

> *When you restate values at a later date (bring them forward in time), the ratio of CPIs will be greater than 1.0 so that the value increases. To restate them in a previous year (take them back in time), the ratio of the CPIs will be less than 1.0, and the value decreases.*

For the Exam: When answering questions about the P/10-year MA(E), important considerations include:

- By restating earnings and prices according to CPI, it considers the effects of inflation.
- By using 10-year average earnings, it captures the effects of business cycles, but by its nature it is backward-looking—current or expected earnings could provide more useful information.
- It does not consider the effects of changes in accounting rules or methods.
- Empirical studies have found that very high or low P/10-year MA(E) ratios have persisted, limiting its usefulness in forming short-run expectations.

---

7. Source: *http://inflationdata.com/inflation/consumer_price_index/historicalcpi.aspx;* accessed August 2011.

Asset-Based Models

Tobin's q compares the current market value of a company to the replacement cost of its assets. The thinking is that the sum of the market (replacement) values of the individual assets should be the same as their aggregate market value, as reflected in the sum of the market values of the firm's debt and equity. The theoretical value of Tobin's q is 1.0. If the current Tobin's q is above (below) 1.0 the firm's stock is presumed to be overpriced (underpriced).

The **equity q** focuses on equity values. It compares the aggregate market value of the firm's equity to the market value of the firm's net worth (i.e., net assets) measured as the market value of its assets less the market value of its liabilities. Again, the expected value of the ratio is 1.0.

Both ratios are considered *mean-reverting*. A q value above 1.0 would be expected to fall because it indicates that the firm's net assets, as measured by the market value of equity, are currently overvalued. Using the opposite argument, a value less than 1.0 would be expected to rise.

$$\text{Tobin's q} = \frac{\text{asset market value}}{\text{asset replacement cost}} = \frac{\text{market value of debt + equity}}{\text{asset replacement cost}}$$

$$\text{equity q} = \frac{\text{market value of equity}}{\text{market value of net worth}} = \frac{\text{\# outstanding shares} \times \text{price per share}}{\text{market value of assets} - \text{market value of liabilities}}$$

Professor's Note: Equity q is similar to the market-to-book ratio. It is not the same, however, because net worth is stated in market value rather than book value terms.

For the Exam: If on the exam, a long-run equilibrium value greater or less than 1.0 is provided for Tobin's q or the equity q, use it to determine whether you would expect the firm or market price to change. If an equilibrium value is not provided, you will be safe in assuming the equilibrium value is 1.0.

When answering questions about Tobin's q or the equity q, important considerations include:

- Both ratios are mean-reverting.
- Both have demonstrated a negative relationship with equity returns. Higher (lower) ratios have forecasted lower (higher) equity returns.
- Replacement costs can be difficult to estimate.
- Empirical studies have found that very high or low ratios have persisted, limiting their usefulness in forming short-run expectations.

KEY CONCEPTS

LOS 19.a

The Cobb-Douglas function (CD) relates real economic output to capital stock and labor as well as factor productivity:

$$Y = AK^{\alpha} L^{\beta}$$

By applying natural logs and making other assumptions, it can be restated to predict changes in output:

$$\frac{\Delta Y}{Y} \cong \frac{\Delta A}{A} + \alpha \frac{\Delta K}{K} + (1-\alpha)\frac{\Delta L}{L}$$

$$\text{Solow residual} = \Delta TFP = \frac{\Delta A}{A} \cong \frac{\Delta Y}{Y} - \alpha \frac{\Delta K}{K} - (1-\alpha)\frac{\Delta L}{L}$$

where:
A = total factor productivity (TFP)
K = capital stock
L = labor input
α = output elasticity of K; the change in Y for a 1-unit change in K ($0 < \alpha < 1$)
β = output elasticity of L; the change in Y for a 1-unit change in L ($\alpha + \beta = 1$)

LOS 19.b

Once we have estimated the growth equation, $\%\Delta Y = \%\Delta A + \alpha \,\%\Delta K + (1 - \alpha) \,\%\Delta L$, we can use the historical growth of capital and labor, along with the estimates of output elasticities for labor and capital, to decompose the growth of GDP in order to evaluate the relative effects of labor growth, capital accumulation, and increases in factor productivity on economic growth.

LOS 19.c,d

We assume the growth rate in corporate earnings and dividends is the same as the growth rate in gross domestic product (GDP). If an economy is expected to grow at a particularly high rate of growth for a number of years and then revert to a sustainable growth rate, we apply the H-model:

$$P_0 = \frac{D_0}{r - g_L}\left[(1 + g_L) + \frac{N}{2}(g_S - g_L)\right]$$

When growth is assumed constant, we can use the constant growth dividend discount model:

$$P_0 = \frac{D_1}{r - \overline{g}} = \frac{D_0(1 + \overline{g})}{r - \overline{g}}$$

LOS 19.e
In a top-down forecast, the analyst utilizes macroeconomic factors to estimate the performance of market-wide indicators. Successive steps include identifying sectors in the market and then individual securities that will perform best, given market expectations.

In a bottom-up forecast, the analyst first takes a microeconomic perspective by focusing on the fundamentals of individual firms. For a macro forecast, the analyst can then aggregate the expected performance of individual securities.

To determine which to use, determine the manager's focus. For example, a macro hedge fund manager who focuses on optimal allocations of global markets or currencies would use a purely top-down approach. An active manager who buys and sells individual securities to capture short-term pricing inefficiency would utilize a bottom-up approach.

LOS 19.f,g
The Fed model assumes the yield on long-term U.S. Treasuries should be the same as the expected operating earnings yield on the S&P 500. When the S&P 500 earnings yield is higher (lower) than the treasury yield, the interpretation is that the index is too low (high).

The Fed model:
- Does not consider the equity risk premium.
- Ignores growth in earnings.
- Compares a real variable (index level) to a nominal variable (Treasury yield).

The Yardeni model assumes investors value total earnings rather than dividends:

$$P_0 = \frac{E_1}{r - g} \Rightarrow \frac{E_1}{P_0} = Y_B - d(LTEG)$$

Important considerations include:
- It uses the yield on A-rated corporate debt as the equity risk premium.
- The risk premium used is actually a measure of default risk, not a true measure of equity risk.
- It relies on an estimate of the value investors place on earnings growth (d), which is assumed to be constant over time.
- The growth rate used in the model (LTEG) might not be a fair estimate of long-term sustainable growth.

P/10-year MA(E): The numerator is the value of the price index, and the denominator is the average of the previous ten years' reported earnings. Both are adjusted for inflation using the consumer price index.

Important considerations include:
- It considers the effects of inflation.
- It captures the effects of business cycles.
- Current or expected earnings could provide more useful information.
- It does not consider the effects of changes in accounting rules or methods.
- Very high or low P/10-year MA(E) ratios can persist, limiting its usefulness in forming short-run expectations.

$$\text{Tobin's q} = \frac{\text{market value of debt } + \text{ equity}}{\text{asset replacement cost}}$$

$$\text{equity q} = \frac{\text{market value of equity}}{\text{market value of assets} - \text{market value of liabilities}}$$

Important considerations include:
- Both ratios are mean-reverting.
- Both have demonstrated a negative relationship with equity returns.
- Replacement costs can be difficult to estimate.
- Very high or low ratios can persist, limiting their usefulness in forming short-run expectations.

CONCEPT CHECKERS

1. While analyzing potential global investments, Gretchen Fenledder, CFA, gathered the data in Table A on emerging Equity Market Index Y:

   Table A: Economic Data for Index Y*

Last dividend (D_0)	150
Forecast earnings per share	600
Current and sustainable long-term growth rate	2.5%
Required return	8.5%
Forward operating yield (E/P)	6.0%

   * Yield on 10-year government bond = 6%

   Based on the data in Table A:
   a. **Determine** the intrinsic price level of the index.
   b. **Determine** whether the market is over- or under-valued using the Fed model.

2. Fenledder also gathered data for Equity Market Index Z as shown in Table B:

   Table B: Economic Data for Equity Market Index Z

Expected growth in total factor productivity	1.5%
Expected growth in labor	3.0%
Expected growth in capital stock, $\alpha = 0.6$	2.2%

   a. **Explain** each of the terms in the Cobb-Douglas production function (CD).
   b. **Calculate** the implied growth (percentage change) in real economic output for Market Z using the data in Table B and the Cobb-Douglas function.
   c. **Define** and **discuss** the Solow residual.

3. **Describe** top-down and bottom-up economic analysis. **Explain** the situations that would imply either a top-down or a bottom-up analysis would be more appropriate and when the use of both would be justified.

4. **Compare** Tobin's q and the equity q for market valuation. **Provide** and **explain** one strength and one weakness of each.

5. **Explain** three weaknesses of the Fed model.

6. **Describe** the Yardeni model. Referring to specific variables in each, **explain** how the Yardeni and Fed models could arrive at different conclusions about the relative value of an equity market.

7.   In the template provided, **indicate** and **explain** the effect on the growth of an
      economy, given the indicated change in the following growth factors:
      i.   Slowing growth of the population.
      ii.   Decrease in the government-mandated retirement age.
      iii. Relaxation of import duties and other trade restrictions.
      iv.   Tax relief to encourage technological innovation.

Template for Question 7:

Factor	Effect on Economic Growth (circle one)	Explanation
i. Slowing growth of the population.	Increase Decrease	
ii. Decrease in the government-mandated retirement age.	Increase Decrease	
iii. Relaxation of import duties and other trade restrictions.	Increase Decrease	
iv. Corporate tax relief to encourage technological innovation.	Increase Decrease	

8.   In the template provided, **determine** whether a top-down or bottom-up forecast would be better indicated for each scenario. **Justify** your selection.

Template for Question 8:

Scenario	Top-Down or Bottom-Up (circle one)	Justification
A global macro-hedge fund takes large positions in foreign currencies.	Top-down Bottom-up	
Portfolio manager Active A employs a market neutral strategy and adds market exposure with equity futures.	Top-down Bottom-up	
Active Investors, LLP, advertises that they earn alpha through stock selection.	Top-down Bottom-up	

ANSWERS – CONCEPT CHECKERS

1.

Last dividend (D_0)	150
Current and sustainable long-term growth rate	2.5%
Required return	8.5%
Forward operating yield (E/P)	6.0%

* Yield on 10-year government bond = 6%

a. We are provided with the long-term sustainable growth rate, the required return, and the current dividend, so we know to use the constant growth dividend discount model to determine the intrinsic value of the index:

$$P_0 = \frac{D_1}{r-g} = \frac{D_0(1+g)}{r-g} = \frac{150(1.025)}{0.085-0.025} = \frac{153.75}{0.06} = 2{,}562.50$$

b. The Fed model compares the operating yield on the index to the yield in the intermediate-term government bond:

Fed model ratio = earnings yield / government yield = 0.06 / 0.06 = 1.0

Based on expected earnings, the market appears to be correctly priced.

If the Fed model produces a ratio greater than 1.0, the earnings yield is considered too high (earnings are high relative to prices), indicating that the market is currently under-valued and would be expected to rise. If the ratio is less than 1.0, the earnings yield is too low, and the market is deemed to be over-valued.

2. a. The CD production function, assuming constant returns to scale, relates the economy's labor and capital inputs to its real economic output:

$$Y = AK^\alpha L^\beta$$

where:
Y = total real economic output
A = total factor productivity (TFP)
K = capital stock
L = labor input
α = output elasticity of K ($0 < \alpha < 1$)
β = output elasticity of L ($\alpha + \beta = 1$)

We can rearrange the CD to state the percentage change in real total economic output in terms of the percentage changes in the factors:

$$\frac{\Delta Y}{Y} \cong \frac{\Delta A}{A} + \alpha \frac{\Delta K}{K} + (1-\alpha)\frac{\Delta L}{L}$$

$\frac{\Delta Y}{Y}$ = % change in real output $(\%\Delta Y)$: growth in GDP

$\frac{\Delta A}{A}$ = % change in total factor productivity $(\%\Delta TFP)$

$\frac{\Delta K}{K}$ = % change in capital stock $(\%\Delta K)$

$\frac{\Delta L}{L}$ = % change in labor $(\%\Delta L)$

The assumption of constant returns to scale implies that $\%\Delta TFP$ is zero, so that equal percentage changes in labor and capital will produce the same percentage change in real output.

b.

Expected growth in total factor productivity	1.5%
Expected growth in labor	3.0%
Expected growth in capital stock, $\alpha = 0.6$	2.2%

$$\frac{\Delta Y}{Y} \cong \frac{\Delta A}{A} + \alpha \frac{\Delta K}{K} + (1-\alpha)\frac{\Delta L}{L}$$

$$\frac{\Delta Y}{Y} \cong 1.5\% + 0.6(2.2\%) + 0.4(3.0\%) = 4.02\%$$

c. The Solow residual is the percentage change in total factor productivity. Given the expected change in the real economic output, expected changes in labor and capital, and the economy's elasticities of capital and labor, we arrange the CD to solve for the Solow residual:

Solow residual $= \%\Delta TFP = \%\Delta Y - \alpha(\%\Delta K) - (1-\alpha)\%\Delta L$

An economy's TFP can change over time due to:
i.   Changing technology.
ii. Changing restrictions on capital flows and labor mobility.
iii. Changing trade restrictions.
iv. Changing laws.
v.   Changing division of labor.
vi. Depleting/discovering natural resources.

As an example of calculating the Solow residual, we use the growth of 4.02% calculated in Question 2 along with the other data provided and solve for %ΔTFP:

$$\%\Delta Y = \%\Delta TFP - \alpha\left(\%\Delta K\right) - \left(1 - \alpha\right)\left(\%\Delta L\right) \Rightarrow$$

$$
\begin{aligned}
\%\Delta TFP\left(\text{Solow residual}\right) &= \%\Delta Y - \alpha\left(\%\Delta K\right) - \left(1 - \alpha\right)\left(\%\Delta L\right) \\
&= 4.02\% - 0.6\left(2.2\%\right) - 0.4\left(3.0\%\right) = 1.5\%
\end{aligned}
$$

3. In a top-down forecast, the analyst utilizes macroeconomic factors to estimate the performance of market-wide indicators, such as the S&P 500. Successive steps include identifying sectors in the market that will perform best given market expectations.

    The analyst starts by comparing the relative values of various market composites to their historical patterns to identify any that appear to be under- or over-priced. Next, the analyst attempts to identify any momentum in the indices. In the final macro-analysis, the analyst compares the expected performance of the indices to general asset classes, such as equities, bonds, and alternatives to identify which class of assets will be expected to under- or out-perform.

    In a bottom-up forecast, the analyst takes a microeconomic perspective by focusing on the fundamentals of individual firms. The analyst starts the bottom-up analysis by looking at an individual firm's product or service development relative to the rest of the industry. The analyst should assess the firm's management and its willingness and ability to adopt the technology necessary to grow or even maintain its standing in the industry. Given the analyst's expectations for the firm, the analyst uses some form of cash flow analysis to determine the firm's investment potential (i.e., expected return).

    The method used depends on the analyst's strategy. A manager who utilizes a long-short, market neutral strategy would probably pursue a purely bottom-up analysis. Another manager's strategy could focus on allocating among markets or industries. In these cases, there is little need for the top-down manager to go any lower or the bottom-up manager to go any higher than the first step.

    When approaching or leaving recessions, manager expectations can be biased. It would be wise in these situations for the bottom-up analyst to also utilize a top-down approach to confirm earnings estimates.

4. Tobin's q compares the current market value of a company to the replacement cost of its assets. The theoretical value of Tobin's q is 1.0. If the current Tobin's q is above (below) 1.0, the firm's stock is presumed to be overpriced (underpriced).

    The equity q compares the aggregate market value of the firm's equity to the market value of the firm's net worth (i.e., net assets) measured as the market value of its assets less the market value of its liabilities. Again, the expected value of the ratio is 1.0.

    Both ratios are considered *mean-reverting*. A q value above 1.0 would be expected to fall because it indicates that the firm's net assets, as measured by the market value of equity, are currently overvalued. Using the opposite argument, a value less than 1.0 would be expected to rise.

$$\text{Tobin's q} = \frac{\text{asset market value}}{\text{asset replacement cost}} = \frac{\text{market value of debt + equity}}{\text{asset replacement cost}}$$

$$\text{equity q} = \frac{\text{market value of equity}}{\text{market value of net worth}} = \frac{\text{market value of equity}}{\text{market value of assets} - \text{market value of liabilities}}$$

Strengths of both models include:
- Both are mean-reverting, so they are easy to use.
- Both have usefulness as demonstrated by a negative relationship with equity returns. Higher (lower) ratios have forecasted lower (higher) equity returns.

Weaknesses include:
- Replacement costs can be difficult to estimate for Tobin's q.
- Empirical studies have found that very high or low ratios have persisted for both, limiting their usefulness in forming short-run expectations.

5. The Fed model does not consider the equity risk premium, it ignores growth in earnings, and it compares a real variable (index level) to a nominal variable (Treasury yield).

    Ignores growth in earnings: It compares the earnings yield on the market index (only a portion of the total return on the index) to the total expected return on the treasury security. It does not include the growth portion of the expected index return.

    Real and nominal variables: The yield on the treasury security includes an inflation premium while earnings are considered a real variable.

6. The Yardeni model is based on the constant growth dividend discount model (CGM), stated in terms of earnings rather than dividends:

$$P_0 = \frac{E_1}{r - g}$$

The earnings yield must be the difference between the required return on equity and expected long-term growth:

$$P_0 = \frac{E_1}{r - g} \Rightarrow r = \frac{E_1}{P_0} + g \Rightarrow \frac{E_1}{P_0} = r - g$$

The model uses the yield on A-rated corporate bonds as the required return on equity. Instead of the long-term growth assumed in the CGM, Yardeni uses a 5-year growth forecast for the S&P 500.

$$\frac{E_1}{P_0} = Y_B - d(LTEG)$$

where:
Y_B = yield on A-rated corporate bonds
d = a weighting factor for the importance of earnings growth; historically around 0.10

If the current market earnings yield is high compared to the Yardeni earnings yield, equities are under-priced. Equities would be expected to rise in value:

$$\text{if } \frac{E_1}{P_0} - \left[Y_B - d(LTEG)\right] > 0 \Rightarrow \text{market is under-valued}$$

$$\text{if } \frac{E_1}{P_0} - \left[Y_B - d(LTEG)\right] < 0 \Rightarrow \text{market is over-valued}$$

The Fed model assumes the expected operating earnings yield on the S&P 500 should be same as the yield on long-term U.S. Treasuries:

$$\text{Fed model ratio} = \frac{\text{S\&P earnings yield}}{\text{Treasury yield}}$$

If the S&P 500 earnings yield is higher than the treasury yield, the index value is low relative to earnings, and the market should increase in value. If the S&P 500 earnings yield is lower than the treasury yield, the index value is high relative to earnings, and the market should drop in value.

In order to discuss circumstances where the two could yield different conclusions about market valuation, we reproduce them as ratios and see that both contain the expected S&P earnings yield in the numerator:

$$\text{Fed model ratio} = \frac{\text{S\&P earnings yield}}{\text{Treasury yield}}$$

$$\text{Yardeni ratio} = \frac{\text{S\&P earnings yield}}{Y_B - d(\text{LTEG})}$$

In situations where $[Y_B - d(\text{LTEG})]$ is dramatically different from the treasury yield, the two ratios can yield conflicting conclusions. For example, Y_B might be historically high while interest rates are historically low (i.e., interest rates are low but risk aversion is high, making the risk premium on A-rated bonds high). In that case, the resulting Yardeni ratio could be less than 1.0 (indicating the market is over-valued) while the Fed model is greater than 1.0 (indicating the market is under-valued).

7.

	Factor	Effect on Economic Growth (circle one)	Explanation
i.	Slowing growth of the population.	Decrease	Increase in labor input slowing.
ii.	Decrease in the government-mandated retirement age.	Decrease	Assuming it induces individuals to retire earlier, reduction in labor input.
iii.	Relaxation of import duties and other trade restrictions.	Increase	Increased international competition; falling prices.
iv.	Corporate tax relief to encourage technological innovation.	Increase	Short-term depression on growth with increased costs and retooling but increased in long-run due to technological improvements.

8.

Scenario	Top-Down or Bottom-Up (circle one)	Justification
A global macro-hedge fund takes large positions in foreign currencies.	Top-down	With their focus on the relative values of global currencies, there is no need for the hedge fund to focus on individual firms.
Portfolio manager Active A employs a market neutral strategy and adds market exposure with equity futures.	Bottom-up	Active A's primary strategy is market neutral. They generate alpha by going long and short in individual stocks expected to out- or under-perform in weights that will drive the ultimate market exposure (systematic risk) to zero. The selection of equity futures is a passive approach to adding market exposure.
Active Investors, LLP, advertises that they earn alpha through stock selection.	Bottom-up	Stock selection represents the stereotypical bottom-up approach. Because they generate alpha through stock selection, the focus is on the valuation of individual stocks, not macro-wide indices or factors.

The following is a review of the Economic Concepts for Asset Valuation in Portfolio Management principles designed to address the learning outcome statements set forth by CFA Institute®. This topic is also covered in:

DREAMING WITH BRICs: THE PATH TO 2050

EXAM FOCUS

In this topic review, focus on the determinants of and potential for economic growth in emerging countries; that is, the characteristics a portfolio manager would look for before investing in a particular emerging market. The potential growth rate in emerging economies is higher than that in the developed world, due to appreciating currencies, technological progress, employment growth, and growth in capital stock. The potential in these markets argues for their inclusion in a well-diversified portfolio.

ECONOMIC POTENTIAL OF THE BRICs

LOS 20.a: Compare the economic potential of emerging markets such as Brazil, Russia, India, and China (BRICs) to that of developed markets, in terms of economic size and growth, demographics and per capita income, growth in global spending, and trends in real exchange rates.

CFA® Program Curriculum, Volume 3, page 187

Potential Economic Size and Growth

In U.S. dollar terms, the size of the BRIC economies as a whole is currently about 15% of that of the G6. However, by the year 2025, they could be more than half the size of the G6. By 2040, the total size of the BRIC economies may surpass that of the G6.

Individually, China's economy is projected to be the largest of the BRICs and might surpass the U.S. economy in 2039. By the year 2050, the largest economies are projected to be China, followed by the United States, India, Japan, Brazil, Russia, the U.K., Germany, France, and Italy, in that order. So, of the six largest economies in 2050, four are projected to be BRIC economies, and only two are from the current G6.

In terms of economic growth, India is projected to have the strongest growth at 5% annually for the next 30 to 50 years. For other BRIC countries, growth will decline more swiftly over time, so that growth will be in the neighborhood of 3% by 2050.

Demographics and Per Capita Income

Although BRIC countries have a relatively young population, they are expected to experience a decline in their working age population, albeit later than that in the G6. The aging will be more rapid in Russia and China and less rapid in India and Brazil.

In terms of per capita income, all the BRIC countries except Russia are expected to remain below that of G6 countries. China is projected to have per capita income similar to the current levels in the G6. By 2050, U.S. income may climb to $80,000 per person.

Growth in Global Spending

Currently, the annual increase in global spending, measured in U.S. dollar terms, is about the same for the G6 and the BRICs as a whole. But by 2025, annual increases in spending could be more than twice as high in the BRIC countries. By 2050, the annual change in spending should be four times larger in the BRIC countries.

Trends in Real Exchange Rates

Real exchange rates in the BRIC countries could strengthen by 300% by 2050. The Chinese yuan could increase by 100% in value over the next ten years if growth remains healthy and the yuan is allowed to float. Note that about one-third of the projected BRIC GDP growth, as measured in U.S. dollar terms, should come from rising exchange rates.

ECONOMIC GROWTH

LOS 20.b: <u>Explain</u> why certain developing economies may have high returns on capital, rising productivity, and appreciating currencies.

CFA® Program Curriculum, Volume 3, page 190

Potential Returns on Capital and Productivity

Developing economies have the potential to increase returns on capital and productivity because they are currently operating below the levels of more mature, developed countries. Because developing countries currently utilize relatively low amounts of capital, an increase in investment capital will result in a relatively high level of output. Furthermore, as developing countries adopt technology available in developed countries, their productivity will increase.

As developing countries mature, their returns on capital and productivity will slow. For example, Japan and Germany had very high rates of growth in the 1960s and 1970s, but their growth slowed in later years. Likewise, China cannot continue to grow at its current rate forever.

Appreciating Currencies

When countries have low per capita income levels, their currencies tend to be weak and below levels predicted by purchasing power parity (PPP). As the developing countries mature and income rises, their currencies appreciate and converge towards the value predicted by PPP.

 Professor's Note: Recall from Level II that PPP states that countries with low prices and low inflation will have stronger currencies than those with higher prices and high inflation.

ELEMENTS OF ECONOMIC GROWTH

LOS 20.c: <u>Explain</u> the importance of technological progress, employment growth, and growth in capital stock in estimating the economic potential of an emerging market.

CFA® Program Curriculum, Volume 3, page 192

The economic growth rate in a country has three elements: (1) *technological progress*, (2) *growth in the capital stock*, and (3) *employment growth*.

Technological Progress

The rate of technological progress in developing countries should eventually catch up to that in developed countries. The wider the income gap between a developing and developed country, the greater the potential for technological progress and the faster the technological growth should be. Stronger technological progress should result in higher economic growth and a stronger currency. When measured in U.S. dollars, economic growth in developing countries will increase as a result of both growth itself and an appreciating currency. Changes in technological progress can have a large impact on economic growth.

In Brazil and India, technological progress is projected to be weaker than in China and Russia over the next 20 years because of a less educated workforce and a weaker infrastructure. Eventually though, technological progress in Brazil and India should converge to that in the developed world.

Growth in Capital Stock

The growth in capital stock is less important for economic growth than it is for technological progress, but it does have an impact on economic growth. Reducing the projected growth in capital stock by 5% would reduce GDP levels by 13% in the BRIC countries in 2050.

China's growth in investment capital is currently a strong 36%. By 2015, however, this growth is projected to gradually decline to the 30% average for Asia.

Employment Growth

The projected growth/decline in working age populations is based on population growth estimates. It will play a more positive role in economic growth in India and Brazil than in the rest of the BRIC countries. In Russia, for example, the working age population is actually projected to decline, as it is in the G6 countries, although this may reverse if decreasing birth rates and life expectancy are just temporary features of a post-communism transition. In the G6, the United States should have the healthiest employment growth, whereas in Japan and Italy an aging population will detract from economic growth.

Note that the projections for employment growth do not account for increases in labor force participation or an extension of the retirement age, both of which could offset the negative effects of a graying population in these countries.

Professor's Note: Recall from Topic Reviews 18 and 19 that economic growth was decomposed into two main components: (1) changes in employment levels and (2) changes in productivity. The latter component was broken down in Topic Review 18 into spending on new capital inputs and total factor productivity growth. The formulation of growth in this topic review is the same except that total factor productivity growth is referred to as technological progress. Also, changes in employment levels were further decomposed into population growth and the rate of labor force participation in Topic Review 18.

THE CONDITIONS FOR SUSTAINED ECONOMIC GROWTH

LOS 20.d: <u>Discuss</u> the conditions necessary for sustained economic growth, including the core factors of macroeconomic stability, institutional efficiency, open trade, and worker education.

CFA® Program Curriculum, Volume 3, page 202

The ability to sustain growth in a country is influenced by its macroeconomic stability, institutional efficiency, open trade, and worker education. These factors are related, and countries that are successful in one area are often successful in another.

Macroeconomic Stability

A stable macroeconomic environment promotes economic growth and is characterized by stable inflation, responsible fiscal policies, stable currency values, and accommodating governmental policies. High inflation hampers growth because it discourages investment in the economy by households and businesses. As such, governmental fiscal and monetary policies should focus on controlling inflation.

Brazil faces significant challenges in this area due to its poor fiscal policies and high inflation. China has had more success, with budget deficits and inflation much lower than Brazil's.

Institutional Efficiency

If the institutions in an economy operate efficiently, an economy can produce goods and services more efficiently. Poorly operating institutions discourage productive enterprise and investment in the economy. The relevant institutions here are the country's financial institutions, markets, legal system, government, health care industry, and educational system. Inefficient institutions are often symptomatic of other chronic problems. BRICs have had trouble in this area, particularly in the case of Russia.

Open Trade

An **open economy** is one in which trade and capital flows freely across its borders. With an open economy, a country gains increased access to technology, inputs, and markets. Research has verified that openness in an economy results in higher growth, with much of the benefit coming at the industry level. BRICs have had varying degrees of success in opening up their economies; India has been particularly slow to do so.

Worker Education

Research has demonstrated that higher levels of education are associated with increased economic growth in a country. The more educated a BRIC's workforce, the faster it can catch up to the technological levels of the developed world. An educated workforce is particularly important for BRICs to enter the next stage of economic growth. Although some BRIC countries have made some progress in this area as demonstrated with increasing school enrollments, the primary and secondary education systems in India are quite poor.

Professor's Note: The discussion in this LOS is similar to that in Study Session 6, Topic Review 18, LOS m and Study Session 8, Topic Review 22, LOS j.

From the former, recall that the risks faced by investors in emerging markets concern the country's fiscal and monetary policies; expected growth; currency valuation; current account deficit; leverage; foreign exchange reserves; and the government's willingness to implement structural reform.

From the latter, recall that the risks particular to emerging markets are unstable political and social environments, undeveloped infrastructure, poor educational systems, and corrupt governments. Also, the emerging markets likely to have higher growth are those with democratic governments, efficient financial regulation, promotion of free enterprise, and effective legal systems.

EMERGING MARKETS IN A PORTFOLIO

LOS 20.e: <u>Evaluate</u> the investment rationale for allocating part of a well-diversified portfolio to emerging markets in countries with above average economic potential.

CFA® Program Curriculum, Volume 3, page 205

The stronger economic growth for emerging markets described previously may result in higher stock returns. Furthermore, the increased growth in these markets will increase the demand for capital, which should strengthen their currency values. As a result, the market capitalization of these markets will increase, further justifying their representation in a well-diversified portfolio.

KEY CONCEPTS

LOS 20.a

In U.S. dollar terms, the size of the BRIC economies as a whole is currently about 15% of that of the G6. However, by the year 2025, they could be more than half the size of the G6. By 2040, the total size of the BRIC economies may surpass that of the G6. By the year 2050, the largest economies are projected to be China, followed by the United States, India, Japan, Brazil, Russia, the U.K., Germany, France, and Italy, respectively. In terms of economic growth, India is projected to have the strongest growth (5% annually) for the next 30 to 50 years. Although BRIC countries have a relatively young population, they are expected to experience a decline in their working age population, albeit later than that in the G6. In terms of per capita income, all the BRIC countries except Russia are expected to remain below that of G6 countries. Currently, the annual increase in global spending, measured in U.S. dollar terms, is about the same for the G6 and the BRICs as a whole. But by 2025, annual increases in spending could be more than twice as high in the BRIC countries. By 2050, BRIC countries should expect a fourfold annual change in spending and a possible strengthening of real exchange rates of 300%.

LOS 20.b

Developing economies have the potential to increase returns on capital and productivity because they are currently operating below the levels of more mature, developed countries. Because developing countries currently utilize relatively low amounts of capital, an increase in investment capital will result in a relatively high level of output. Furthermore, as developing countries adopt technology available in developed countries, their productivity will increase.

As developing countries mature, their returns on capital and productivity will slow. For example, Japan and Germany had very high rates of growth in the 1960s and 1970s, but their growth slowed in later years. Likewise, China cannot continue to grow at its current rate forever.

When countries have low per capita income levels, their currencies tend to be weak and below levels predicted by Purchasing Power Parity (PPP). As the developing countries mature and income rises, their currencies appreciate and converge towards the value predicted by PPP.

LOS 20.c

The rate of technological progress in developing countries should eventually catch up to that in developed countries. The wider the income gap between a developing and developed country, the greater the potential for technological progress and the faster the technological growth should be; this will result in higher economic growth and a stronger currency. Changes in technological progress can have a large impact on economic growth.

The growth in capital stock is less important for economic growth than it is for technological progress, but it does have an impact on economic growth. Reducing the projected growth in capital stock by 5% would reduce GDP levels by 13% in the BRIC countries in 2050.

The projected growth/decline in working age populations is based on population growth estimates. It will play a more positive role in economic growth in India and Brazil than in the rest of the BRIC countries. For example, in Russia the working-age population is projected to decline, as it is in the G6 countries. In the G6, the United States should have the healthiest employment growth, whereas an aging population in Japan and Italy will detract from economic growth.

LOS 20.d

A stable macroeconomic environment promotes economic growth and is characterized by stable inflation, responsible fiscal policies, stable currency values, and accommodating governmental policies. High inflation hampers growth because it discourages investment in the economy by households and businesses. As such, governmental fiscal and monetary policies should focus on controlling inflation.

If the institutions in an economy operate efficiently, an economy can produce goods and services more efficiently. Poorly operating institutions discourage productive enterprise and investment in the economy. The relevant institutions are financial institutions, markets, the legal system, government, health care industry, and educational system.

An open economy is one in which trade and capital flows freely across its borders. With an open economy, a country gains increased access to technology, inputs, and markets that will stimulate higher growth.

Research has demonstrated that higher levels of education are associated with increased economic growth in a country.

LOS 20.e

The stronger economic growth for emerging markets previously described may result in higher stock returns. Furthermore, the increased growth in these markets will increase the demand for capital, thereby strengthening their currency values. As a result, the market capitalization of these markets will increase, further justifying their representation in a well-diversified portfolio.

CONCEPT CHECKERS

1. **Compare** the expected economic health of the BRIC countries to that of the G6 in the year 2050.

2. Relative to developed countries, why should developing countries have higher returns on capital and stronger productivity?

3. **Assess** the contribution of employment growth to economic growth in India and Brazil, relative to that in Russia.

4. How is the educational level in a country related to an emerging country's economic growth rate?

5. **Discuss** the reasons why an investor should consider including emerging stocks in a well-diversified portfolio.

ANSWERS – CONCEPT CHECKERS

1. On the positive side, the BRIC countries as a whole should have a larger economy, stronger increases in annual spending, and currencies that have quadrupled in value. Although their population will age, the decline in workforce-age population will occur later than that in the G6 countries.

    On the negative side, all the BRIC countries except Russia should have lower per capita incomes than that in the G6.

2. Currently, developing countries underutilize capital and technology. Increased utilization of capital and technology in developing countries will result in relatively high levels of output. Developing countries will also see the value of their currencies increase as per capita income increases.

3. In India and Brazil, employment growth will have a positive impact on economic growth. In Russia, employment growth is actually projected to decline because the population is projected to decline. Note, however, that this projected decline in employment growth may reverse itself. Furthermore, this projected employment growth does not account for increases in labor force participation or an extension of the retirement age, which would counteract a decline in population growth.

4. For an emerging economy to enter into the more advanced stages of economic growth, it must have a more educated workforce. To catch up to the technological level of a developed country, the emerging economy workforce must be skilled. The more skilled the workforce, the faster the country can catch up to that level and the faster its economy can grow.

5. The potentially higher growth in these markets could result in higher stock returns. The higher growth will require additional capital. This will increase emerging currency values and market capitalization. These forces argue for a portfolio allocation to emerging markets.

SELF-TEST: ECONOMIC CONCEPTS

Use the following information for Questions 1 through 6.

Economist James Jones prepares economic forecasts for Global Bancorp, one of the world's largest investment banks. The markets have been volatile, and a change in the party in power in Washington has many investors worried about the future. Jones has been tasked with projecting what will happen in the year ahead.

Jones begins by looking at interest rates in the hopes of offering some help to Global's bond department. He knows the yield curve is flat, but wants more insight on the future direction of interest rates. Jones finds the Taylor rule useful for predicting the Federal Reserve's action, so he attempts to calculate a short-term interest rate target based on the following data:

Current short-term rate target:	4.15%
Neutral rate:	3.57%
Target inflation rate:	2.00%
Expected inflation rate:	0.60%
Expected GDP growth, current year:	3.84%
Long-term estimated GDP growth rate:	3.27%
Risk-free rate:	4.11%

Jones also performs some analysis of the U.S. economy from an equity perspective. The stock market has been going up, and sales and profit growth are on the increase. P/E ratios are very high, but wage growth is very low.

While emerging markets are not Jones' area of expertise, he has also been asked to make a recommendation regarding investment in Venvakia. In his research, Jones learns the following information:

Venvakia's population is rising at a 5.2% rate, while the rate of participation in the labor force is rising at a 0.9% clip. The country's population is younger than the average of its region. Over the last year, GDP increased 7.5%. The world's GDP rose 3%. In an effort to boost development, the government aggressively funds businesses, taking equity stakes in small companies in exchange for expansion capital. Also in an effort to boost growth, the government keeps tariffs high and funds high-quality colleges to improve the versatility of the Venvakian workforce.

The budget deficit stands at 5% of GDP, as the government has opted to borrow rather than raise taxes. Venvakia's government is uncommonly steady relative to that of other countries in its part of the world. The country's tax rate is quite low, and there are very few deductions allowed for either consumers or businesses. Spending on raw materials is expected to fall 1.5% this year, though total factor productivity is expected to rise 0.4%. The inflation rate is currently 1.3% and expected to stay at that level this year. Consumer consumption is expected to rise 3.4% this year, and an expected appreciation in Venvakian currency should boost buying power.

After collecting data on Venvakia, Jones submits his investment recommendation to Global's foreign desk.

1. What is the *most likely* current blend of fiscal and monetary policy?

	Monetary policy	Fiscal policy
A.	Restrictive	Expansive
B.	Expansive	Restrictive
C.	Restrictive	Restrictive

2. The target short-term interest rate using the Taylor rule is *closest* to:
   A. 3.15%.
   B. 2.74%.
   C. 3.73%.

3. If Jones' inflation forecast is incorrect, which types of accounts are *most* at risk?
   A. Defined-benefit plans.
   B. Individual investors.
   C. Property-and-casualty insurers.

4. Based on Jones' forecasts, what action should the bond portfolio managers take?
   A. Increase duration.
   B. Decrease duration.
   C. Underweight cyclicals.

5. Venvakia's long-term economic growth forecast is *closest* to:
   A. 3.7%.
   B. 5.0%.
   C. 7.1%.

6. Should Global invest in Venvakian businesses?
   A. No, because government policies are not likely to enhance growth.
   B. Yes, because economic growth is likely to remain higher than the global average.
   C. No, because economic growth is likely to fall below the global average.

SELF-TEST ANSWERS: ECONOMIC CONCEPTS

1. **A** The key piece of data here is the fact that the yield curve is flat. When fiscal policy is expansive but monetary policy is restrictive, the yield curve is more or less flat. No other mix is likely to cause a flat yield curve.

2. **A** To calculate the target interest rate, use the following equation. Target rate = neutral rate + 0.5 × (expected GDP – GDP trend) + 0.5 × (expected inflation – target inflation). Target rate = 3.57% + 0.5 × (3.84% – 3.27%) + 0.5 × (0.6% – 2.0%) = 3.15%.

3. **B** Jones is forecasting that inflation will fall. If it rises, individual investors are the most susceptible. Their expenses will rise, while they often have few options for increasing their investment to compensate.

4. **A** Jones projects a target short-term interest rate of 3.15% (see Question 2), lower than the current rate. To take advantage of the likely rate reduction, bond managers should increase duration. A mix of high stock valuations, a rising market, strong sales and profit growth, and modest growth in labor costs suggests the economy is in the early expansion phase, historically a good time to invest in (i.e., over-weight) cyclicals.

5. **B** The components of a long-term growth forecast are population growth, labor market participation, capital input spending, and total factor productivity. The sum of those four inputs is 5.0% (= 5.2 + 0.9 – 1.5 + 0.4).

6. **A** Economic growth is slowing but likely to remain higher than the global average. While high-growth economies are better than low-growth economies all else being equal, all else is rarely equal. The political system is stable, but the Venvakian government interferes with the economy through its control of business, borrows too heavily, and stifles foreign competition, earning negative marks in three of the four major areas of concern despite an attractive tax structure.

ASSET ALLOCATION

Study Session 8

EXAM FOCUS

Strategic asset allocation is the part of the portfolio management process that deals with allocating money to different asset classes. Strategic asset allocation is the targeted portfolio weights with a long-term perspective and is consistent with the investor's IPS. You should be able to (1) find the portfolio on the efficient frontier using weights on the corner portfolios and (2) interpret the asset class exposures.

STRATEGIC ASSET ALLOCATION

LOS 21.a: Explain the function of strategic asset allocation in portfolio management and discuss its role in relation to specifying and controlling the investor's exposures to systematic risk.

CFA® Program Curriculum, Volume 3, page 223

Strategic asset allocation combines capital market expectations (formally represented by the efficient frontier) and the investor's risk, return, and investment constraints (from the IPS). Strategic asset allocation is long-term in nature, and hence the weights are called *targets* and the portfolio represented by the strategic asset allocation is called the *policy portfolio*. Short-term deviation from the strategic asset allocation may be based on short-term capital market expectations and would be the result of active management.

Each asset class has its own quantifiable systematic risk, and strategic asset allocation is a conscious effort to gain the desired exposure to systematic risk via specific weights to individual asset classes. Each asset class represents relatively similar investments (e.g., long-term corporate bonds) with similar systematic risk factors. Exposure to specific asset classes in specific proportions enables portfolio managers to effectively monitor and control their systematic risk exposure. In other words, strategic asset allocation reflects the investor's desired systematic risk exposure.

TACTICAL ASSET ALLOCATION

LOS 21.b: Compare strategic and tactical asset allocation.

CFA® Program Curriculum, Volume 3, page 225

Tactical asset allocation is the result of active management wherein managers deviate from the strategic asset allocation to take advantage of any perceived *short-term* opportunities in the market. Hence, tactical asset allocation introduces additional risk, which should be justified by additional return (i.e., positive alpha).

LOS 21.c: Discuss the importance of asset allocation for portfolio performance.

CFA® Program Curriculum, Volume 3, page 226

Asset allocation is performed as two distinct processes: (1) strategic and (2) tactical asset allocation. The first, strategic allocation, responds to the interaction of the investor's long-term strategic (policy) needs and long run capital market expectations. The allocation itself is typically specified in a range of percentages (e.g., a strategic allocation for domestic equity of 30% to 40%), and if the actual percentage wanders outside that range, the portfolio is rebalanced.

It should be remembered that the strategic allocation is based upon the investor's long-run goals and long-run capital market (systematic) expectations. When the market experiences short-term disruptions or the portfolio manager recognizes opportunities, she can change the allocation for short periods (tactical allocation). The question is, because portfolio managers are the *experts* at seeking out these opportunities, why should strategic allocation even be performed?

The first response to this question is to provide discipline, that is, to maintain focus on objectives and constraints. Without a clearly defined strategic allocation based upon systematic risk factors, it is not clear that the portfolio would accurately reflect the investor's desires with respect to risk and return. Also, over the long run, asset classes seem to respond somewhat homogeneously to systematic (macroeconomic) factors. That is, the investor can expect general classes of assets in the portfolio to respond similarly to interest rate changes and other macro factors.

Without even considering the benefits of discipline in keeping the investor's goals clearly in focus, the importance of long-run (strategic) asset allocation has been well established empirically. One study shows that 94% of the variability of total portfolio returns is explained by the strategic asset allocation.[1] Another study by the Vanguard Group[2] shows that, using long-term Strategic Asset Allocation as the benchmark, the returns to market timing and security selection (tactical allocation) are minimal at best and at worst insufficient to cover the associated operating expenses and trading costs.

LOS 21.d: Contrast the asset-only and asset/liability management (ALM) approaches to asset allocation and discuss the investor circumstances in which they are commonly used.

CFA® Program Curriculum, Volume 3, page 228

ALM strategic asset allocation is determined in conjunction with modeling the liabilities of the investor. For investors with specific liabilities (e.g., defined benefit pension

---

1. Brinson, Gary P., L. Randolph Hood, and Gilbert L. Beebower. 1986. "Determinants of Portfolio Performance." *Financial Analysts Journal*, vol. 42, no. 4 (July/August).
2. The Vanguard Group Inc. July 2003. "Sources of Portfolio Performance: The Enduring Importance of Asset Allocation."

plans or insurance companies), asset allocation is tailored to meet liabilities and to maximize the surplus given an acceptable level of risk. This usually results in a relatively high allocation to fixed-income assets. Strategic asset allocation involves specifically modeling liabilities and determining the asset allocation appropriate to fund them. Even for those investors who don't have specific (contractual) liabilities, future obligations (e.g., retirement living expenses for an individual investor) can be modeled as liabilities, and an ALM approach to strategic asset allocation can be applied.

In *asset-only* strategic asset allocation, the focus is on earning the highest level of return for a given (acceptable) level of risk without any consideration for liability modeling. The liability (explicit or implied from future expected cash outflows) is indirectly taken into consideration through the required rate of return. Because the asset-only approach does not specifically model liabilities, the risk of not funding liabilities is not accurately controlled.

DYNAMIC AND STATIC ASSET ALLOCATION

LOS 21.e: Explain the advantage of dynamic over static asset allocation and discuss the trade-offs of complexity and cost.

CFA® Program Curriculum, Volume 3, page 229

Dynamic asset allocation takes a multi-period view of the investment horizon. In other words, it recognizes that asset (and liability) performance in one period affects the required rate of return and acceptable level of risk for subsequent periods. *Static asset allocation* ignores the link between optimal asset allocations across different time periods. For example, the manager using a static approach might estimate the necessary mean-variance inputs at a point in time and then construct the long-term portfolio accordingly. The manager using dynamic allocation allows for changing parameters over time using such techniques as Monte Carlo simulation. This allows the manager to build in expected changes to inputs as well as model unanticipated changes in macroeconomic factors.

Dynamic asset allocation is difficult and costly to implement. However, investors who have significant liabilities, especially those with uncertain timing and/or amount (e.g., non-life insurance companies), find the costs acceptable. Investors who undertake an asset-liability approach to strategic asset allocation typically prefer dynamic asset allocation to static asset allocation.

LOS 21.f: Explain how loss aversion, mental accounting, and fear of regret may influence asset allocation policy.

CFA® Program Curriculum, Volume 3, page 237

Recall that **loss aversion** makes investors focus on gains and losses rather than risk and return as prescribed by modern portfolio theory. Loss aversion can lead an investor to take increasingly greater risk in an attempt to recover from a loss. This *risk-seeking behavior* in turn can lead to highly concentrated or otherwise riskier portfolios.

Mental accounting is the tendency for individuals to identify and immunize individual goals rather than use a diversified portfolio to meet all goals considered together. This can be thought of as a pyramiding approach. The base of the pyramid represents the largest and most critical goals, such as retirement living expenses and children's educations. The investor focuses on immunizing these goals with very low risk investments, such as Treasuries and high-grade corporate bonds. Once the most important goals are met, the investor looks at the goals that are secondary in importance and uses somewhat riskier investments to meet them. In this fashion, the individual moves in a step-wise manner, identifying and immunizing goals of continually decreasing importance.

Regret is the feeling of disappointment or shame that investors feel from having to admit making a poor investment decision. A feeling of regret can be avoided if the investor does not have to actually recognize a loss. For example, an investor will hold an investment, even though it has fallen in value, in hopes that it will return to its previous, higher level. If the investor instead sold the investment at a loss, the investor would feel the resulting stigma of having made a bad investment.

Fear of regret can make investors avoid taking actions that could lead to regret. For example, the investor holding the losing investment will continue holding the asset rather than sell it. The result could obviously be an even greater loss. From the opposite perspective, an investor fearing regret will tend to hold a winner too long. Fearing selling a rising stock too soon and losing out on even higher returns, the investor will continue holding the stock, possibly until it begins to fall in value. Thus, fear of regret leads investors to hold both losing and winning investments too long.

Fear of regret can also lead to investing only in "comfortable" investments, such as domestic stocks and bonds. By deliberately excluding some asset classes, such as foreign investments, the investor avoids the possibility of making uninformed and possibly poor investment decisions he could later regret. Thus, fearing making a poor decision, the investor fails to hold investments that could improve the return/risk characteristics of the portfolio.

SPECIFYING RISK AND RETURN OBJECTIVES

LOS 21.g: <u>Evaluate</u> return and risk objectives in relation to strategic asset allocation.

CFA® Program Curriculum, Volume 3, page 230

Return and risk objectives are determined in accordance with the investor's specified constraints. The **return objective** for an individual's or institution's portfolio, for example, is based upon the size of the portfolio, long-term spending (liquidity) needs, the time horizon, and maintenance of the principal. Unless specifically stated otherwise, we always assume the investor will maintain the principal, so the portfolio must not only meet spending needs, it must also cover expected inflation. For example, assume the before-tax required return is estimated at 4% and inflation is expected to average 3%. The nominal before-tax required return for the portfolio is 7.12%:

$$R_{\text{before-tax}} = (1.04)(1.03) - 1 = 0.0712 = 7.12\%$$

> **For the Exam:** Always pay close attention to the wording in the exam question. Recent morning cases have asked for the investor's required after-tax return, but either could be asked.

The investor's **risk objective** should be specified in light of the investor's risk aversion. In Study Sessions 4 and 5, we classified investors as having below-average, average, or above-average *risk tolerance*. Investors can be placed into numerical categories using this very rough approximation or through answers to questionnaires. One possible numerical rating scheme might be to score investors from 1 to 10 based upon their tolerance for risk. Those with below-average risk tolerance (highly risk-averse investors) are given a score of 7 to 10, while those who are highly tolerant of risk (low risk aversion) are given a score of 1 to 3.

Then, using a well accepted quantitative relationship, we can determine the *utility-adjusted* return the investor will realize from the portfolio:

$$U_P = \hat{R}_P - 0.005(A)\left(\sigma_P^2\right)$$

where:
U_P = the investor's utility from investing in the portfolio
(i.e., the investor's utility-adjusted return)
$\hat{R}_P$ = the portfolio expected return
A = the investor's risk aversion score
σ_P^2 = the portfolio variance

> **For the Exam:** The command word **evaluate** could imply that you can be asked to perform the utility-adjusted return calculation.

Using the formula, we can test various allocations to determine which is best for the investor. For example, assume we have determined the investor's required before-tax return is 8% and his risk aversion score is 7. We can place him in one of two portfolio allocations, A or B, which meet his required return and risk (standard deviation) objectives.

- Allocation A (Portfolio A) has an expected return of 8.5% and a standard deviation of 9%.
- Allocation B (Portfolio B) has an expected return of 8.8% and a standard deviation of 10%.

Using the formula, we can determine that the investor would be better off with Allocation A. Even though it has a somewhat lower expected return, its risk-adjusted return is actually higher.

$$U_A = \hat{R}_A - 0.005(A)\left(\sigma_A^2\right) = 8.5\% - 0.005(7)(9\%)^2 = 5.67\%$$
$$U_B = \hat{R}_B - 0.005(A)\left(\sigma_B^2\right) = 8.8\% - 0.005(7)(10\%)^2 = 5.30\%$$

 Professor's Note: Using 0.005 on the right-hand side of the equation, you insert return and standard deviation in percentage form (i.e., 25% is denoted 25%) as we did. To enter the return and standard deviation in decimal form (i.e., 25% is denoted 0.25), you need to use 0.5 on the right side of the equation. For example, using 0.5 for the previous calculations:

$$U_A = \hat{R}_A - 0.5(A)\left(\sigma_A^2\right) = 0.085 - 0.5(7)(0.09)^2 = 0.0567 = 5.67\%$$
$$U_B = \hat{R}_B - 0.5(A)\left(\sigma_B^2\right) = 0.088 - 0.5(7)(0.10)^2 = 0.0530 = 5.30\%$$

Now we'll determine the risk-adjusted returns assuming the investor has a risk aversion score of 2:

$$U_A = \hat{R}_A - 0.005(A)\left(\sigma_A^2\right) = 8.5\% - 0.005(2)(9\%)^2 = 7.69\%$$
$$U_B = \hat{R}_B - 0.005(A)\left(\sigma_B^2\right) = 8.8\% - 0.005(2)(10\%)^2 = 7.80\%$$

Now Allocation B is preferred. There are at least two implications of these results:

1. When choosing from a set of assets with the same risk and return rankings (Portfolio B has both a higher expected return and higher standard deviation than A), the choice is driven by the investor's risk aversion.

2. As risk aversion increases (denoted with a higher risk aversion score), the deduction for (adjustment for) risk increases.

Roy's Safety-First Measure

In addition to standard deviation as a measure of risk (volatility), the acceptable level of risk can be stated in terms of *downside risk* measures such as shortfall risk, semivariance, and target semivariance. **Shortfall risk** is the risk of exceeding a maximum acceptable dollar loss. **Semivariance** is the *bottom half* of the variance (i.e., the variance calculated using only the returns below the expected return). **Target semivariance** is the semivariance using some target minimum return, such as zero.

Roy's Safety-First Measure is one of the oldest and most cited measures of downside risk. The measure is stated as a ratio of *excess return* to risk:

$$RSF = \frac{\hat{R}_P - R_{MAR}}{\sigma_P}$$

where:

$\hat{R}_P$ = portfolio expected return

R_{MAR} = the investor's minimum acceptable return

σ_P = portfolio standard deviation

The *excess return* in Roy's measure is the expected return in excess of the investor's minimum acceptable return. Dividing excess return by the portfolio standard deviation tells us how many standard deviations the minimum acceptable return lies below the portfolio expected return.

For example, we will assume our investor in the previous example also requires that the portfolio not lose any money (i.e., the minimum acceptable return is 0). Applying Roy's Safety-First Measure to Allocations A and B, we determine that Allocation A is preferred:

$$RSF_A = \frac{\hat{R}_P - R_{MAR}}{\sigma_P} = \frac{8.5 - 0}{9} = 0.94$$

$$RSF_B = \frac{\hat{R}_P - R_{MAR}}{\sigma_P} = \frac{8.8 - 0}{10} = 0.88$$

For the Exam: You will notice that the two measures, utility-adjusted return and Roy's Safety-First Measure, chose the same allocation for the first investor (aversion score of 7) but not the second investor (aversion score of 2). This could be because the safety first ratio is linear while the utility measure is quadratic. In any case, if you should have to use them on the exam, you will no doubt be able to do so without a conflict in their results.

SPECIFYING ASSET CLASSES

LOS 21.h: Evaluate whether an asset class or set of asset classes has been appropriately specified.

CFA® Program Curriculum, Volume 3, page 240

Throughout our discussion of strategic and tactical asset allocation, we have assumed that asset classes are correctly identified. We assumed that the manager has appropriately placed assets into groups according to their descriptions and characteristics such as risk and return. For example, including emerging markets equities and domestic equities in a single class labeled *equities* would be appropriate only from a general description standpoint; their risk and return characteristics are obviously significantly different. A primary factor to consider in determining whether asset classes are properly defined is whether the classes held together will produce the desired diversification.

In addition to their descriptions and characteristics, we should ensure that the classes are not highly correlated. A high correlation between classes would indicate that the classes are related from a risk and return standpoint and would defeat the purpose of holding separate classes in an allocation (lack of diversification).

Individual assets should be defined clearly within a single classification. If it can be legitimately argued that assets can be placed in more than one class, the descriptions of the classes are too vague (have not been correctly specified). Again, this defeats the purpose of placing assets into classes for allocation purposes.

In addition to the desired diversification effect, the asset classes should define the majority of all possible investable assets. This not only increases the set of investable assets, but also pushes up the efficient frontier (i.e., increases return at all levels of risk). Remember that the domestic efficient frontier for equities is shifted upward with the inclusion of international equities and that the frontier is pushed even farther up with the inclusion of other asset classes.

Depending upon the strategy employed, the manager will want to rebalance the portfolio to the original strategic allocation, whether the allocation has varied due to performance or tactical allocation. This implies that the asset classes should have sufficient liquidity.

To sum up, asset classes have been appropriately specified if:

- Assets in the class are similar from a descriptive as well as a statistical perspective.
- They are not highly correlated so they provide the desired diversification.
- Individual assets cannot be classified into more than one class.
- They cover the majority of all possible investable assets.
- They contain a sufficiently large percentage of liquid assets.

Some well accepted asset classes include domestic equity, domestic fixed income, global equity, global fixed income, cash and equivalents, and alternative investments, which may be further divided into classes, such as real estate, private equity, etc.

 Professor's Note: LOS 21.i is discussed later with LOS 21.n.

Inflation-Adjusted Securities, Global Securities, and Alternative Investments

LOS 21.j: <u>Evaluate</u> the theoretical and practical effects of including additional asset classes in an asset allocation.

CFA® Program Curriculum, Volume 3, page 240

As you consider additional asset classes, keep in mind the goals to allocating assets to classes and combining them in a portfolio; the manager seeks the risk and return characteristics provided by each class. **Inflation-protected securities**, for example, provide the obvious characteristic of helping guard against the potential effects of rising or falling inflation. They also provide a practical function by automatically increasing or decreasing portfolio cash flows with inflation and deflation. U.S. Treasury Inflation Protected Securities (TIPS) are highly liquid and virtually risk-free.

The theoretical justification for adding **global securities** is the potential to increase return at all levels of risk. The practical implications of including global securities relate to other concerns associated with global investing that are not experienced in a domestic-only setting. For example, in a global setting the investor faces currency risk and the usual concerns associated with political, legal, tax, free float, and other issues. In addition, there has been some debate about the consistent diversification effects of global securities. Some argue that during economic downturns, exactly when the investor needs the diversification effects the most, emerging and developed markets tend to be highly correlated.

Alternative investments, as we see in Study Session 13, include real estate, private equity, hedge funds, etc. The primary benefit to including alternative investments in an asset allocation is the diversification benefit. Each category of alternative investments on its own can be considered fairly risky, but in a portfolio they bring the potential of significantly increased returns. The practical drawbacks to investing in alternative investments include the typically large amount of capital required and the need to carefully select out-performers. In some cases, information on alternative investments can be sparse or even nonexistent.

Determining Whether to Add an Investment to the Portfolio

To determine whether adding a new asset, i, to a portfolio would be beneficial, the portfolio manager can analyze the relationship of the new investment's Sharpe ratio, the current portfolio Sharpe ratio, and the correlation of the returns on the two.[3] If the Sharpe ratio of the new investment is greater than the current portfolio Sharpe ratio multiplied by the correlation of the new investment's returns with the portfolio's returns, adding the investment to the portfolio will improve the portfolio Sharpe ratio:[4]

$$\text{if } S_i > S_p \times \rho_{i,p} \text{ adding the investment will improve the portfolio Sharpe ratio}$$

where:
S_i = Sharpe ratio of proposed investment
S_p = current portfolio Sharpe ratio
$\rho_{i,p}$ = correlation of the returns on the proposed investment with the portfolio returns

---

3. This methodology can be applied to individual assets or asset classes.

4. Because it relies on Sharpe ratios, which in turn rely on standard deviations, this methodology is inappropriate for analyzing assets with skewed returns distributions.

Example 1: Will adding the asset improve the portfolio Sharpe ratio?

A manager is considering adding an investment to his diversified portfolio, but he is unsure of the correlation of the new investment with his portfolio. **Determine** the maximum correlation between the new investment and his portfolio that would make the new investment acceptable (risk-free rate = 3%).

	Portfolio	*New Investment*[1]
Expected return	12%	12%
Standard deviation	18%	30%
Sharpe ratio	(12 – 3) / 18 = 0.50	(12 – 3) / 30 = 0.30

[1.] Remember, the proposed investment could have been an asset class. For example, a manager might be considering adding a class of foreign investments to a domestic portfolio.

Answer 1: Calculate the correlation coefficient that makes the equation an identity.

$$S_i = S_p \times \rho_{i,p}$$

$$0.30 = 0.50 \times \rho_{i,p} \Rightarrow \rho_{i,p} = \frac{0.30}{0.50} = 0.60$$

- If the correlation of the new investment with the portfolio is 0.60, then $S_i = S_p \times \rho_{i,p}$, and adding the new investment will leave the portfolio Sharpe ratio unchanged.
- If the correlation is less than 0.60, then $S_i > S_p \times \rho_{i,p}$, and adding the investment will *increase* the portfolio Sharpe ratio.
- If the correlation is greater than 0.60, then $S_i < S_p \times \rho_{i,p}$, and adding the investment will *decrease* the portfolio Sharpe ratio.

Example 2: Selecting an asset for the portfolio

A portfolio manager is considering three investments, only one of which he will add to his portfolio. Data on the investments and his portfolio are provided in the table. Based on the data provided, **determine** which investment the manager should select.

	Portfolio	Investment 1	Investment 2	Investment 3
Sharpe ratio[1]	0.41	0.30	0.31	0.19
Correlation with current portfolio, ρ		0.77	0.80	0.40

1. $S_i = \dfrac{\hat{R}_i - R_F}{\sigma_i}$

Answer 2: Follow these steps:

1. If Sharpe ratios are not presented, you would be provided with expected returns, standard deviations, and the risk-free rate.

2. Multiply the portfolio Sharpe ratio by the correlation of each asset with the portfolio.

3. If the Sharpe ratio of an investment is greater than the respective product in #2, the investment is acceptable.

    if $S_i > S_p \times \rho_{i,p} \Rightarrow$ the investment will increase the portfolio Sharpe ratio
    $S_1 = 0.30; \quad S_p \times \rho_{1,p} = 0.41 \times 0.77 = 0.316; \quad S_1 < S_p \times \rho_{i,p}$
    $S_2 = 0.31; \quad S_p \times \rho_{2,p} = 0.41 \times 0.80 = 0.328; \quad S_2 < S_p \times \rho_{i,p}$
    $S_3 = 0.19; \quad S_p \times \rho_{3,p} = 0.41 \times 0.40 = 0.164; \quad S_3 > S_p \times \rho_{i,p}$

We see from the calculations that only Investment 3 would increase the portfolio Sharpe ratio. Even though it has the lowest Sharpe ratio of the three investments, it also has the lowest correlation with the portfolio.

STEPS IN ASSET ALLOCATION

LOS 21.k: <u>Explain</u> the major steps involved in establishing an appropriate asset allocation.

CFA® Program Curriculum, Volume 3, page 246

The asset allocation process is basically the portfolio management process we have identified throughout the CFA curriculum (i.e., construct the portfolio, monitor its progress, and revise the portfolio as necessary).

As we saw in Study Sessions 4 and 5, the asset allocation process starts with determining the investor's return requirement and risk tolerance, subject to the investor's current wealth and constraints. The manager formulates long-term capital market expectations and their potential effects on the various asset classes. The job is then to determine the mix of assets (allocation) that best meets the objectives defined in the IPS, subject to any other limitations specified by the investor. For example, an investor might strictly forbid investment in cigarette companies or companies that do business with certain countries.

Once the strategic allocation has been implemented, it should be monitored regularly as specified in the IPS. The monitoring process should contain a feedback loop so that changes in long-term market factors can be incorporated back into the "model" and an assessment made to determine whether adjustments to the strategic allocation are justified. If the market changes are only short-term in nature, the manager should consider implementing tactical allocation measures, which have been approved in the IPS.

MINIMUM VARIANCE FRONTIER AND EFFICIENT FRONTIER

LOS 21.l: <u>Discuss</u> the strengths and limitations of the following approaches to asset allocation: mean–variance, resampled efficient frontier, Black–Litterman, Monte Carlo simulation, ALM, and experience based.

CFA® Program Curriculum, Volume 3, page 249

For the Exam: Notice that the LOS asks you to discuss the strengths and weaknesses of the methods. It does not ask you to perform any calculations. For the exam, you should be able to discuss and compare the methods.

The mean-variance approach to strategic asset allocation is a static approach (versus a multi-period dynamic approach). The mean-variance frontier is the *outer edge* of a graphical plot of all possible combinations of risky assets. The efficient frontier is the portion of the mean-variance frontier which contains portfolios (combinations) with the highest expected return at each level of risk. Figure 1 shows an example of a mean-variance frontier and the efficient frontier.

The horizontal axis represents risk as measured by standard deviation. The vertical axis represents portfolio expected return. All portfolios below the efficient frontier, even those on the mean-variance frontier but below the global minimum variance portfolio, are sub-optimal. This is because there is a portfolio (on the efficient frontier) that has a higher expected return for the same amount of risk.

Figure 1: Mean-Variance (Efficient) Frontier

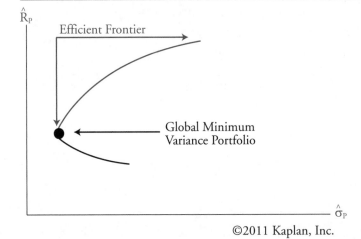

Efficient portfolios are essentially portfolios with varying allocations to the available asset classes. To determine an efficient portfolio with an expected return of *k* and given that there are *j* asset classes, we find the allocation that has the lowest standard deviation, such that:

$$\hat{R}_P = \sum w_i \left(\hat{R}_i \right) = k \text{ for i = 1 through j}$$

where:
$\hat{R}_P$ = expected return on the portfolio
w_i = weight of class i and $\sum w_i = 1$
$\hat{R}_i$ = expected return for class i

This essentially identifies a minimum variance allocation (the portfolio with lowest standard deviation from all the portfolios with the same expected return) that has an expected return of *k* such that the weights of all asset classes sum to one.

Once we have determined the composition of *any* two efficient portfolios on the efficient frontier, we can determine any portfolio on the same efficient frontier as a weighted average of the two.

Example: Efficient frontier

Assume only four asset classes combined into Portfolio A (w_1 = 0.25, w_2 = 0.15, w_3 = 0.20, w_4 = 0.40) and Portfolio B (w_1 = 0.30, w_2 = 0.20, w_3 = 0.35, w_4 = 0.15), which lie on the efficient frontier. Portfolio A has an expected return of 10%, and Portfolio B has an expected return of 15%. **Calculate** the asset class weightings (combination of Portfolios A and B) for the efficient portfolio with an expected return of 11%.

Answer:

We solve for *w* in the following equation:

$$\hat{R}_P = w_A \hat{R}_A + w_B \hat{R}_B \Rightarrow \text{letting } w_B = (1 - w_A)$$
$$0.11 = w_A (0.10) + (1 - w_A)(0.15)$$
$$w_A = 0.80, \text{ so } w_B = 0.20$$

Thus, the weights of the individual asset classes in the resulting efficient portfolio allocation with an expected return of 11% are:

Asset class 1: $(0.80 \times 0.25) + (0.20 \times 0.30) = 0.26$
Asset class 2: $(0.80 \times 0.15) + (0.20 \times 0.20) = 0.16$
Asset class 3: $(0.80 \times 0.20) + (0.20 \times 0.35) = 0.23$
Asset class 4: $(0.80 \times 0.40) + (0.20 \times 0.15) = \underline{0.35}$
$$\sum = 1.00$$

Resampled Efficient Frontier

A significant drawback to generating an efficient frontier through traditional mean-variance optimization methods is the *sensitivity* of the frontier to changes in the inputs. And because the inputs themselves (e.g., expected returns, covariances) are estimates, reliance on an efficient frontier developed through a traditional, single mean-variance optimization is questionable.

In response, Michaud[5] developed a simulation approach utilizing historical means, variances, and covariances of asset classes, which, combined with capital market forecasts, assumes they are fair representations of their expectations. His *resampling* technique is based on a Monte Carlo simulation that draws from the distributions to develop a simulated efficient frontier. Because the simulation is run thousands of times, the efficient portfolio at each return level, and hence the resulting efficient frontier, is the result of an averaging process.

Rather than a single, sharp curve, the resampled efficient frontier is a blur. At each level of return, the most efficient of the simulated efficient portfolios is at the center of a distribution (think of the expected return at the center of a normal distributions' bell-shaped curve). The composition of the portfolio changes as you move away from the center. In stark contrast, the traditional mean variance optimization yields a single portfolio with very specific asset class weights at each level of return.

By utilizing this resampling technique, a portfolio manager is able to judge the need for rebalancing. For example, if the manager's portfolio is within a 90% confidence interval of the most efficient portfolio, it could be considered *statistically equivalent*. That is, rebalancing to the most optimal weights would not produce a statistically significant change in its risk-return profile.

Resampling has two major *advantages* over its traditional counterpart. First, because it utilizes an averaging process, the generated efficient frontier is more stable than a traditional mean variance efficient frontier; small changes in the input variables result in only minor changes in the REF. Next, portfolios generated through this process tend to be better diversified. The biggest *disadvantage* of resampling is its lack of a sound theoretical basis. There is simply no theoretical reasoning to support the contention that a portfolio constructed through resampling should provide superior performance relative to another constructed through traditional mean variance analysis.

Black-Litterman

With the same motivations as Michaud (resampling), Black and Litterman developed two models for dealing with the problems associated with estimation error, especially expected return: (1) the unconstrained Black-Litterman model (UBL) and (2) the Black-Litterman model (BL). We mention the UBL, but the assigned reading focuses primarily on the BL.

---

5. Michaud, Richard, 1989. "The Markowitz Optimization Enigma: Is Optimized Optimal?" *Financial Analysts Journal*, January.

The **unconstrained Black-Litterman model** (UBL) draws weights of asset classes from a global index. Applying a Bayesian process, the manager increases or decreases the weights based upon her views of expected asset class returns and the strengths of those views with no constraint against short sales (negative weights are allowed).

The **(constrained) Black-Litterman model** (BL), which allows no negative asset weights, also produces well-diversified portfolios that incorporate the manager's views on asset class returns. In a process which amounts to the reverse of mean-variance optimization, the manager inputs *world-wide* asset class weights and covariances and solves for the returns. Because the returns are drawn from a well-diversified global portfolio, they represent average (i.e., market) expectations.

As in the UBL, the manager incorporates her views on the asset class returns into the model and adjusts the expected returns accordingly. Using these adjusted returns, the manager runs the mean variance optimization. If the manager has no particular expectations about asset class performance, she would weight her portfolio the same as world-wide asset class weights. If she uses the world-wide asset class weights, this would imply she has *average risk tolerance*. That is, she is willing to accept the risk and return of the market.

Example: Asset allocation using BL

A portfolio manager has no particular views on expected asset class returns. World-wide weights for seven asset classes are shown in Table A.

For the Exam: In an exam question, asset class weights will most likely be given as global indexes for different regions (or countries) of the globe.

Table A: Global Asset Class Weights

Assets	Class 1	Class 2	Class 3	Class 4	Class 5	Class 6	Class 7
Amount	10,000	15,000	5,000	25,000	20,000	10,000	15,000
%	10%	15%	5%	25%	20%	10%	15%

a. Assuming the manager has *average risk tolerance* and is constrained to investing in only those seven asset classes, **determine** the optimal portfolio allocation.

b. Now, assuming the manager has above- or below-average risk tolerance, **explain** how the optimal asset allocation would be achieved.

Answer:

a. If the manager has no particular expectations or is otherwise uncomfortable adjusting asset class expected returns, she would weight the asset classes in the portfolio the same as their global weights: 1–10%; 2–15%; 3–5%; 4–25%; 5–20%; 6–10%; and 7–15%. Because the manager is constrained to holding only those asset classes, she is effectively holding her *market portfolio*. In capital market theory, the investor who holds the market portfolio has average risk tolerance.

b. We know from capital market theory that an investor with average risk tolerance will hold (invest all funds in) the market portfolio. In other words, the investor will hold all of the assets in the market portfolio and in their respective market value weights. To take on more or less risk, an investor can combine the market portfolio with the risk-free asset to move left or right of the market portfolio on the Capital Market Line (CML).

If the manager has *below-average* risk tolerance, she would invest a portion of her funds in the market portfolio and put the rest of her funds in the risk-free asset. The greater the percentage of total funds invested in the risk-free asset, the lower the portfolio standard deviation and expected return.

If the manager has *above-average* risk tolerance, she would borrow at the risk-free rate (short the risk-free asset) and invest the funds in the market portfolio to move right along the CML, above the market portfolio. This produces a portfolio with a greater expected return and higher standard deviation.

Monte Carlo Simulation

This computer process utilizes inputs specified by the manager. Using different strategic allocations (including the investor's current allocation), the program incorporates the effects of various assumed capital market factors (inflation, yield spreads, recession, etc., and their expected changes) in the next period as well as their compounding effects *over several future periods*. This way the model overcomes the static (1-period) nature of the typical mean-variance analysis. The model can even incorporate varying tax rates associated with increased or decreased income or the need to readjust the allocation by selling and purchasing assets. The manager selects the strategic allocation that yields the best long-run (strategic) results with respect to the investor's objectives.

 Professor's Note: Mean-variance analysis typically incorporates 1-year expected returns and standard deviations and assumes they will be constant over future periods.

Asset-Liability Management

The allocation methodologies discussed thus far attempt to identify the strategic allocation that achieves the best long-run results (i.e., the best asset-only allocation).

Asset-liability management (ALM), on the other hand, considers the allocation of assets with respect to a given liability or set of liabilities. The ALM approach searches for the set of allocations, which maximize the *difference* (the *surplus*) between assets and liabilities at each level of risk (much like the efficient frontier represents the maximum return at each level of risk).

Figure 2 shows an example of an ALM efficient frontier[6] for a generic defined benefit pension plan.

Figure 2: The Asset Liability Management (ALM) Efficient Frontier

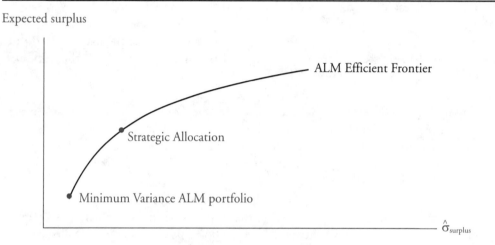

The vertical axis in Figure 2 is the value of the expected surplus (assets minus liabilities), and the horizontal axis represents the associated risk, measured by standard deviation. As with any *efficient* frontier, there is a minimum-variance portfolio (allocation), which has the minimum expected surplus. As you move to the right on the frontier, both the expected surplus and the risk of the allocation increase. Management can (more or less arbitrarily) select any allocation along the frontier, realizing they accept more and more risk as they move out on the frontier. In Figure 2, management has selected the allocation labeled *Strategic Allocation*.

Professor's Note: Occasionally you will see the ALM efficient frontier presented in terms of the funding ratio (i.e., the value of plan assets divided by the value of plan liabilities). In that case, the ratio is presented along the vertical axis, as either a percent or a ratio, and risk is plotted along the horizontal axis. Other than the way the vertical axis is labeled, the procedure is the same.

As with other optimization procedures, ALM requires estimations of all associated mean-variance parameters and thus suffers from estimation bias. To help avoid this problem, the manager can utilize a resampling technique or the Black-Litterman approach.

---

6. The ALM efficient frontier is sometimes referred to as the *surplus* efficient frontier.

Experience-Based Techniques

Rather than being based on sound investment theory, experience-based techniques have come about through decades of experience. For example, one accepted guideline is that investors with long time horizons can tolerate more risk (we employ this guideline in Study Session 4 when we determined the risk objective for an individual). The young professional, for example, should be invested heavily in riskier, higher return assets such as equities. The thought is that the investor's portfolio has sufficient time to recover from temporary declines in value. On the other hand, as individuals approach retirement, they can tolerate less risk and should be moved into high-quality corporate bonds and Treasuries.

Another accepted guideline is the 60/40 rule (60% diversified equities and 40% diversified bonds). This long-accepted rule is considered a starting point in all individual allocations because it is considered a neutral approach. The equities in the portfolio provide long-term growth potential, and the bonds provide income and risk reduction. A guideline that can be applied to adjust this allocation is the *100 – age* rule. You simply subtract the investor's age from 100 to arrive at the preferred allocation to equities, which falls as the investor ages.

Figure 3 contains strengths and weaknesses for the asset allocation approaches discussed.

Figure 3: Strengths and Limitations of Asset Allocation Approaches

Asset Allocation Approach	*Strengths*	*Limitations*
Mean–variance (MV)	• Optimization programs used to generate the efficient frontier are inexpensive and readily available. • Identifies portfolios with the highest expected return at each level of risk. • Any efficient portfolio (i.e., combination of risk and return) can be created by combining the tangency portfolio with the risk-free asset. • Widely understood and accepted.	• The number and nature of estimates (i.e., expected returns, variances, covariances) can be overwhelming. • Expected returns are subject to estimation bias. • Static (one-period) approach. • Can yield under-diversified (concentrated) portfolios, including the tangency portfolio.
Resampled efficient frontier	• EF more stable than traditional MV. ◆ Small changes in inputs produce only minor changes. • Portfolios tend to be better diversified than traditional MV.	• No theoretical support that a portfolio constructed through resampling should provide superior performance relative to another portfolio constructed through traditional mean variance analysis.

Black–Litterman	• **UBL:** Takes asset class weights from global index.
	• Adjust based on strength of views.
	  ◆ Stable efficient frontier.
	  ◆ Portfolios well-diversified.
	• **BL:** Reverse optimization process.
	  ◆ Allows portfolio constraints, such as no negative weights or limited asset classes.
	  ◆ Well-diversified portfolios.
	  ◆ Stable efficient frontier.
		• **UBL:** Allows no constraints.
		  ◆ Relies on historical returns, standard deviations, and covariances.
		  ◆ Uses MV optimization.
		• **BL:** Relies on historical standard deviations and covariances.
		  ◆ Uses MV optimization.
		  ◆ Relies on capital market theory.

Figure 3: Strengths and Limitations of Asset Allocation Approaches (cont.)

Asset Allocation Approach	Strengths	Limitations
Monte Carlo simulation	• Overcomes the static nature of the typical MV analysis. • Incorporates the effects of various assumed capital market factors. • Can be used to generate a distribution of probabilities of meeting liabilities (e.g., ALM).	• Can be complex to implement. • Can generate false confidence; the output is only as accurate as the inputs.
ALM	• Considers the allocation of assets with respect to liabilities. • Can generate an ALM frontier that shows the combinations of risk and return and their probability of meeting liabilities.	• Suffers from estimation bias (e.g., expected returns). • Static approach unless combined with Monte Carlo or some other multi-period methodology.
Experience based	• Incorporates decades of asset allocation experience. • Easy to understand. • Inexpensive to implement.	• Not based on sound investment theory. • Allocation rules may be too simple for some investors.

CONSTRAINTS AGAINST SHORT SALES

LOS 21.m: Discuss the structure of the minimum-variance frontier with a constraint against short sales.

CFA® Program Curriculum, Volume 3, page 251

Remember that mean-variance optimization identifies portfolios that have the highest expected return for a given level of risk (efficient portfolios). Each efficient portfolio represents weights on each of the asset classes. The only constraint was that the sum of all the weights should be equal to one. If we add an additional constraint of no short sales, we restrict the value of the weights to be greater than or equal to zero. Our optimization (to determine each efficient portfolio with an expected return of k given that there are j asset classes) changes as follows:

$$\hat{R}_P = \sum w_i \hat{R}_i = k \text{ for } i = 1 \text{ through } j$$
$$\sum w_i = 1 \text{ and all } w_i \geq 0$$

Here we have an additional constraint that the weight of each asset class be *non-negative*.

In case of a *constrained optimization* (no short sales in this case), the minimum-variance frontier consists of corner portfolios. A **corner portfolio** is formed when the weight of an asset class changes from zero to positive or from positive to zero.

Professor's Note: In the unconstrained optimization used in developing the Capital Market Line or Security Market Line, all investors are assumed to hold the market portfolio in combination with the risk-free asset. To increase expected return above the expected return on the market portfolio, investors can short sell the risk-free asset (borrow) and invest more than 100% of their total assets in the market portfolio. In other words, moving to the right along the capital market line or security market line, the weight of the risk-free asset decreases, goes to zero at the market portfolio, and then turns negative as you pass the market portfolio. In the constrained optimization, the weights of some assets in the portfolio go from positive to zero and the weights of others go from zero to positive as you "pass" a corner portfolio.

Figure 4 shows an example of an efficient frontier with seven corner portfolios. Portfolio A is the global minimum-variance (GMV) portfolio, which is always included as one of the corner portfolios. To determine any portfolio on the efficient frontier, we only need the two *adjacent* corner portfolios. For example, Portfolio C is a weighted average of Portfolios L and D. The only difference here is that instead of any two efficient portfolios, we now need knowledge of the *adjacent* corner portfolios.

Figure 4: Efficient Frontier with Corner Portfolios

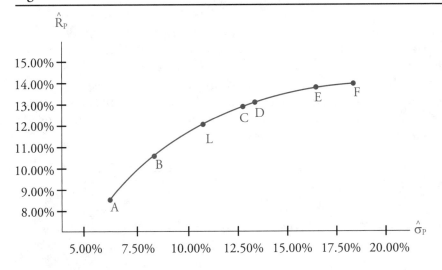

Corner Portfolios

Mathematically, calculating the standard deviation of an efficient portfolio, given the adjacent corner portfolios' standard deviations, is identical to the calculations we use when we calculate the weights of a portfolio necessary to achieve an expected return.

Example: Standard deviation using corner portfolios

From the efficient frontier example in LOS 21.k where we computed the weights of two portfolios such that the expected return is 11%, **compute** the portfolio's approximate standard deviation. We will assume that Portfolios A and B from that example are corner portfolios and further assume their standard deviations are 12% and 16%, respectively.

Answer:

We know from the previous example that the weight of Portfolio A is 0.80 and the weight of Portfolio B is 0.20.

$$\hat{R}_P = w_A\hat{R}_A + w_B\hat{R}_B \Rightarrow \text{letting } w_B = (1 - w_A)$$
$$0.11 = w_A(0.10) + (1 - w_A)(0.15)$$
$$w_A = 0.80, \text{ so } w_B = 0.20$$
$$\sigma_P = 0.80(\sigma_A) + 0.20(\sigma_B)$$
$$\sigma_P = 0.80(0.12) + 0.20(0.16) = 0.128 = 12.8\%$$

Professor's Note: Any time you estimate a value as a weighted average of other values, you assume a linear relationship. By estimating standard deviation in this way, we assume no diversification benefits (i.e., the portfolio lies on a straight line between Portfolios A and B). Because we assume no diversification effect, the estimated standard deviation actually represents the maximum standard deviation when the portfolios are combined in certain weights (i.e., an upper limit to the standard deviation).

LOS 21.i: <u>Select</u> and <u>justify</u> an appropriate set of asset classes for an investor.

CFA® Program Curriculum, Volume 3, page 240

LOS 21.n: <u>Formulate</u> and <u>justify</u> a strategic asset allocation, given an investment policy statement and capital market expectations.

CFA® Program Curriculum, Volume 3, page 257

Professor's Note: Discussion related to these LOS is continued in the discussion of LOS 21.o as well as in Study Sessions 4 and 5.

Example: Strategic asset allocation

Jim Sheehan is the portfolio manager for the $200 million Brent Industries defined benefit pension fund. Jim is planning on making a presentation to the trustees of the pension plan. His firm has come up with the long-term capital market expectations as shown in the following figure.

Capital Market Expectation

Asset Class	Expected Return	Expected Std. Dev.	Correlations				
			1	2	3	4	5
U.S. equity	12.00%	16.00%	1.00				
U.S. bonds	8.25%	6.50%	0.32	1.00			
Int'l equities	14.00%	18.00%	0.46	0.22	1.00		
Int'l bonds	9.25%	12.25%	0.23	0.56	0.32	1.00	
Alternative inv.	11.50%	21.00%	0.25	0.11	0.08	0.06	1.00

Using the capital market expectations, Jim identifies an efficient frontier with the six corner portfolios (see the following graphic) with the characteristics shown in the following table.

Corner Portfolio	Expected Return	Expected Std. Dev.	Sharpe Ratio	Asset Class Weights				
				U.S. Equity	U.S. Bonds	Int'l Equities	Int'l Bonds	Alt. Inv
1	14.00%	18.00%	0.639	0.00%	0.00%	100.00%	0.00%	0.00%
2	13.66%	16.03%	0.696	0.00%	0.00%	85.36%	0.00%	14.64%
3	13.02%	13.58%	0.775	21.69%	0.00%	56.56%	0.00%	21.75%
4	12.79%	13.00%	0.792	21.48%	0.00%	52.01%	5.24%	21.27%
5	10.54%	8.14%	0.988	9.40%	51.30%	26.55%	0.00%	12.76%
6	8.70%	6.32%	0.981	0.00%	89.65%	4.67%	0.00%	5.68%

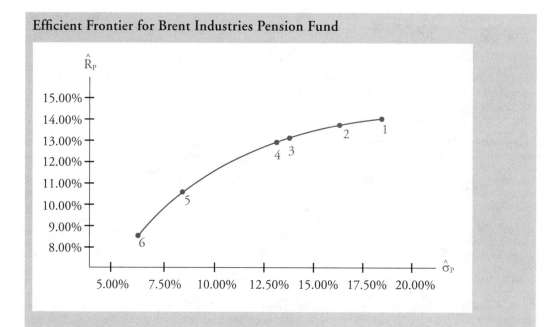

Efficient Frontier for Brent Industries Pension Fund

The following additional information is available about the pension fund:

1. The trustees have established a spending rate of 8.50%. Inflation is expected to be 2% per year, and the cost of managing the fund is expected to be 0.40%. The trustees would like to preserve the purchasing power of the fund.

2. The majority of plan participants are young, so additional liquidity needs are minimal.

3. The trustees would like to limit risk (as defined by standard deviation) to no more than 10% per year.

Calculate the fund's required rate of return and **determine** the appropriate strategic asset allocation.

Answer:

The required return is 11.11% [=(1.085)(1.02)(1.004) − 1], which lies between Corner Portfolios 4 and 5 with their expected returns of 12.79% and 10.54%. We solve for w in the following equation:

$$0.1111 = w_4(0.1279) + (1 - w_4)(0.1054)$$

$$w_4 = 0.25 \Rightarrow w_5 = 0.75$$

In other words, the efficient portfolio with an expected return of 11.11% has 25% weight of Corner Portfolio 4 and 75% weight of Corner Portfolio 5. With respect to asset classes, the weights are then derived as follows:

U.S. equity $= (0.25)(0.2148) + (0.75)(0.0940) = 0.1242 = 12.42\%$

U.S. bonds $= (0.25)(0.0000) + (0.75)(0.5130) = 0.3848 = 38.48\%$

Int'l equity $= (0.25)(0.5201) + (0.75)(0.2655) = 0.3292 = 32.92\%$

Int'l bonds $= (0.25)(0.0524) + (0.75)(0.0000) = 0.0131 = 1.31\%$

Alt. invest. $= (0.25)(0.2127) + (0.75)(0.1276) = 0.1489 = 14.89\%$

In the above computation for U.S. equity, 0.25 (the weight of Corner Portfolio 4) is multiplied by 21.48% (the proportion of U.S. equity in Corner Portfolio 4). Similarly, 0.75 (the weight of Corner Portfolio 5) is multiplied by 9.40% (the proportion of U.S. equity in Corner Portfolio 5). We then add these together to arrive at 12.42% as the weight of U.S. equity in the efficient portfolio with an expected return of 11.11%. We repeat the same process for each asset class.

Math check:

1. Sum of weights should be 100%:

$$0.1242 + 0.3848 + 0.3292 + 0.0131 + 0.1489 = 1.00 = 100\%$$

2. Also, check that the sum of the weights of each asset class multiplied by their expected returns add up to 11.11%:

$$\hat{R}_P = (0.1242)(0.12) + (0.3848)(0.0825) + (0.3292)(0.14)$$
$$+ (0.0131)(0.0925) + (0.1489)(0.1150)$$
$$= 0.1111 = 11.11\%$$

Also note that the standard deviation of this portfolio is (approximately) the weighted average of the standard deviations of Corner Portfolios 4 and 5, which satisfies the risk requirement of the fund:

$$\sigma_P = (0.25)(0.13) + (0.75)(0.0814) = 0.09355 = 9.36\%$$

Special Considerations

Sometimes the IPS may specifically provide for some cash flow needs in the short-term. For example, an individual investor may consider providing for retirement her primary investment goal. However, she may have a secondary goal of taking a vacation in six months and wants to have $50,000 available toward that planned expense. In such a situation, the present value of the projected cash flow should be invested in cash equivalents (because it is short-term). The remainder of the portfolio is allocated according to the weights previously established.

Example: Planned cash outflow

In the previous example of the $200 million pension fund (the risk-free rate is given at 2.5%), the pension fund has a planned cash outflow of $20 million in one year to fund retiree pension buyouts. **Determine** the appropriate strategic asset allocation for the fund.

Answer:

Because $20 million is a planned cash outflow one year from today, the fund should invest $\frac{\$20,000,000}{1.025} = \$19,512,195$ in T-bills at 2.50%. One year from today, that money will grow to $20 million, providing for the planned cash outflow.

The remaining $180,487,805 (= $200,000,000 − $19,512,195) should be allocated to the five asset classes in the same proportion as before (12.42%, 38.48%, 32.92%, 1.31%, 14.89%).

For the Exam: You will not have to worry about setting aside the present value of planned, short-term expenditures. Just be sure that the selected portfolio has an allocation to cash sufficient to meet the expenditure with enough left to meet emergency needs (e.g., three to six months' living expenses).

The Capital Allocation Line

The capital allocation line (CAL) is the straight line drawn from the risk-free rate to the tangency portfolio on the efficient frontier, where the tangency portfolio is the corner portfolio with the highest Sharpe ratio. If the investor's required rate of return is lower than the expected return on the tangency portfolio, the investor will invest a portion of the funds in a risk-free asset and the remainder in the tangency portfolio.

If, on the other hand, the investor's required rate of return is higher than the tangency portfolio's expected rate of return, the investor will use margin (borrow at the risk-free rate) to leverage the return. If the IPS specifically prohibits borrowing, then we select different corner portfolios above the tangency portfolio. The new corner portfolios will be the ones that bracket the investor's required rate of return.

For the Exam: In the following example, we assume the manager is limited to combining the risk-free asset with one corner portfolio. An alternative is finding a combination of corner portfolios that generates the required return (in this example, we would use corner portfolios 4 and 5). Be sure to check out the Level III library volume on corner portfolios.

Example: Determining the tangency portfolio

Continuing the previous example (the figure from the previous example is reproduced for your convenience).

Corner Portfolio	Expected Return	Expected Std. Dev.	Sharpe Ratio	Asset Class Weights				
				U.S. Equity	U.S. Bonds	Int'l Equities	Int'l Bonds	Alt. Inv
1	14.00%	18.00%	0.639	0.00%	0.00%	100%	0.00%	0.00%
2	13.66%	16.03%	0.696	0.00%	0.00%	85.36%	0.00%	14.64%
3	13.02%	13.58%	0.775	21.69%	0.00%	56.56%	0.00%	21.75%
4	12.79%	13.00%	0.792	21.48%	0.00%	52.01%	5.24%	21.27%
5	10.54%	8.14%	0.988	9.40%	51.30%	26.55%	0.00%	12.76%
6	8.70%	6.32%	0.981	0.00%	89.65%	4.67%	0.00%	5.68%

1. **Determine** which portfolio is the most suitable candidate for the tangency portfolio.

2. Assuming no constraint against leverage and a risk-free rate of 2.5%, **determine** the asset allocation for the pension fund if management chooses an available corner portfolio.

3. Assume you are not allowed to leverage. **Determine** the asset allocation if management chooses an available corner portfolio.

Answers:

1. Corner Portfolio 5 with an expected return of 10.54%, has the highest Sharpe ratio (0.988) and would be the most suitable candidate for the tangency portfolio. Because it has the highest Sharpe ratio, Portfolio 5 is the tangency portfolio for the capital allocation line. If allowed to borrow and lend at the risk-free rate, the investor will combine Portfolio 5 with the risk-free asset to attain the desired expected return.

2. The fund's required rate of return is 11.11%, the risk-free rate is 2.50%, and the expected return of the tangency portfolio is 10.54%. Let w_{RF} denote the weight of the risk-free asset and $(1 - w_{RF})$ denote the weight of the tangency portfolio:

$$
\begin{aligned}
0.1111 &= (w_{RF})0.0250 + (1 - w_{RF})0.1054 \\
0.1111 &= 0.0250w_{RF} + 0.1054 - 0.1054w_{RF} \\
0.0804w_{RF} &= -0.0057 \\
w_{RF} &= -0.07; (1 - w_{RF}) = 1.07
\end{aligned}
$$

Therefore, we borrow 7% and invest 107% in the tangency portfolio.

3. In the situation where using margin is not allowed (i.e., cannot borrow at the risk-free rate), the investor will combine the two corner portfolios adjacent to the required return. We will assume the investor has a required return of 11.11% and no borrowing is allowed. In this situation, Corner Portfolios 4 and 5 (expected returns of 12.79% and 10.54%, respectively) will be combined.

Let w_4 be the weight of Corner Portfolio 4 in the combination of 4 and 5:

$$
\begin{aligned}
11.11 &= w_4(12.79) + (1 - w_4)(10.54) \\
11.11 &= 12.79w_4 + 10.54 - 10.54w_4 \\
0.57 &= 2.25w_4 \\
w_4 &\approx 0.25 \\
w_5 &\approx 0.75
\end{aligned}
$$

Investing 25% of our funds in Corner Portfolio 4 and 75% in Corner Portfolio 5, the asset class weights in the final portfolio are:

Asset class weight	$= (w_4)$(wt in 4)	$+ (w_5)$(wt in 5)	
U.S. equity	$= (0.25)(21.48)$	$+ (0.75)(\ 9.40)$	$= 12.42\%$
U.S. bonds	$= (0.25)(\ 0.00)$	$+ (0.75)(51.30)$	$= 38.48\%$
International equity	$= (0.25)(52.01)$	$+ (0.75)(26.55)$	$= 32.91\%$
International bonds	$= (0.25)(\ 5.24)$	$+ (0.75)(\ 0.00)$	$= 1.31\%$
Alternative investments	$= (0.25)(21.27)$	$+ (0.75)(12.76)$	$= 14.89\%$

STRATEGIC ASSET ALLOCATION ISSUES

LOS 21.o: <u>Compare</u> the considerations that affect asset allocation for individual investors versus institutional investors and <u>critique</u> a proposed asset allocation in light of those considerations.

CFA® Program Curriculum, Volume 3, page 260

For the Exam: Much of what this LOS asks for is also covered in the Concept Checkers for Study Sessions 4 and 5. There are some testable morsels in the following discussion, however, that you will not find in those Study Sessions.

Institutional investors. The typical institutional investor is concerned more with meeting liabilities than with generating wealth, although of course, increasing wealth is usually also a goal. An insurance company, for example, must be concerned first and foremost with immunizing its liabilities (with a fixed-income portfolio). Once that is accomplished, the company tries to generate wealth (surplus) through an actively managed portfolio (usually equities). Banks have their liabilities, also, but as we saw in Study Session 5, they manage securities portfolios with the intent of generating income, maintaining liquidity, managing the duration gap, etc. In other words, institutions tend toward an ALM allocation.

Individuals. Individuals' goals include meeting living expenses, funding children's educational expenses, funding retirement, setting up trusts, etc. In other words, the individual typically looks primarily at wealth accumulation to meet required as well as *desired* expenditures.

Another primary difference between an individual investor and an institutional investor is the patterns of income generation and wealth accumulation. Unlike the institutional investor, the typical individual's wealth is accumulated over many years, while the ability to generate income reaches a peak and falls to zero at retirement. The individual's *human capital* (the total present value of future employment income), therefore, is greatest at an early age, while his financial capital (accumulated wealth) increases over time and reaches a maximum at retirement.

The individual's human capital can be a major component of her total assets and must be considered in determining an appropriate strategic asset allocation. Think of the individual's human capital as an allocation to bonds (i.e., return comes in the form of income and isn't as risky as equities). As the young professional starts out, her earnings potential (human capital) is considerable and more than likely comprises the vast majority of her total portfolio (human capital plus financial capital).

At younger ages, then, she has a considerable allocation to *bonds* (her human capital) and the allocation of her financial assets should be toward riskier, higher-return assets like equities. As she ages and accumulates financial capital, her human capital becomes a smaller and smaller component of her total portfolio, and the financial assets require more protection (i.e., an allocation to safer assets).

Another factor that separates individuals from institutions is **longevity risk**. This is the possibility of living longer than planned. For example, the individual might do a very good job of planning for a 25-year retirement at the age of 60 and then live to be older than 100. In this situation, the accumulated wealth is probably not going to be sufficient to fund the extra years. The inverse (sort of) of longevity risk is **mortality risk**; the risk of dying younger than expected. Mortality risk is usually mitigated by purchasing life insurance. Note that the individual bears at least part of the longevity risk, but the individual's spouse and other heirs bear the mortality risk.

Figure 5 presents hypothetical asset allocations for an individual according to age ranges. The important thing is that the allocation is tied to wealth creation in earlier years and protection in later years.

Figure 5: Mix of Human and Financial Capital and Financial Asset Allocation by Age*

Age	25–35	50–Retirement	Retirement Years
Human capital	90–100%	40–50%	0–5%
Financial capital	0–10%	50–60%	95–100%
Equities	100%	25–50%	0–10%
Safer assets	0%	50–75%	90–100%

* Allocation and age ranges are for demonstration purposes. They are not hard-and-fast rules.

Note that even though the actual allocations and age ranges in Figure 5 are subject to some debate, the gradual transition to bonds as the investor ages is indisputable. For example, if on the exam, you see a 50–50 allocation advised for a 25-year-old professional, this is probably incorrect. Because the individual's human capital is probably at its highest level, the allocation of financial assets should be nearly 100% equity. As the individual ages and approaches retirement, the allocation should gradually shift toward nearly 100% bonds.

Professor's Note: Throughout this discussion, we implicitly assumed the individual's income (human capital) was not correlated with the capital markets. If this assumption is not correct, the individual's financial asset allocation should consider safer assets, even in the earlier years.

Defined benefit pension plans. Defined benefit pension plans are concerned foremost with meeting pension obligations, so an ALM process is generally employed. The pension fund manager estimates the minimum acceptable (inflation-adjusted) return and then searches for the appropriate strategic allocation. Any future changes to the strategic allocation for the pension fund are based on several factors.

• The proposed allocation must meet the plan's risk and return objectives. Potential allocations are often compared on a risk-adjusted basis using the Sharpe ratio.
• The volatility of the plan surplus must be maintained within established bounds.
• The allocation must meet liquidity requirements.

Models, such as Monte Carlo simulation, can be employed to determine the long-term effects of the proposed allocation.

Endowments. The primary goal of an endowment is meeting spending requirements while protecting the fund principal. Note that the relevant rate of inflation for an endowment is the rate that affects its institutional beneficiary. For example, a university's costs typically rise at a higher rate than the overall economy, so its endowment fund must incorporate this higher rate into return calculations. Risk is a very important concern for an endowment because its funding is usually critical to the beneficiary.

Because bonds, especially Treasuries, are incapable of meeting their long-term return requirements, endowments usually allocate to a mix of debt for income and stability and equity for long-term returns and growth.

 Professor's Note: When you think about a successful university endowment, you realize that the endowment must (1) meet a portion of the university's current spending needs, (2) keep up with inflation to protect the fund's principal, and (3) meet increased future needs caused by enrollment increases.

Foundations. Although not usually tied to a single beneficiary, foundations are formed to provide grants to individuals, communities, and/or organizations. Depending upon their legal status, foundations are required to make minimum annual payouts based on a percentage of fund assets. The primary goal is to cover the spending requirement while protecting the fund's principal. From a strategic asset allocation standpoint, foundations and endowments are very similar. On the exam, be sure to select an allocation that meets the spending requirements, covers expected inflation, and provides for sufficient growth to fund anticipated growth.

Insurance companies. The characteristic that distinguishes insurance companies from most other institutional investors is the need to *segment* their portfolio. The portfolio is segmented along product lines, as each line has risk and return objectives related to its specific constraints.

Portfolio constraints can differ significantly across segments. For example, if the segment funds fixed-annuity products, the fund should be allocated in fixed-income securities. A segment that funds variable annuities and variable life products indexed to equity markets should be allocated to equities. Of course, as we discussed in Study Session 5, the surplus portfolio is usually invested heavily in equities to provide necessary growth.

The bottom line for insurance companies is that each portfolio segment must meet its objectives and constraints as specified by the characteristics of the insurance products funded by that segment.

For the Exam: On the exam, the specifics of the individual segments would have to be provided and you would select a suitable allocation for each based on its return and risk objectives and its constraints. Tax laws vary considerably from country to country, so any tax differences will have to be clearly noted for you on the exam.

Banks. The strategic allocation for banks is determined by their product mix and the goals of the securities portfolio. As we discussed in Study Session 5, the primary goals for a bank's securities portfolio are:

1. Provide liquidity.
2. Manage credit risk.
3. Manage duration (gap management).
4. Generate income.

Of the listed goals, managing duration (interest rate risk) is the most important, although managing credit risk and providing a source of liquidity are also very important. The strategic allocation is determined through an ALM process. You saw in Study Session 5 that bank portfolios are allocated primarily to fixed-income securities, and the equity (surplus) duration (asset duration minus liability duration) is managed by altering the duration of the securities portfolio.

TACTICAL ALLOCATION

LOS 21.p: <u>Formulate</u> and <u>justify</u> tactical asset allocation (TAA) adjustments to strategic asset class weights, given a TAA strategy and expectational data.

CFA® Program Curriculum, Volume 3, page 316

Tactical asset allocation (TAA) involves short-term deviations from the strategic asset allocation in an attempt to capitalize on capital market disequilibria (mispricing). It can be accomplished by trading assets or (more commonly) through a *derivative overlay* (as you will see in Study Session 15). In either case, the process can be performed at infrequent intervals or as part of a regular tactical allocation program that monitors market conditions, sectors, or asset classes and reacts accordingly. TAA can be performed by internal personnel or by outside firms that specialize in TAA.

As you will see in Study Session 15, the manager might change the allocation to equities, for example, if she feels that equities are undervalued. She can actually sell bonds and buy equities or, to avoid the associated analysis and trading costs, apply an equity index overlay to the portfolio with equity index futures. In reaction to overpricing, the manager can reduce the exposure to equities by selling equity index futures.

Another common reason for tactical allocation is changing interest rates. If the manager feels that interest rates will change more than is currently reflected in asset prices, she can change the duration of the bond portfolio accordingly (i.e., lengthen the duration if rates are expected to fall and shorten the duration if rates are expected to rise). As you will see in Study Session 15, just about any change in allocation can be performed with a derivative overlay.

KEY CONCEPTS

LOS 21.a

Strategic asset allocation combines capital market expectations (formally represented by the efficient frontier) and the investor's risk, return, and investment constraints [from the investment policy statement (IPS)]. Strategic asset allocation is long-term in nature, and hence the weights are called *targets* and the portfolio represented by the strategic asset allocation is called the *policy portfolio*.

Each asset class has its own quantifiable systematic risk. Strategic asset allocation is a conscious effort to gain the desired exposure to systematic risk via specific weights to individual asset classes. Each asset class represents relatively similar investments (e.g., long-term corporate bonds) with similar systematic risk factors. Exposure to specific asset classes in specific proportions enables portfolio managers to effectively monitor and control their systematic risk exposure. In other words, strategic asset allocation reflects the investor's desired systematic risk exposure.

LOS 21.b

Tactical asset allocation is the result of active management wherein managers deviate from the strategic asset allocation to take advantage of any perceived *short-term* opportunities in the market. Hence, tactical asset allocation introduces additional risk, which should be justified by additional return (i.e., positive alpha).

LOS 21.c

Strategic allocation responds to the interaction of the investor's long-term strategic needs and long-run capital market expectations. The investor's goals are in terms of investment policy statement (IPS) objectives and constraints.

It should be remembered that the strategic allocation is based on long-run goals and capital market expectations. Tactical allocation may be used if the market experiences short-term disruptions or the manager recognizes mispriced assets, whereby they can change the allocation for short periods.

Because managers are the *experts* at selecting investments, the question is whether strategic allocation is worth the time and effort. The first response is that without a clearly defined strategic allocation, the portfolio may not reflect the investor's desires. Also, the importance of strategic asset allocation has been well-established empirically. One study by the Vanguard Group shows that *more than* 100% of the long-term performance of a portfolio is explained by its strategic asset allocation. Another study puts this number at 94%.

LOS 21.d

ALM strategic asset allocation is determined in conjunction with modeling the liabilities of the investor. For investors with specific liabilities (e.g., defined benefit pension plans or insurance companies), asset allocation is tailored to meet liabilities and to maximize the surplus, given an acceptable level of risk. This usually results in a relatively high allocation to fixed-income assets. Strategic asset allocation involves specifically modeling liabilities and determining the asset allocation appropriate to fund them. Even for those investors who don't have specific (contractual) liabilities, future obligations (e.g., providing for post-retirement living expenses for an individual investor) can be modeled as liabilities, and an ALM approach to strategic asset allocation can be applied.

In asset-only strategic asset allocation, the focus is on earning the highest level of return for a given (acceptable) level of risk without any consideration for liability modeling. The liability (explicit or implied from future expected cash outflows) is indirectly taken into consideration through the required rate of return. Because the asset-only approach does not specifically model liabilities, the risk of not funding liabilities is not accurately controlled.

LOS 21.e

Dynamic asset allocation takes a multi-period view of the investment horizon. In other words, it recognizes that asset performance in one period affects the required rate of return and acceptable level of risk for subsequent periods. Dynamic asset allocation is difficult and costly to implement. However, investors who have significant liabilities, especially those with uncertain timing and/or amount, find the cost acceptable. Usually, investors who undertake the asset-liability approach to strategic asset allocation prefer dynamic asset allocation.

Static asset allocation ignores the link between optimal asset allocation across different time periods. For example, the manager using a static approach might estimate the necessary mean-variance inputs at a point in time and then construct the long-term portfolio accordingly. The manager using dynamic allocation allows for changing parameters over time using such techniques as Monte Carlo simulation. This allows the manager to build in expected changes to inputs as well as model unanticipated changes in macroeconomic factors.

LOS 21.f

Individuals display *loss aversion* rather than risk aversion and approach investing from a segmented perspective. Because of *mental accounting,* they meet goals one at a time. Their overall asset allocation is likely to be different from their optimal strategic allocation and inconsistent with their risk tolerance.

LOS 21.g

The portfolio's return objective is based on portfolio size, liquidity needs, time horizon, and maintenance of the principal. Unless stated otherwise, we always assume the investor will maintain the principal, so the portfolio must not only meet spending needs but expected inflation and management fees as well.

The risk objective should be specified in light of the investor's risk aversion. Investors can be classified using a numerical scheme, such as scoring investors from 1 to 10 based on their risk tolerance, with 1 indicating very high tolerance and 10 indicating very low tolerance.

The utility-adjusted (risk-adjusted) return the investor will realize from the portfolio can be found by using the following equation:

$$U_P = \hat{R}_P - 0.005(A)\left(\sigma_P^2\right)$$

where:
$\hat{R}_P$ = portfolio expected return
A = investor's risk aversion score
σ_P^2 = portfolio variance

In addition to standard deviation as a measure of risk (volatility), the acceptable level of risk can be stated in terms of *downside risk* measures such as shortfall risk, semivariance, and target semivariance.

LOS 21.h

Asset classes have been appropriately specified if:
- Assets in the class are similar from a descriptive as well as a statistical perspective.
- They are not highly correlated, so they provide the desired diversification.
- Individual assets cannot be classified into more than one class.
- They cover the majority of all possible investable assets.
- They contain a sufficiently large percentage of liquid assets.

LOS 21.i, n

The capital allocation line (CAL) is the straight line drawn from the risk-free rate to a tangency portfolio on the efficient frontier, where the tangency portfolio is the corner portfolio with the highest Sharpe ratio. If the investor's required rate of return is lower than the expected return on the tangency portfolio, she will invest a portion of the funds in a risk-free asset and the remainder in the tangency portfolio.

If, on the other hand, the investor's required rate of return is higher than the tangency portfolio expected rate of return, she will use margin (borrow at the risk-free rate) to leverage the return. If the IPS specifically prohibits borrowing, then we select different corner portfolios above the tangency portfolio. The new corner portfolios will be the ones with the highest Sharpe ratios that bracket the investor's required rate of return.

For example, an endowment's return objective is 7% with a maximum standard deviation of 11%, and no risk-free asset is available.

Given the corner portfolio returns below, determine the standard deviation and asset weights for the portfolio that will meet their objective.

Corner Portfolio	E(R)	σ	Sharpe Ratio	Asset A Weight	Asset B Weight	Asset C Weight
1	9.0%	16.0%	0.438	100%	0%	0%
2	7.5%	11.5%	0.478	80%	20%	0%
3	5.5%	7.7%	0.455	0%	40%	60%
4	5.3%	7.6%	0.434	0%	0%	100%

7% lies between corner portfolios 2 and 3. Solving for the weights of corner portfolios 2 and 3: $7.0 = W_2(7.5) + (1 - W_2)(5.5)$, $7.0 = 7.5W_2 + 5.5 - 5.5W_2$, $7.0 - 5.5 = 2W_2$, $1.5 = 2W_2$, $1.5 / 2 = W_2$, .75 or 75% $= W_2$ and .25 or 25% $= W_3$.

The approximate standard deviation of the portfolio is a weighted average of the standard deviations of Corner Portfolios 2 and 3:

$$\sigma_p = 0.75(0.115) + 0.25(0.077) = 0.1055 = 10.55\% \text{ (less than the maximum of 11\%)}$$

To calculate how much the strategic portfolio invests in assets A, B, and C, use the 75/25 weights in corner portfolios 2 and 3:
- Portfolio 2 has weights 80/20/0 in assets A, B, and C.
- Portfolio 3 has weights 0/40/60 in assets A, B, and C.

Our portfolio has weights in A, B, and C of:

Asset A: $0.75(80) + 0.25(0) = 60\%$

Asset B: $0.75(20) + 0.25(40) = 25\%$

Asset C: $0.75(0) + 0.25(60) = 15\%$

LOS 21.j
There are advantages and disadvantages to adding different asset classes to a portfolio:
- Inflation-protected securities provide protection against inflation and automatically increase or decrease portfolio cash flows with inflation and deflation. U.S. Treasury Inflation Protection Securities (TIPS) are highly liquid and virtually risk free.
- The theoretical justification for adding global securities is the potential to increase return at all levels of risk. The practical implications of including global securities relate to other concerns associated with global investing that are not experienced in a domestic-only setting.
- The primary benefit to including alternative investments in an asset allocation is the diversification benefit. However, the practical drawbacks include the typically large amount of capital required and the need to carefully select out-performers.
- In some cases, information on alternative investments can be sparse or even nonexistent.

LOS 21.k
The asset allocation process is essentially the portfolio management process that has been identified throughout the CFA curriculum. The steps are as follows:
- Determine the investor's return requirement and risk tolerance, subject to the investor's current wealth and constraints.
- Formulate long-term capital market expectations and their potential effects on the various asset classes.
- Determine the asset allocation that best meets the objectives defined in the investment policy statement (IPS), subject to any other limitations specified by the investor.
- Monitor the portfolio regularly as specified in the IPS. A feedback loop should be included so changes in long-term market factors can be incorporated into the *model* and to determine whether adjustments to the strategic allocation are justified. If market changes are short-term, tactical allocation measures should be considered.

©2011 Kaplan, Inc.

LOS 21.l

Mean-Variance Approach

The **mean-variance approach** to strategic asset allocation is a static approach. Efficient portfolios are essentially portfolios with varying allocations to the available asset classes.

Resampled Efficient Frontier

There can be many different combinations (by varying the weights) of a given set of assets that will yield the same expected return and standard deviation, so the computer is asked for many sets of mean-variance efficient portfolios (a resampled efficient frontier) using the same set of returns and standard deviations.

The average weights for each asset are used to represent the weights of the assets in the resampled efficient frontier.

Black-Litterman

The Black-Litterman measure uses asset returns implied by a value-weighted global market index. The analyst can then adjust the model-generated returns using personal return expectations (and confidence in those expectations).

Monte Carlo Simulation

Using different strategic allocations (including the investor's current allocation), the program incorporates the effects of various assumed capital market factors (inflation, yield spreads, recession, etc., and their expected changes) in the next period as well as their compounding effects *over several future periods*. This way the model overcomes the static (1-period) nature of the typical mean-variance analysis.

Asset-Liability Management

Asset-liability management considers the allocation of assets with respect to a given liability or set of liabilities. The ALM approach searches for the set of allocations, which maximize the *difference* (the *surplus*) between assets and liabilities at each level of risk.

Experience-Based Techniques

Experience-based techniques have come about through decades of experience.

LOS 21.m

Each efficient portfolio represents weights on each of the asset classes. The only constraint was that the sum of all the weights should be equal to one. If we add an additional constraint of no short sales, we restrict the value of the weights to be greater than or equal to zero.

Here we have an additional constraint that the weight of each asset class be *non-negative*. In the case of a *constrained optimization* (no short sales in this case), the minimum-variance frontier changes from a smooth curve to one with corner portfolios.

LOS 21.o

Institutional investors. The typical institutional investor is concerned more with meeting liabilities than with generating wealth.

Individuals. Individuals' goals include meeting living expenses, funding children's educational expenses, funding retirement, setting up trusts, etc. In other words, the individual typically looks primarily at wealth accumulation to meet required as well as *desired* expenditures.

Unlike the institutional investor, the typical individual's wealth is accumulated over many years, while the ability to generate income reaches a peak and falls to zero at retirement. The individual's *human capital*, therefore, is greatest at an early age, while his financial capital increases over time and reaches a maximum at retirement.

At younger ages, then, he has a considerable allocation to *bonds* (his human capital) and the allocation of his financial assets should be toward riskier, higher-return assets like equities. As he ages and accumulates financial capital, his human capital becomes a smaller and smaller component of his total portfolio, and the financial assets require more protection (i.e., an allocation to safer assets).

Two other factors that separate individuals from institutions are **longevity risk** and **mortality risk**.

LOS 21.p

Tactical asset allocation (TAA) involves short-term deviations from the strategic asset allocation in an attempt to capitalize on capital market disequilibria (mispricing). It can be accomplished by trading assets or (more commonly) through a *derivative overlay*. In either case, the process can be performed at infrequent intervals or as part of a regular tactical allocation program that monitors market conditions, sectors, or asset classes and reacts accordingly. TAA can be performed by internal personnel or by outside firms that specialize in TAA.

For example, a manager might change the allocation to equities if she feels equities are undervalued. Another common reason for tactical allocation is changing interest rates. If the manager feels interest rates will change more than as currently reflected in asset prices, she can change the duration of the bond portfolio accordingly.

Study Session 8

CONCEPT CHECKERS

1. Jack Manning, CFA, and Tess Brown, CFA, have just joined a financial planning firm. They will work as a team assessing and managing the portfolios of individual clients. Manning will specialize in forming long-term capital market expectations. Brown will assess each client's risk and return objectives as well as constraints. Based upon this, we would define the focus of:
    A. both Manning and Brown as tactical asset allocation.
    B. both Manning and Brown as strategic asset allocation.
    C. Manning as strategic asset allocation and Brown as tactical asset allocation.

2. Deviation from strategic asset allocation due to short-term capital market expectations is called:
    A. active risk assessment.
    B. tactical asset allocation.
    C. policy reallocation.

3. North East Fellowship University's endowment fund has $20 million in assets. The fund has a targeted spending rate of 4.50%. The fund has been incurring 0.75% as management costs. The trustees would like to preserve the purchasing power of the fund and curtail the risk in terms of standard deviation to no more than 10%. Inflation expectation is 2% per year over the foreseeable future. The fund's required rate of return is *closest* to:
    A. 7.25%.
    B. 7.39%.
    C. 8.02%.

4. Tom Wright is evaluating the following portfolios for his retirement. The risk-free rate is 3%, and Wright is moderately risk averse with a numerical ranking of 5.

Portfolio	Return	Std. Dev.
A	15.50%	19%
B	10.85%	12%
C	8.50%	14%
D	14.25%	16%

    The utility adjusted return for the portfolio Wright will *most likely* accept is *closest* to:
    A. 6.48%.
    B. 7.25%.
    C. 7.85%.

Use the following information to answer Question 5.

Portfolio	Exp. Return	Std. Dev.	Asset Class Weights			
			1	2	3	4
A	12.00%	10.50%	65%	–20%	35%	20%
B	16.50%	15.00%	15%	20%	50%	15%
C	18.00%	20.00%	30%	20%	25%	25%
D						

5. Given that Portfolio D is composed of 35% Portfolio A and 65% Portfolio B, the asset class weights in Portfolio D (in percent) are *closest* to:

	1	2	3	4
A.	32.50	20.00	30.75	16.75
B.	14.85	6.00	32.50	46.65
C.	32.50	6.00	44.75	16.75

Use the following information to answer Questions 6 through 9.

Alpa Singh, 56, was recently widowed. She was married to Robert Singh, MD, for 29 years and has two daughters, a 26-year-old and a 23-year-old. Upon the death of her husband, Mrs. Singh received $2 million from his life insurance policy. The Singhs had also set aside $1,350,000 towards their retirement. Mrs. Singh has no income of her own and was dependent on her husband. They lived comfortably, and Mrs. Singh estimates that she would need about $100,000 next year, after taxes. Even though her daughters are not dependent on her, she would like to gift them each $15,000 next year out of the after-tax return on the portfolio. She also would like to be able to pay $200,000 for the younger daughter's wedding in one year. As she will set aside the appropriate amount in T-bills, it will not be considered part of her investable portfolio. Her house is completely paid for, and she would like to leave it to her daughters upon her death as part of their inheritance. She would also like to leave a sizable inheritance for her grandchildren.

Mrs. Singh would like to keep her investments in the United States and not use any leverage in her portfolio. She considers herself to be moderately risk averse but recognizes that she has a long-term time horizon after taking gifts to her grandchildren into account. Her numerical risk aversion is 6. Her tax bracket is 30%, and inflation is estimated to be 1.50% per year.

David Wells has been the financial adviser for the Singhs. To plan for changes in her portfolio and to invest the proceeds from the life insurance policy, he has prepared the following long-term capital market expectations:

	Asset Class	Expected Return	Exp. Std. Dev.	Correlations			
				1	2	3	4
1	U.S. Lg Cap	14.23%	14.74%	1.00			
2	U.S. Sm Cap	13.36%	17.32%	0.793406	1.00		
3	U.S. LT corp	9.47%	6.90%	0.317803	0.097134	1.00	
4	U.S. LT Gov	9.55%	8.99%	0.325103	0.075176	0.95754	1.00

The risk-free rate is assumed to be 2%. Using the long-term capital market expectations, the mean-variance optimization yields four corner portfolios as follows:

Corner Portfolio	Expected Return	Exp. Std. Dev.	Sharpe Ratio	Asset Class Weights			
				1	2	3	4
1	9.90%	6.60%	1.197	0.00%	11.10%	88.90%	0.00%
2	10.06%	6.64%	1.214	0.00%	14.90%	85.10%	0.00%
3	12.10%	9.58%	1.054	55.22%	0.00%	44.78%	0.00%
4	14.23%	14.74%	0.830	100.00%	0.00%	0.00%	0.00%

The efficient frontier from the same data is shown in the following graph:

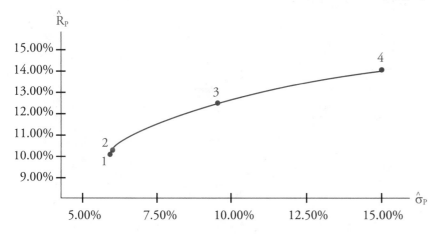

6. Assuming Mrs. Singh wants to protect the real value of her portfolio, the required nominal, before-tax rate of return her portfolio must generate to meet her combined expenses next year is *closest* to:
    A. 6.21%.
    B. 7.45%.
    C. 9.13%.

7. Suppose that Mrs. Singh agrees with her adviser to seek a required rate of return of 11%. Wells then calculates the asset class weights of the efficient portfolio that has an expected return of 11%. His results are *closest* to (with weights given in percentages):
    A. weights = 35.43; 6.32; 58.25; 0.00.
    B. weights = 27.26; 7.25; 65.49; 0.00.
    C. weights = 25.44; 8.03; 66.52; 0.00.

8. Wells then determines the efficient portfolio that provides the highest level of utility for Mrs. Singh and calculates the utility she will derive from it. He decides on:
    A. Portfolio 2 with U_2 = 0.0879.
    B. Portfolio 3 with U_3 = 0.0935.
    C. Portfolio 1 with U_1 = 0.0859.

9.   Using Roy's Safety-First Measure, **determine** which of the corner portfolios is the *most appropriate* given that the minimal acceptable return on the portfolio is 6%.

10.   **Explain** the key assumption of the Black-Litterman approach in forming market expectations and how an analyst uses that assumption to form the expectations. **Explain** one of the benefits that the final results generally exhibit when using this approach over other methods.

©2011 Kaplan, Inc.

Use the following information to answer Questions 11 and 12.

Bill Mosley is the Chief Investment Officer for Trinity Endowment Fund. The trustees of the fund have asked Bill to recommend a strategic asset allocation for the fund. The trustees have determined that the required rate of return for the fund should be 12% and that the fund standard deviation should not exceed 15%. Further, the fund should be diversified in broad asset categories including foreign equities and precious metals. The fund charter does not allow negative weights in any asset classes.

Bill has developed the following long-term capital market expectations:

| | Asset Class | Expected Return | Exp. Std. Dev. | Correlations | | | | |
				1	2	3	4	5
1	U.S. LT Corp	9.47%	6.90%	1.00				
2	U.S. LT GOV	9.55%	8.99%	0.96	1.00			
3	MSCI Eur	13.34%	16.13%	0.15	0.18	1.00		
4	MSCI PAC	12.51%	24.37%	0.03	0.02	0.55	1.00	
5	MSCI U.S.	14.29%	14.65%	0.32	0.33	0.67	0.25	1.00
6	Gold	2.04%	12.27%	−0.24	−0.24	−0.14	0.13	−0.32

The risk-free rate is assumed to be equal to 1.50%.

Based on the above capital market expectations, Bill ran a constrained optimization, and the results are shown below:

| Corner Portfolio | Expected Return | Exp. Std. Dev. | Sharpe Ratio | Asset Class Weights | | | | | |
				1	2	3	4	5	6
1	7.86%	5.05%	1.259	59.59%	0.00%	4.90%	0.00%	6.87%	28.63%
2	8.52%	5.18%	1.355	61.11%	0.00%	6.56%	0.00%	9.74%	22.58%
3	10.88%	7.23%	1.297	66.65%	0.00%	7.47%	4.78%	20.78%	0.32%
4	14.10%	13.96%	0.903	0.00%	0.00%	4.75%	8.22%	87.03%	0.00%
5	14.18%	14.19%	0.894	0.00%	0.00%	0.07%	6.33%	93.60%	0.00%
6	14.29%	14.65%	0.873	0.00%	0.00%	0.00%	0.00%	100.00%	0.00%

The efficient frontier is shown below.

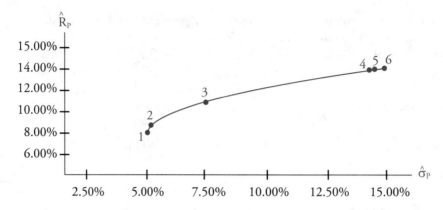

11. What would be the asset class weights of the efficient portfolio that would be recommended for the endowment fund?
    A. Weights = (43.47%; 0%; 6.52%; 5.98%; 43.82%; 0.21%).
    B. Weights = (35.22%; 0%; 6.23%; 5.67%; 21.71%; 0.32%).
    C. Weights = (45.98%; 0%; 6.21%; 5.45%; 33.72%; 0.21%).

12. **Discuss** and **contrast** asset-only versus asset-liability portfolio management.

13. **Describe** expected return estimation bias associated with traditional mean-variance allocation and **describe** a method that can be used to help solve the problem.

ANSWERS – CONCEPT CHECKERS

1. **B** Strategic asset allocation uses long-term capital market expectations as well as the client's risk and return objectives and constraints.

2. **B** Short-term deviations from the strategic asset allocation to take advantage of short-term capital market expectations are called tactical asset allocation.

3. **B** Required rate of return = $(1.045)(1.02)(1.0075) - 1 = 0.0739 = 7.39\%$

   Ordinarily, either adding or compounding the components would be acceptable. In this case, the curriculum specifies the compounding method.

4. **C** $U_A = \hat{R}_A - 0.5(R_Z)(\sigma_A^2) = 0.1550 - 0.5(5)(0.19)^2 = 0.0648$
   $U_B = \hat{R}_B - 0.5(R_Z)(\sigma_B^2) = 0.1085 - 0.5(5)(0.12)^2 = 0.0725$
   $U_C = \hat{R}_C - 0.5(R_Z)(\sigma_C^2) = 0.0850 - 0.5(5)(0.14)^2 = 0.0360$
   $U_D = \hat{R}_D - 0.5(R_Z)(\sigma_D^2) = 0.1425 - 0.5(5)(0.16)^2 = 0.0785$

   Because U_D is the highest of all four, Tom gets the highest utility by investing in Portfolio D with a utility-adjusted return of 7.85%.

5. **C** Investing 35% of our funds in Corner Portfolio A and 65% in Corner Portfolio B, the asset class weights in Portfolio D are:

   $$\text{asset class weight} = (w_A)(\text{wt in A}) + (w_B)(\text{wt in B})$$
   $$\text{weight of } 1 = (0.35)(65) + (0.65)(15) = 32.50\%$$
   $$\text{weight of } 2 = (0.35)(-20) + (0.65)(20) = 6.00\%$$
   $$\text{weight of } 3 = (0.35)(35) + (0.65)(50) = 44.75\%$$
   $$\text{weight of } 4 = (0.35)(20) + (0.65)(15) = 16.75\%$$
   $$\sum_{i=1}^{4} W_i = 100\%$$

6. **B** The total value of Singh's portfolio is $3,350,000 ($2,000,000 life insurance proceeds + $1,350,000 retirement portfolio). To provide $200,000 in one year, she will set aside the present value of $200,000 at 2% = $196,078 in T-bills. Therefore, she has an investable portfolio of $3,350,000 – $196,078 = $3,153,922.

   Singh's after-tax living expenses and gifts over the coming year total $130,000. This equates to $130,000 / (1 – 0.30) = $185,714 in before-tax dollars and represents a before-tax spending rate of $185,714 / $3,153,922 = 5.89%. Adding 1.5% inflation to protect the real value of the portfolio, the required before-tax nominal return becomes 7.39% (1.0589 × 1.015 – 1 = 7.48% geometric).

7. **C** The expected return of 11% lies between Corner Portfolios 2 and 3 with expected returns of 10.06% and 12.10%, respectively. We solve for w in the following equation:

   $$0.11 = w_2(0.1006) + (1 - w_2)(0.1210)$$
   $$w_2 = 0.5392; \quad w_3 = 1 - 0.5392 = 0.4608$$

In other words, the efficient portfolio with an expected return of 11% has 53.92% weight in Corner Portfolio 2 and 46.08% weight in Corner Portfolio 3. With respect to asset classes, the weights then are derived as follows:

US Lg Cap	$= (0.5392)(0)+(0.4608)(0.5522)$	$= 0.2544 = 25.45\%$
US Sm Cap	$= (0.5392)(0.149)+(0.4608)(0)$	$= 0.0803 = 8.03\%$
US LT Corp bonds	$= (0.5392)(0.851)+(0.4608)(0.4478)$	$= 0.6652 = 66.52\%$
US LT Gov bonds	$= (0.5392)(0)+(0.4608)(0)$	$= 0\%$

Note: The approximate standard deviation of the efficient portfolio with 11% expected return is the weighted average standard deviations of Corner Portfolios 2 and 3.

Standard deviation = $(0.5392)(0.0664) + (0.4608)(0.0958) = 0.08 = 8\%$

8. **B** Risk aversion is 6.

$$U_1 = \hat{R}_1 - 0.5(R_Z)\left(\sigma_1^2\right) = 0.0990 - 0.5(6)(0.0660)^2 = 0.0859$$

$$U_2 = \hat{R}_2 - 0.5(R_Z)\left(\sigma_2^2\right) = 0.1006 - 0.5(6)(0.0664)^2 = 0.0874$$

$$U_3 = \hat{R}_3 - 0.5(R_Z)\left(\sigma_3^2\right) = 0.1210 - 0.5(6)(0.0958)^2 = 0.0935$$

$$U_4 = \hat{R}_4 - 0.5(R_Z)\left(\sigma_4^2\right) = 0.1423 - 0.5(6)(0.1474)^2 = 0.0771$$

Portfolio 3 has the highest utility for Mrs. Singh.

9. Corner Portfolio 3 is the most appropriate. Roy's Safety-First criterion for Portfolio 3 is:

$$RSF_{P3} = \frac{\hat{R}_P - R_{MAR}}{\sigma_P} = \frac{12.1\% - 6\%}{9.58\%} = 0.637$$

Portfolio	Expected Return	Std. Dev.	Roy's Safety First Measure
1	9.90%	6.60%	0.591
2	10.06%	6.64%	0.611
3	12.10%	9.58%	0.637
4	14.23%	14.74%	0.558

10. *Key assumption*: Financial markets are in equilibrium.

Using this assumption and current market data, the analyst backs out the implied market risk premium and covariances of the assets from a value-weighted global market index. In other words, it gives the equilibrium values implied by the existing market prices. Also, the analyst can adjust the results using personal expectation.

Resulting benefit: Because the analyst uses a global index, the Black-Litterman approach tends to yield portfolios that are more diversified than those determined using other methods. It also yields returns for each asset, helping to avoid the associated input bias.

11. **A**   The required rate of return of 12% lies between Corner Portfolios 3 and 4 with expected returns of 10.88% and 14.10% respectively. We solve for w_3 in the following equation:

$$0.12 = w_3(0.1088) + (1 - w_3)(0.1410)$$

$$w_3 = 0.6522$$

65.22% is in Corner Portfolio 3 and 34.78% is in Corner Portfolio 4, so the asset class weights are:

US LT Corp:	$(0.6522)(0.6665) + (0.3478)(0)$	$= 0.4347 = 43.47\%$
US LT Gov:	$(0.6522)(0) + (0.3478)(0)$	$= 0$
MSCI Europe:	$(0.6522)(0.0747) + (0.3478)(0.0475)$	$= 0.0652 = 6.52\%$
MSCI Pacific:	$(0.6522)(0.0478) + (0.3478)(0.0822)$	$= 0.0598 = 5.98\%$
MSCI US:	$(0.6522)(0.2078) + (0.3478)(0.8703)$	$= 0.4382 = 43.82\%$
Gold:	$(0.6522)(0.0032) + (0.3478)(0)$	$= 0.0021 = 0.21\%$

12.   Asset-liability portfolio management allocates assets within the framework of funding liabilities. The optimal allocation is the one that maintains risk within an acceptable range while providing the return necessary to meet the liabilities. The manager can employ an ALM efficient frontier framework. The ALM frontier plots surplus at various levels of risk, and the manager selects the allocation on the frontier that produces an acceptable mix of expected surplus and risk.

   In contrast, asset-only allocation looks solely at risk and return with the goal of maximizing return for the acceptable level of risk. Although liabilities can be modeled into the required return, the surplus (assets minus liabilities) is not specifically considered. To avoid the estimation uncertainty associated with projecting expected returns, the Black-Litterman approach can be employed in an asset-only allocation.

13.   The inputs to the traditional mean-variance allocation include expected returns, standard deviations, and correlations. Historical standard deviations and correlations are frequently employed in a traditional analysis and usually do not have an associated bias (i.e., the historical values of these inputs do not consistently over- or underestimate their future values). The expected return bias arises from the requirement to estimate expected returns, which must be done by an analyst. Whenever an individual starts from zero in forming an estimate, there is always the possibility of intentional or unintentional bias.

   To overcome the need to form these estimates, the analyst/manager can utilize the Black-Litterman approach. In this methodology, the inputs are the historical standard deviations, weights, and correlations of assets in a world index. Using a reverse optimization process, the analyst backs out the equilibrium returns implied by these inputs. Then, based upon expectations and their associated confidence, the analyst changes some of the returns. The returns are then used as inputs to a traditional mean-variance analysis to determine an efficient frontier for the assets being considered.

The following is a review of the Asset Allocation principles designed to address the learning outcome statements set forth by CFA Institute®. This topic is also covered in:

THE CASE FOR INTERNATIONAL DIVERSIFICATION

EXAM FOCUS

Several issues involving international diversification are covered in this topic review, including expected returns, asset risk, currency risk, and correlations for developed and emerging market investors. With the continuing globalization of the Level III curriculum, any or all of this material could show up on the exam. For insight into forms the questions could take, pay close attention to the command words in the LOS. Most are qualitative in nature (e.g., explain, justify, distinguish, summarize). LOS 22.a and c, however, asks you to *evaluate*, so related material is likely to require calculations. Remember that calculations can be required for item set as well as constructed response essay questions. Also, if part of an essay question, be sure to show your calculations, including the formulas, so the grader can award partial credit if your answer is not numerically correct.

GLOBAL DIVERSIFICATION

LOS 22.a: <u>Discuss</u> the implications of international diversification for domestic equity and fixed-income portfolios, based on the traditional assumptions of low correlations across international markets.

CFA® Program Curriculum, Volume 3, page 350

There are two primary reasons why an investor would want to diversify globally:

1. Risk reduction.
2. Return enhancement.

An investor can decrease risk by investing in foreign assets with low correlations. The lower correlations from foreign assets also indicate that higher returns are sometimes available abroad. If correlations are low, asset markets tend to move independently of one another. This means that there may be higher returns available in foreign markets when U.S. markets experience low returns.

Global Portfolio Risk and Return

Professor's Note: For simplicity, we take the perspective of the U.S. investor; therefore, the U.S. dollar is the domestic currency in the examples that follow.

The volatilities of international markets are similar to those in the United States. However, the total risk of a foreign asset measured in U.S. dollars is often higher than that of U.S. securities, because foreign asset risk has two components:

1. The volatility of the foreign asset.
2. The volatility of the foreign currency.

Even though the total risk of foreign assets is often higher, adding a foreign asset to a portfolio will reduce portfolio risk if the correlations are sufficiently low.

Recall the formulas for calculating the portfolio expected return and portfolio variance for a portfolio with two assets:

$$\widehat{R}_P = w_A \widehat{R}_A + w_B \widehat{R}_B$$

$$\sigma_P^2 = w_A^2 \sigma_A^2 + w_B^2 \sigma_B^2 + 2w_A w_B \sigma_A \sigma_B \rho_{A,B}$$

where:

$\widehat{R}_P$	= expected return on a portfolio
w_A	= proportion invested in Asset A
$\widehat{R}_A$	= expected return on Asset A
w_B	= proportion invested in Asset B
$\widehat{R}_B$	= expected return on Asset B
σ_P^2	= variance of a portfolio
σ_A and σ_A^2	= standard deviation and variance of Asset A
σ_B and σ_B^2	= standard deviation and variance of Asset B
$\rho_{A,B}$	= correlation of returns between Asset A and Asset B

Note: $\sigma_A \sigma_B \rho_{A,B} = Cov_{A,B}$

From the formula, we see that the portfolio's expected return is a weighted average of the individual asset returns. That is not the case with the portfolio's expected risk, however. Note that for portfolio risk, the first two terms represent weighted averages of individual asset risk, but a third term is added to account for the co-movement between the two assets.

The measures we can use to measure co-movement are either the covariance or the correlation, as in the above formula. Recall that correlation will always be between −1.0 and +1.0. If the correlation is low, investing in foreign assets will reduce the risk of the overall portfolio.

Example: Calculating the return and standard deviation of a global portfolio

The domestic stock has an expected return of 10% and a standard deviation of 25%. The foreign asset has an expected return of 15% and a standard deviation of 35%. The correlation between the two assets is 0.40.

Assuming the portfolio has 30% invested in the domestic asset and the remainder in the foreign asset, **calculate** the portfolio's expected return and standard deviation.

Answer:

$$\hat{R}_P = 0.30(0.10) + 0.70(0.15) = 0.135 = 13.5\%$$

$$\sigma_P^2 = (0.30)^2(0.25)^2 + (0.70)^2(0.35)^2 + 2(0.30)(0.70)(0.25)(0.35)(0.40)$$
$$\sigma_P^2 = 0.005625 + 0.060025 + 0.0147 = 0.0804$$

The standard deviation is just the square root of the variance so the portfolio standard deviation is:

$$\sigma_P = \sqrt{0.0804} = 0.2835 = 28.35\%$$

Note that because the correlation is less than 1.0, the portfolio standard deviation of 28.35% is less than the weighted sum of individual assets' standard deviations [0.3(25%) + 0.7(35%) = 32%]. It is also less than the risk of the foreign asset (35%).

If you need practice calculating expected portfolio return and risk, you should note that if we instead invest 50% in each asset, the return and risk will change. In this case, the portfolio return will drop to 12.5% and the portfolio standard deviation will drop to 25.25%.

The portfolio risk will also change as the correlation changes. Using the original 30/70 asset weighting, the portfolio standard deviation will drop to 27.69% if the correlation decreases to 0.30.

> *Professor's Note: Although it is often assumed that correlations are constant, they can be quite variable over time. The investor is exposed to the risk that correlations will increase subsequent to investment and decrease the diversification benefits.*

International Equity Market Correlations

All countries will be affected to some degree by changes in the world economy. However, the correlations between country stock returns will be low when countries pursue economic and governmental policies that are independent of one another and high when they are closely related. For example, we would expect the countries of the G 7 (Canada, France, Germany, Italy, Japan, the United Kingdom, and the United States) to have high stock market correlations because they meet regularly to coordinate economic policy.

The factors that cause economies to behave independently and their resulting correlations to be low are:

- Government regulations.
- Technological specializations.
- Fiscal policies.
- Monetary policies.
- Cultural and sociological differences.

For example, if a government regulates capital flows, the stock markets will be less affected by developed-world stock market crashes. Countries with unique technologies (e.g., consumer-related and production technologies) will also have low correlations with other markets. In the case of fiscal and monetary policy, there is a great deal of variety among countries. As such, national economies and stock markets will move independently of one another. Lastly, differences in cultural and societal behaviors will isolate countries and the economies from international trends.

Even among countries with similar government regulations, fiscal policies, and monetary policies (e.g., the G 7 countries), the correlations can be sufficiently low to offer diversification opportunities.

International Bond Market Correlations

The factors that cause bond market correlations to be low are differing government fiscal and monetary policies. If a government has unusually high budget deficits or extremely high or low interest rates, the country's bond market and currency will tend to move independently of other countries. Hence, the correlation between domestic and foreign bonds will tend to be low, especially when foreign bond returns are measured in U.S. dollar terms.

INTERNATIONAL EFFICIENT FRONTIER

LOS 22.d: <u>Discuss</u> the impact of international diversification on the efficient frontier.

CFA® Program Curriculum, Volume 3, page 353

The correlations between U.S. and foreign markets are low enough that adding foreign investments to a domestic portfolio could result in opportunities for lower risk. Higher returns are also possible, as many foreign markets will outperform the U.S. market from time to time. The benefits from foreign diversification are illustrated in Figure 1.

Figure 1: The Global Efficient Frontier

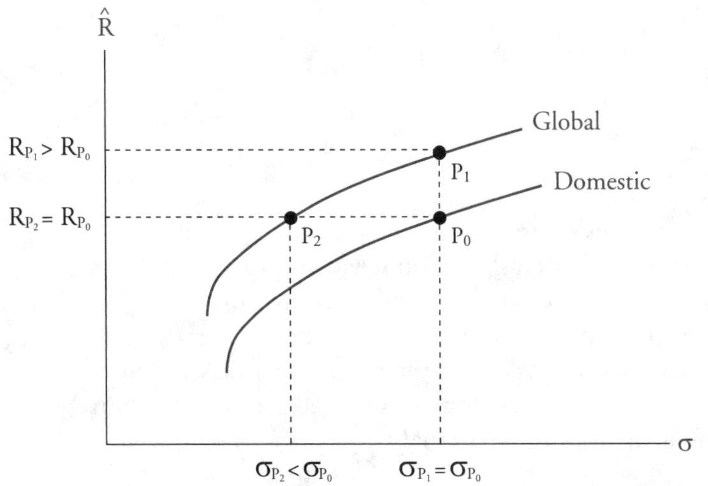

The upper curve in Figure 1 represents portfolios that include investments throughout the world, and it clearly dominates the domestic-only efficient frontier by offering a higher return for the same amount of risk and a lower level of risk for a given amount of return.

BENEFITS OF DIVERSIFICATION

LOS 22.e: Evaluate the potential performance and risk-reduction benefits of adding bonds to a globally diversified stock portfolio.

CFA® Program Curriculum, Volume 3, page 357

Due to generally low correlations of monetary and budgeting policies, which affect interest rates and prices, global bond markets tend to have low correlations with one another. Further, bond markets tend to have low correlations with stock markets. The result is increased diversification potential from adding global bonds to a well-diversified portfolio of global stocks.

However, although a naïve diversification strategy using global bonds can produce positive results for the diversified stock investor, one should be aware of "pockets" of high correlation. For example, although the U.S. bond market shows correlations of less than 0.50 with almost all other global markets, it has a higher correlation with Canada. Likewise, bond markets in the countries of the European Union have correlations approaching 1.0.[1]

Further, one must consider currency-hedging. For example, when considering an unhedged investment, the Canadian bond market has a correlation of 0.41 with U.S. equity, whereas if the currency is hedged, the correlation is 0.26. The correlation of the

---

1. Source: Exhibit 3, page 355, 2012 CFA Level III Curriculum, Volume 3, Reading 22, *The Case for International Diversification*.

Canadian and U.S. bond markets changes from 0.49 to 0.64 when the investor hedges the currency exposure.[2]

As shown in Figure 2, plotting ex-post data indicates a general benefit to adding global bonds to a well-diversified portfolio of global stocks. The effectiveness for the individual portfolio manager, however, will be determined by:

1. The correlations of the global bond markets under consideration.

2. The correlations of those global bond markets with the stock portfolio.

3. Whether currency exposures will be hedged.

Figure 2: Risk and Returns for International Bond Markets

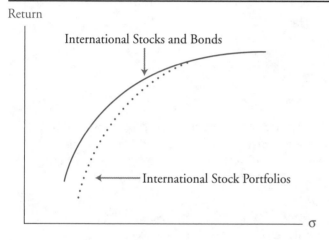

CURRENCY RETURN

LOS 22.b: **Distinguish** between the asset return and currency return for an international security.

CFA® Program Curriculum, Volume 3, page 351

For an investor who invests overseas, the return from a foreign asset is:

$$R_\$ = R_{LC} + S + (R_{LC})(S)$$

where:
$R_\$$ = return on the foreign asset in U.S. dollar terms
R_{LC} = return on the foreign asset in local currency terms
S = percentage change in the foreign currency

2. Ibid.

Professor's Note: The local currency in the preceding formula is the currency local to the asset (i.e., the currency in which the foreign asset is denominated). Don't confuse this with the domestic currency, which refers to the currency of the investor.

In the preceding formula, note that in addition to the return on the asset and return on the foreign currency, the U.S. investor also earns (or suffers) the third term on the right-hand side, the currency appreciation (or depreciation) on the foreign asset's return.

Example: Calculating the domestic return on an international security

The foreign asset return in local currency terms is 6%. Assuming the foreign currency appreciates by 10%, **calculate** the return to the U.S. investor.

Answer:

Using the preceding formula:

$$R_\$ = 0.06 + 0.10 + (0.06)(0.10) = 0.166 = 16.6\%$$

The return to the U.S. investor is composed of the return to the foreign asset in foreign currency terms (6%), the return from the currency appreciation (10%), plus the currency appreciation on the foreign asset return (0.6%). In this example, the appreciation of the foreign currency increased the U.S. investor's return.

Note that a foreign currency *depreciation* would have the opposite effect (i.e., decrease the U.S. investor's return). For example, if the foreign currency were to depreciate by 10% in our example, the return to the U.S. investor would be:

$$R_\$ = 0.06 + (-0.10) + (0.06)(-0.10) = -0.046 = -4.6\%$$

Instead of earning a return higher than the foreign asset return of 6% as in the previous example, the U.S. investor suffers a loss of −4.6%.

CURRENCY RISK

LOS 22.c: <u>Evaluate</u> the contribution of currency risk to the volatility of an international security position.

CFA® Program Curriculum, Volume 3, page 351

When investing in a foreign asset, the U.S. investor is exposed to both the risk of the foreign asset and the foreign currency risk. Just as we had with the 2-asset portfolio above, we also consider the co-movement between the asset return and the currency. The formula for the risk of a foreign asset is much the same as for portfolio risk, except that we *omit the weights* from the formula. That is, the weights of both the asset and the currency are 1.0, so they can be dropped from the equation.

$$\sigma_\$^2 = \sigma_{LC}^2 + \sigma_S^2 + 2\sigma_{LC}\sigma_S\rho_{LC,S}$$

where:

$\sigma_\$^2$ = variance of the returns on the foreign asset in U.S. dollar terms

$\sigma_{LC}^2, \sigma_{LC}$ = variance and standard deviation of the foreign asset in local currency terms

σ_S^2, σ_S = variance and standard deviation of foreign currency

$\rho_{LC,S}$ = correlation between returns for the foreign asset in local currency terms and movements in the foreign currency

With the correlation never greater than +1.0, the standard deviation in U.S. dollar terms will never be greater than the sum of the foreign asset and currency standard deviations:

$$\sigma_\$ \le \left(\sigma_{LC} + \sigma_S\right)$$

The difference between the risk of the investment in U.S. dollar terms and in local currency terms is referred to as the contribution of currency risk:

$$\text{contribution of currency risk} = \sigma_\$ - \sigma_{LC}$$

For the Exam: The Level III exam is less about "plug and chug" (i.e., simply plugging numbers into an equation) than about the effects on portfolio risk and return of taking certain actions. The added risk of having an investment denominated in a foreign currency, therefore, is exactly the type of question that is likely to appear on the exam. Be sure you are able to perform the related calculations.

Example: Calculating the contribution of currency risk

The foreign stock has a standard deviation of 14% in local currency terms and the foreign currency has a standard deviation of 6%. If the correlation between the foreign stock returns and the foreign currency is 0.1, what is the standard deviation in U.S. dollar terms and what is the contribution of currency risk?

Answer:

Using the preceding formula:

$$\sigma_\$^2 = \left(0.14\right)^2 + \left(0.06\right)^2 + 2\left(0.14\right)\left(0.06\right)\left(0.1\right) = 0.0249$$

$$\sigma_\$ = \sqrt{0.0249} = 0.1577 = 15.77\%$$

contribution of currency risk = 15.77% − 14.00% = 1.77%

Note that in the preceding example the risk in U.S. dollar terms (15.77%) is not a great deal higher than the 14% in local currency terms. This is due to the relatively low standard deviation of the foreign currency and the low correlation between the foreign asset return and the currency changes. Indeed, the contribution of currency risk is only 1.77%.

CURRENCY RISK AND VOLATILITY

LOS 22.f: Explain why currency risk should not be a significant barrier to international investment.

CFA® Program Curriculum, Volume 3, page 366

The reasons currency risk only slightly magnifies the volatility of foreign investments are:

- Currency risk is about half that of foreign *stock* risk.
- Foreign asset risk and currency risk are not additive (due to correlations of less than one).
- Currency risk can be hedged.
- Currency risk will be diversified away in a portfolio of many foreign assets.

Currency risk is about half the risk of foreign stocks when measuring risk by standard deviation. In the case of foreign *bonds*, however, currency risk is *greater* by a factor of about two.

Second, as seen in the previous example, asset risk and currency risk are not additive because the correlation between them is usually low and sometimes negative. This results in the contribution of currency risk being quite low, usually about 10% of the foreign asset risk in local currency terms.

Third, currency risk can be hedged by using forwards, futures, options, or by taking a loan in the foreign currency. Lastly, if an investor holds many different country assets, much of the currency risk will be diversified away. The foreign currency risk that remains will also help diversify domestic fiscal and monetary policies.

INTERNATIONAL DIVERSIFICATION SHOULD NOT WORK

LOS 22.g: Critique the traditional case against international diversification.

CFA® Program Curriculum, Volume 3, page 367

For the Exam: This material on currency risk (LOS 22.f) and international diversification (LOS 22.g) is ideal for an essay question. A very likely question would ask you to agree or disagree with a statement made by a portfolio manager or analyst and explain your decision if you disagree. Keep in mind as you continue that LOS 22.g and 22.h could be covered in the same question or set of questions.

©2011 Kaplan, Inc.

Changing correlations among international economies can have very undesirable effects. For example, if we create an international portfolio based upon historical correlations and those correlations subsequently increase, we will have overestimated the benefits of international diversification.

The increasing correlations argument against international diversification states that the benefits of international diversification are generally overstated because:

- Correlations have increased over time.
- Correlations among markets increase during periods of increased volatility.

According to proponents, correlations have been *increasing* over time because:

- Free trade among nations has increased.
- Capital markets are becoming integrated into the world economy as they are deregulated and opened up.
- Corporations have increased exports, foreign operations, and foreign mergers and acquisitions. As the nationality of a corporation becomes less indicative of their global reach, the opportunities for diversification lessen. For example, in an effort to diversify internationally, a U.S. investor may have invested in Daimler Benz in the 1980s. Although still representing large foreign investments, Daimler-Chrysler is much less effective today as a diversification tool.
- The mobility of capital has increased with institutional investors more active in international markets, particularly in developed countries.

In addition to correlations increasing over time, correlations between markets appear to increase when volatility increases in international markets. For example, in October 1987, most of the world's markets were down sharply. At precisely the time when an investor needs diversification, the association between markets increased.

A Statistical Aberration

The problem with estimating correlation during periods of rising volatility is that the calculated correlation will be biased upwards when in fact it has not changed. If we take a sample of data and split the sample in half based on the absolute value of returns, the high-return half (with an accompanying higher volatility) will have a higher measured correlation, whereas the low-return half will have a lower measured correlation. So although the true correlation might be about 0.40, the higher volatility of the first sample exhibits higher correlation. This phenomenon is due to the econometrics of the correlation measure. Higher volatility in returns equates with higher measured correlations.

Academic research has found that the previously reported increases in correlation during volatile stock markets were, for the most part, manifestations of the higher volatility and not increases in the true correlations. An alternative to the correlation for measuring co-movement of assets during volatile periods would be to plot the *cross-section* of the returns of several global markets at several points over time. If the plotted returns tend to wander, the markets are moving independently. If instead they tend to follow a pattern, they are highly correlated.

BARRIERS TO INTERNATIONAL INVESTING

LOS 22.h: <u>Discuss</u> the barriers to international investments and their impact on international investors.

CFA® Program Curriculum, Volume 3, page 371

Capital market theory incorporates the assumption of a "market" portfolio that encompasses all available risky assets. The weights of the individual risky assets in the market portfolio correspond to their weights in the economy (i.e., their total market values). If the market value of a company amounts to 1/1000 of the total market value of all risky assets in the market, for example, its weight should also be 1/1000 of the market portfolio.

Unfortunately, from a risk and return perspective, international investments are not included at their full economic values in the *global market portfolio*. Although empirical studies have repeatedly demonstrated the risk (i.e., diversification benefits) and return benefits of adding international investments to a domestic portfolio, investors are hesitant to fully incorporate international investments into their portfolios due to barriers such as *transactions costs, regulations, taxes, currency risk, political risk, market efficiency,* and *lack of familiarity*.

> **For the Exam:** Be able to list and discuss several barriers to international investing, including a discussion of the different transactions costs.

Transactions costs. Compared to the United States, trading costs in general tend to be larger in foreign markets. *Brokerage commissions*, for example, are typically higher and can be variable. In some cases, when brokerage costs are fixed by regulation, stamp taxes are applied to trades. In addition to these direct trading costs, investors must be aware of *price impact costs*, which can be significant for trades by large portfolio managers wishing to trade significant blocks of individual securities.

International investors must also be aware of possibly higher *custodial costs* and *record-keeping costs*. International investors, for example, are often faced with a double layer of custodians, composed of a master custodian who oversees a set of "sub-custodians," one in each country. Then, because investments are usually denominated in several different currencies, all transactions, cash flows, and their associated accounting must be performed and managed using several different accounting systems. Even though the efficiency of the systems varies significantly by foreign market, associated costs can amount to several (e.g., 10–12) basis points.

Management costs can also be higher for several reasons. For example, costs associated with researching and monitoring (e.g., foreign databases, collection of data, communication) as well as the time and expense of maintaining a working knowledge of many different accounting systems can be significant and add a few basis points to management fees.

To avoid some of the added expenses of international investing, individual investors can limit foreign investments to those listed as ADRs. This is typically not an efficient

Study Session 8

mechanism for large asset managers, however, whose trades can cause extensive price reactions and are thus best placed on the larger local markets.

Regulations. Both domestic and foreign regulations can limit foreign investment. Many U.S. pension plans, for example, are limited in the amount of any single international investment in their portfolios as well as foreign investments in total. In addition, some foreign markets limit investment by international investors. Again, the extent or even the presence of these restrictions varies greatly by market.

Most emerging markets, for example, impose limitations on the percentage of any individual firm (i.e., equity) that can be held by foreign investors. Even some developed markets limit foreign ownership, even though there is an extensive world-wide movement to remove any ownership discrimination. The European Union, for example, prohibits any ownership discrimination among its members.

 Professor's Note: Even though emerging market governments often apply restrictions on foreign ownership of equities, those same governments often rely on foreign ownership of their bonds and force their domestic companies to purchase only domestic bonds.

Taxes. Income taxes on dividends are commonly withheld by local governments. Even though the withheld taxes are usually paid out to foreign investors after several months, there is an opportunity cost associated with the period of time they are lost. Having a considerable amount of cash continually tied up in withheld taxes is a definite disincentive to institutional portfolio managers. In some cases, investors are allowed to claim a portion of withheld taxes as tax credits in their home countries, but this opportunity obviously holds no value for tax-exempt investors.

For the Exam: The CFA Program is neither a law program nor a tax program. On the exam you will not be expected to discuss either international laws or tax codes at length, but be sure you can briefly discuss these barriers.

Currency risk. The primary concerns here are the extra *costs* associated with having to deal in many different currencies (e.g., accounting, trading). As we have already discussed, there are risks associated with international currencies, but those can be partially or mostly eliminated through hedging strategies.

For the Exam: The currency risk associated with international investing has been a long standing favorite of CFA Institute. Currency risk is a very logical barrier to international investing and would readily qualify as part of a list of barriers you are asked to create and discuss on the exam. However, if asked to discuss it as part of a list of barriers, do not limit your discussion to the associated costs. Include a discussion of the increased return volatility (i.e., uncertainty) caused by the volatility of the currency itself, even though it can and often is managed through hedging strategies.

Political risk. This refers to uncertainty in foreign investments related to the local country itself. For example, an emerging market might experience a change in its political climate and become more hostile toward foreign investment or its local currency might experience significant devaluation.

Market efficiency. A major concern in international investing is the *liquidity* of the individual markets, which can be quite variable. In those situations where a portfolio manager has a relatively large holding of a foreign company, for example, liquidating the position might be accompanied by a significant decline in the price. Although rare in developed economies, some emerging markets also limit the amount of capital that can be repatriated by the investor. In other words, even if the position is liquidated, the investor might not be able to remove all of the funds from the economy.

Another concern for international investors is a potential *lack of reliable information*. In some developed and emerging markets, for example, available information can be slow in coming (i.e., late), inaccurate, or even managed through insider trading and/or price manipulating.

Lack of familiarity. Although limited somewhat to individuals and small institutional investors, a lack of familiarity with foreign business practices can make the investor hesitant to make international investments. Also, this lack of familiarity usually leads these investors to perceive foreign investments as riskier than domestic investments.

GLOBAL VS. INTERNATIONAL INVESTING

LOS 22.i: Distinguish between global investing and international diversification and discuss the growing importance of global industry factors as a determinant of risk and performance.

CFA® Program Curriculum, Volume 3, page 377

It is possible to invest globally without achieving international diversification. Until recently, the traditional approach to international diversification was to decide on the countries and then find stocks headquartered within those countries to invest in. Increasingly, though, corporations are not defined by where they are incorporated, given increased international trade, cross-border acquisitions, and other financial activity. Instead of domestic conglomerate diversification, corporations are concentrating on their core business and expanding their operations across countries.

Hence, country factors are not as important as they once were—stock returns are less dependent on the country where the firm is based and more dependent on the industries in which the firm operates. Industry factors become more important as corporations become more global and more narrowly focused on a single industry. The implication for investors is that diversification should include industry diversification as well as country diversification.

Global investing diversifies across industries as well as countries, in contrast to traditional international diversification that only considers country diversification. Although industry factors have become more important and country factors less important, an investor should not assume that diversifying across borders is no longer necessary. Consider, for example, an Italian investor. If she were to diversify across industries but invest only in Italian companies, she would still be exposed to the Italian country-factor risk. Further, not all industries will be present in Italy and those that are may not be the best investment. Thus, the contemporary investor would be wise to diversify across both countries and industries (global investing) instead of just diversifying across countries (international investing).

EMERGING MARKETS

LOS 22.j: Discuss the basic case for investing in emerging markets, as well as the risks and restrictions often associated with such investments.

CFA® Program Curriculum, Volume 3, page 380

Emerging markets offer opportunities for higher returns. In the recent past, emerging markets have had higher returns than developed world markets. Although the stand-alone risk of emerging markets is higher, much of this risk is diversified away in a global portfolio due to the low correlations with developed world markets. In the following sections, we will discuss how the expected returns from emerging markets are high relative to the incremental risk from adding emerging markets to a global portfolio.

The return volatility in emerging markets is much higher than that in developed markets. Furthermore, the distribution of emerging market returns is negatively skewed, so there is a higher probability of a large negative return than that inferred from a normal distribution. The use of the standard deviation, which assumes normality, is not an appropriate risk measure for emerging market returns.

Risks unique to emerging markets include:

- Unstable political and social environments.
- Undeveloped infrastructure.
- Poor educational systems.
- Corrupt governments.

The return correlations among emerging markets can be high in times of crisis, depending on the cause of the crisis. If the crisis is due to local factors, it does not usually spread to other emerging markets. If it is caused by outside factors, however, the crisis can be contagious, and crises in emerging markets are usually more prolonged than in developed countries. Emerging market crises do not usually spread to developed markets, which accounts for the low correlation between emerging and developed markets.

 Professor's Note: A crisis in emerging markets can also be caused by recessions in the developed markets with which the emerging markets trade. Obviously, in this situation, the returns to the developed and emerging markets are highly correlated.

In a portfolio, the inclusion of emerging markets should result in higher expected returns due to their higher expected economic growth. Many analysts expect higher growth for emerging markets in the future due to low labor costs, low levels of unionization, and higher demand for their products. In addition, increased trade, increased capital flows, and outsourcing of production worldwide by developed nations could have impacts on the development of emerging nations. Those emerging countries likely to do particularly well are those with democratic political systems, efficient financial regulation, promotion of free enterprise, and effective legal systems.

Although the stand-alone risk of emerging markets can be quite high, the incremental risk from adding emerging markets to a portfolio should be reasonable, as the correlations with developed world markets are typically quite low.

In emerging markets, currencies are more volatile than in developed markets. Currency devaluations are common and the central banks are usually weak. A currency devaluation would weaken the dollar return to the U.S. investor.

In developed countries, the correlation between stock returns and currency movements is usually negative, the explanation usually being that a weakening currency makes the local corporations' products more competitive on the world markets. Thus, currency risk and asset risk often offset one another to reduce the risk to a U.S. investor.

This is not the case, though, in emerging markets, where the stock returns and currency returns are usually positively correlated. In the case of a downturn, the emerging markets investor usually suffers twice, with decreasing asset returns and decreasing foreign exchange value. In times of crisis, emerging market currencies are frequently devalued and local stocks fall in value as foreign investors lose their faith in the emerging market economy.

Investability

Although the returns from emerging markets can appear quite attractive, the foreign investor may not be able to exploit these returns for several reasons:

- Some emerging countries restrict the amount of stock that can be held by foreigners.
- Free float (the proportion of stock publicly traded) can be low because the government is often the primary owner of stock.
- Repatriation of invested capital is often restricted, especially in times of crisis.
- Discriminatory taxes are sometimes applied to foreign investors.
- Convertibility of foreign currency is often restricted, which is a problem for the foreign investor who wants to convert the local currency denominated investment back to the domestic currency.
- Authorized investors are sometimes the only investors able to invest in local firms. These are often institutional investors.
- Liquidity in emerging markets is often quite low, so that the price impact of a trade reduces the return.

With the liberalization of financial markets, these issues are decreasing in importance and the investability of emerging markets is increasing. *Investable* or *free* emerging market stock indexes are constructed to reflect the investability of these markets.

Segmentation and Integration of Emerging Markets

If markets were integrated throughout the world, capital would flow freely across borders and assets of the same risk would have the same expected returns. On the other hand, if markets are segmented, assets of the same risk will not always offer the same expected return.

There is evidence that emerging markets are segmented. Emerging market returns are not priced according to their risk contribution to a world portfolio. Instead, emerging market returns correspond more closely to local risks, which results in high expected returns. The implication is that emerging markets make an attractive addition to a global portfolio because the expected returns are high but the increase in portfolio risk is not large, due to the low correlations between emerging and developed country markets.

KEY CONCEPTS

LOS 22.a

There are two primary reasons why an investor would want to diversify globally:
- Risk reduction.
- Return enhancement.

An investor can decrease risk by investing in foreign assets with low correlations. If correlations are low, asset markets tend to move independently of one another. This means that there may be higher returns available in foreign markets when U.S. markets experience low returns.

Correlations between country stock returns will be low when countries pursue economic and governmental policies that are independent of one another and high when they are closely related.

Even among countries with similar government regulations, fiscal policies, and monetary policies, the correlations can be sufficiently low to offer diversification opportunities.

The factors that cause bond market correlations to be low are differing government fiscal and monetary policies. If a government has unusually high budget deficits or extremely high or low interest rates, the country's bond market and currency will tend to move independently of other countries.

LOS 22.d

The correlations between U.S. and foreign markets are low enough that adding foreign investments to a domestic portfolio could result in opportunities for lower risk. Higher returns are also possible, as many foreign markets will outperform the U.S. market from time to time as illustrated in the following figure.

The Global Efficient Frontier

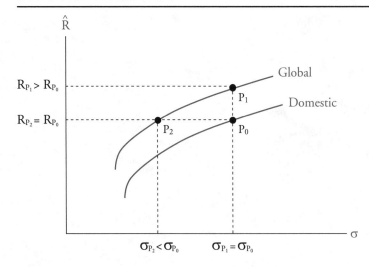

©2011 Kaplan, Inc.

LOS 22.e

The correlations between international bond markets are often lower than that between international stock markets. Therefore, adding international bonds to a global portfolio offers opportunities for lower risk and higher return, as illustrated in the following figure.

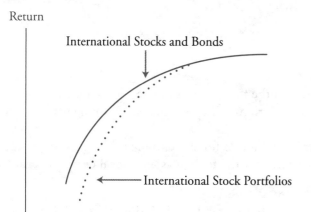

LOS 22.b

For an investor who invests overseas, the return from a foreign asset is:

$$R_\$ = R_{LC} + S + (R_{LC})(S)$$

where:
$R_\$$ = return on the foreign asset in U.S. dollar terms
R_{LC} = return on the foreign asset in local currency terms
S = percentage change in the foreign currency

In the preceding formula, note that in addition to the return on the asset and return on the foreign currency, the U.S. investor also earns (or suffers) the third term on the right-hand side, the currency appreciation (or depreciation) on the foreign asset's return.

LOS 22.c

When investing in a foreign asset, the U.S. investor is exposed to both the risk of the foreign asset and the foreign currency risk. Just as we had with the two-asset portfolio before, we also consider the co-movement between the asset return and the currency. The formula for the risk of a foreign asset is much the same as for portfolio risk except that the weights for the asset and the currency are 1.0.

$$\sigma_\$^2 = \sigma_{LC}^2 + \sigma_S^2 + 2\sigma_{LC}\sigma_S\rho_{LC,S}$$

where:

$\sigma_\$^2$ = variance of the returns on the foreign asset in U.S. dollar terms

$\sigma_{LC}^2, \sigma_{LC}$ = variance and standard deviation of the foreign asset in local currency terms

σ_S^2, σ_S = variance and standard deviation of foreign currency

$\rho_{LC,S}$ = correlation between returns for the foreign asset in local currency terms and movements in the foreign currency

With the correlation never greater than +1.0, the standard deviation in U.S. dollar terms will never be greater than the sum of the foreign asset and currency standard deviations:

$$\sigma_\$ \leq (\sigma_{LC} + \sigma_S)$$

The difference between the risk of the investment in U.S. dollar terms and in local currency terms is referred to as the contribution of currency risk:

$$\text{contribution of currency risk} = \sigma_\$ - \sigma_{LC}$$

LOS 22.f

The reasons currency risk only slightly magnifies the volatility of foreign investments are:
- Currency risk is about half that of foreign *stock* risk.
- Foreign asset risk and currency risk are not additive (due to correlations of less than one).
- Currency risk can be hedged.
- Currency risk will be diversified away in a portfolio of many foreign assets.

Currency risk is about half the risk of foreign stocks when measuring risk by standard deviation. In the case of foreign *bonds*, however, currency risk is *greater* by a factor of about two.

LOS 22.g

The increasing correlations argument against international diversification states that the benefits of international diversification are generally overstated because:

- Correlations have increased over time.
- Correlations among markets increase during periods of increased volatility.

According to proponents, correlations have been *increasing* over time because:

- Free trade among nations has increased.
- Capital markets are becoming integrated into the world economy as they are deregulated and opened up.
- Corporations have increased exports, foreign operations, and foreign mergers and acquisitions are becoming more global, lessening the opportunities for diversification.
- The mobility of capital has increased with institutional investors being more active in international markets.

LOS 22.h

Investors are hesitant to fully incorporate international investments into their portfolios due to barriers such as:

- **Transactions costs.** Compared to the United States, trading costs in general tend to be larger in foreign markets.
- **Regulations.** Both domestic and foreign regulations can limit foreign investment.
- **Taxes.** Income taxes on dividends are commonly withheld by local governments. The withheld taxes are usually paid out to foreign investors after several months. There is an opportunity cost associated with the period of time they are lost.
- **Currency risk.** The primary concerns here are the extra *costs* associated with having to deal in many different currencies (e.g., accounting, trading).
- The increased return volatility (i.e., uncertainty) is caused by the volatility of the currency itself.
- **Political risk.** This refers to uncertainty in foreign investments related to the local country itself.
- **Market efficiency.** A major concern in international investing is the *liquidity* of the individual markets, which can be quite variable and a potential *lack of reliable information.*
- **Lack of familiarity.** Although limited somewhat to individuals and small institutional investors, a lack of familiarity with foreign business practices can make the investor hesitant to make international investments.

LOS 22.i

Increasingly, corporations are not defined by where they are incorporated, given increased international trade, cross border acquisitions, and other financial activity due to their expanding operations across countries.

Stock returns are less dependent on the country where the firm is based and more dependent on the industries in which the firm operates. Industry factors become more important as corporations become more global and more narrowly focused on a single industry.

Global investing diversifies across industries as well as countries, in contrast to traditional international diversification that only considers country diversification. Although industry factors have become more important and country factors less important, an investor should not assume that diversifying across borders is no longer necessary. Thus, the contemporary investor would be wise to diversify across both countries and industries (global investing) instead of simply diversifying across countries (international investing).

LOS 22.j

Emerging markets offer opportunities for higher returns. In the recent past, emerging markets have had higher returns than developed world markets. Although the stand-alone risk of emerging markets is higher, much of this risk is diversified away in a global portfolio due to the low correlations with developed world markets.

Risks unique to emerging markets include:
- Unstable political and social environments.
- Undeveloped infrastructure.
- Poor educational systems.
- Corrupt governments.

In developed countries, the correlation between stock returns and currency movements is usually negative, the explanation usually being that a weakening currency makes the local corporations' products more competitive on the world markets.

In emerging markets, the stock returns and currency returns are usually positively correlated. In the case of a downturn, the emerging markets investor usually suffers twice, with decreasing asset returns and decreasing foreign exchange value.

Although the returns from emerging markets can appear quite attractive, the foreign investor may not be able to exploit these returns for several reasons:
- Some emerging countries restrict the amount of stock that can be held by foreigners.
- The proportion of stock publicly traded can be low.
- Repatriation of invested capital is often restricted.
- Discriminatory taxes are sometimes applied to foreign investors.
- Convertibility of foreign currency is often restricted.
- Liquidity in emerging markets is often quite low.

CONCEPT CHECKERS

Use the following data to answer Questions 1 and 2.
- The domestic stock has an expected return of 12% and a standard deviation of 30%.
- The foreign stock has an expected return of 15% and a standard deviation of 50%.
- The investor will place 60% of her funds in the foreign stock and the remainder in the domestic stock.
- The correlation in returns between the two stocks is 0.30.

1. The expected return of the portfolio is *closest* to:
    A. 13.20%.
    B. 13.80%.
    C. 21.00%.

2. As measured by its standard deviation, the risk of the portfolio is *closest* to:
    A. 12.60%.
    B. 17.64%.
    C. 35.50%.

Use the following data about a U.S. investor making an international investment to answer Questions 3 through 5.
- The return on the stock in foreign currency terms was 17%.
- The foreign currency has depreciated by 6%.
- The standard deviation of stock returns was 31% and the standard deviation of the foreign currency was 11%.
- The correlation between the stock returns and the currency is 0.20.

3. The return to the U.S. investor was *closest* to:
    A. 9.98%.
    B. 11.00%.
    C. 23.00%.

4. The risk of the portfolio in U.S. dollar terms as measured by its standard deviation is *closest* to:
    A. 12.18%.
    B. 17.64%.
    C. 34.91%.

5. The contribution of currency risk to the risk of the portfolio is *closest* to:
    A. 3.91%.
    B. 11.00%.
    C. 12.61%.

6. Which of the following factors would be *least likely* to result in low correlations between stock markets?
    A. Strict government regulations.
    B. Cultural and sociological heterogeneity.
    C. Monetary policies coordinated among countries.

7.   Which of the following statements regarding currency risk is *least accurate*?
      A. The amount of currency risk in a foreign stock is about equal to its actual stock-specific risk.
      B. Currency risk is diversified away in a foreign asset portfolio.
      C. Foreign asset risk and currency risk are not additive if the correlation between them is less than one.

8.   Which of the following factors would be the *most likely* cause of increased correlations between stock markets?
      A. Capital markets have become more segmented.
      B. Free trade between nations has increased due to trade treaties.
      C. The mobility of capital has been increasingly restricted by government regulations.

9.   Which of the following statements regarding global and international investing is *most accurate*?
      A. Global investing is achieved through diversifying a portfolio across countries.
      B. Bonds do not improve the mean variance efficiency of an international stock portfolio.
      C. Real economic growth and economic flexibility both positively influence stock market performance.

10.   Which of the following factors would be *least likely* to limit the investability of emerging markets?
      A. Liquidity is often low.
      B. Free float increases currency volatility.
      C. Repatriation of capital is often restricted.

11.   Which of the following statements regarding emerging markets is *most accurate*?
      A. Emerging markets appear to be integrated with the world economy.
      B. The return on emerging markets does not justify their risk in a portfolio.
      C. The use of the standard deviation is not an appropriate measure of emerging market risk.

ANSWERS – CONCEPT CHECKERS

1. **B** Portfolio return is a weighted average of the two asset returns:

   0.40(12%) + 0.60(15%) = 13.80%.

2. **C** Portfolio risk includes individual asset risk as well as the correlation between the assets. The calculation is:

   $$\sigma_P^2 = (0.40)^2 (0.30)^2 + (0.60)^2 (0.50)^2 + 2(0.40)(0.60)(0.30)(0.50)(0.30)$$

   $$\sigma_P^2 = 0.0144 + 0.0900 + 0.0216 = 0.1260$$

   $$\sigma_P = \sqrt{0.1260} = 0.3550 = 35.50\%$$

3. **A** To obtain the return in U.S. dollar terms, use the following formula that considers the return in local currency terms as well as the exchange rate change:

   $$R_\$ = 0.17 + (-0.06) + (0.17)(-0.06) = 0.0998 = 9.98\%$$

4. **C** We will use the formula for portfolio risk that considers the risk of the asset in foreign currency terms, the risk of the foreign currency, and the correlation between the two:

   $$\sigma_\$^2 = \sigma_{LC}^2 + \sigma_S^2 + 2\sigma_{LC}\sigma_S\rho_{LC,S}$$

   $$\sigma_\$^2 = (0.31)^2 + (0.11)^2 + 2(0.31)(0.11)(0.2) = 0.1218$$

   $$\sigma_\$ = \sqrt{0.1218} = 0.3491 = 34.91\%$$

5. **A** The contribution of currency risk measures the risk incremental to foreign asset risk after considering currency risk, and is the difference between the asset risk in domestic currency terms minus the risk of the foreign asset in foreign currency terms:

   contribution of currency risk = 34.91% – 31.00% = 3.91%

6. **C** Government regulations, technological specialization, heterogeneity in fiscal and monetary policies, and heterogeneous cultures all result in low correlations. Homogeneous or coordinated monetary polices would likely cause correlations to increase.

7. **A** Currency risk is actually about half that of foreign stock risk, which is one of the reasons currency risk only slightly magnifies the volatility of foreign currency denominated investments. The other reasons are that foreign currency risk and foreign asset risk are not additive, currency risk can be hedged, and it is diversified away in a portfolio of many foreign assets.

8. **B** As free trade increases between nations, economies become more interdependent and correlations increase. Other factors for increasing correlations are that capital markets are becoming more integrated as they are deregulated, the mobility of capital has increased as institutional investors have become more active in international investing, and corporations have become more globally oriented.

9. **C**   The higher the real economic growth and economic flexibility, the higher the stock market performance. Global investing requires diversification across both countries *and* industries, and adding international bonds to an international stock portfolio will result in a lower level of risk for a given amount of return.

10. **B**   Free float refers to the amount of stock that is publicly traded, which is often low in emerging markets as governments often hold a large portion of the stock. Other factors limiting the investability of emerging markets include: restrictions on the amount of stock that can be held by foreigners, discriminatory taxes are often applied to foreign investors, repatriation of capital and convertibility of currency are often restricted, restrictions are placed so that only authorized investors can purchase stock, and liquidity is often low.

11. **C**   There is a higher probability of a large loss with emerging markets than that inferred from a normal distribution, so the standard deviation is not an appropriate measure of risk. Emerging markets appear to be segmented. Although emerging markets have high stand-alone risk, the returns are higher than what is expected, given their contribution to portfolio risk. The relatively low contribution to portfolio risk results from the low correlations with developed markets.

Use the following information for Questions 1 through 6.

Tyler Robinson, CFA, a senior analyst at RNC Investments, is reviewing the investment policy statements (IPS) of two new RNC clients. The first client, Bob Carlson, is a 45-year-old seasoned investor who prefers to take a strategic approach to allocating his assets. The second client, Rick Olsen, is a 22-year-old recent college graduate who believes in monitoring his portfolio on a daily basis and capitalizing on perceived mispricings.

Carlson has just moved his account from Aggressive Investments (AI) to RNC because he was uncomfortable with the 12% return AI was promising their clients. Carlson knew that this return was only achievable with an increased level of risk-taking. Robinson interviews Carlson over the phone and inquires about his spending rate and his risk aversion score on a scale of 1 to 10, with 10 indicating the lowest tolerance for risk. Carlson thinks that a 3% after-tax return should cover his spending needs on an annual basis and believes that his risk aversion score would be 8 out of 10.

Olsen has just opened up his first investments account through RNC. RNC services were recommended to him by one of his college finance professors who has a son working at RNC. Although he would like to manage his own investments, Olsen's new job requires him to work 60 hours a week leaving him little time to day trade for his own account. For this reason, Olsen has handed investing responsibilities to RNC and consequently, Robinson. Robinson asks Olsen the same two questions that he asked Carlson. Olsen thinks a 5% after-tax return is enough to cover his spending needs and rates his risk aversion score at 2 out of 10.

Robinson begins to select a static asset allocation for each investor given the information he gathered from both interviews. His first step entails specifying asset classes. Robinson believes that the set of asset classes should provide a high level of diversification and they should have a large percentage of liquid assets. However, he does not think that a majority of all possible investable assets need to be included in a given portfolio or that assets need to be classified into more than one class. A drawback to Robinson's asset allocation approach is that the number of estimates needed is overwhelming. Robinson evaluates the following asset classes as possible investments for Carlson and Olsen:

Asset Class	Expected Return	Expected Standard Deviation
U.S. Large-Cap	8.5%	15%
U.S. Small-Cap	12%	20%
U.S. Fixed Income	5.5%	3%
Real Estate	7.0%	12%

Robinson then creates four portfolios with the previous asset classes and calculates their expected returns, standard deviations, and Sharpe ratios. The portfolios are as follows:

Corner Portfolio	Exp. Return	Exp. Std. Dev.	Sharpe Ratio	Asset Class Weights %			
				A	B	C	D
1	6.50%	5.95%	0.756	12	13	5	70
2	7.25%	8.30%	0.633	22	5	21	52
3	8.00%	11.15%	0.538	32	18	15	35
4	8.75%	14.25%	0.474	42	21	22	15

1. Assuming inflation of 2% and a marginal tax rate of 25% for Carlson and Olsen, their required, before-tax nominal returns are *closest* to:

Carlson	Olsen
    A. 6.0%   8.7%
    B. 6.5%   9.5%
    C. 7.1%   9.9%

2. Assuming Robinson recommended Portfolio 1 to Carlson and Portfolio 4 to Olsen, the utility-adjusted returns for both investors would be *closest* to:
    A. 5.08% for Carlson and 6.72% for Olsen.
    B. 6.72% for Olsen and 6.26% for Carlson.
    C. 6.26% for Carlson and 8.61% for Olsen.

3. Has Robinson appropriately specified the set of asset classes?
    A. No, because a set of asset classes does not need to provide a high level of diversification.
    B. No, because a set of asset classes does not need to contain a large percentage of liquid assets.
    C. No, because a set of asset classes should cover a majority of all possible investable assets.

4. What approach to asset allocation is Robinson *most likely* using?
    A. Resampled efficient frontier.
    B. Mean-variance optimization.
    C. Black-Litterman.

5. Given the four corner portfolios that Robinson developed, the standard deviation of a portfolio that is capable of achieving an expected return of 7.5% is *closest* to:
    A. 9.73%.
    B. 9.51%.
    C. 9.24%.

6.   Assuming a risk-free rate of 2.5% and no constraint against leverage, determine the weights that should be invested in the risk-free asset and the tangency portfolio to achieve an expected return of 7.5%.

A.   The risk-free asset would be –20% and the tangency portfolio would be 120%.

B.   The tangency portfolio would be 75% and the risk-free asset would be 25%.

C.   The risk-free asset would be –25% and the tangency portfolio would be 125%.

SELF-TEST ANSWERS: ASSET ALLOCATION

1. **A** Carlson's real, after-tax required return is 3%, which equates to 0.03 / 0.75 = 4.0% before tax. His nominal before-tax return is 4% + 2% = 6% (6.08% geometric).

    Olsen's real, after-tax spending rate is 5%. Before tax this equates to 0.05 / (1 − 0.25) = 6.67%. Thus, his nominal before-tax required return is 6.67% + 2% = 8.67% (8.80% geometric).

2. **A** Portfolio 1 has an expected return of 6.5% and an expected standard deviation of 5.95%. Given Carlson's risk aversion score of 8, his utility-adjusted return would be:

    $U_P = 6.5\% - 0.005(8)(5.95^2) = 5.08\%$

    Portfolio 4 has an expected return of 8.75% and an expected standard deviation of 14.25%. Given Olsen's risk aversion score of 2, his utility-adjusted return would be:

    $U_P = 8.75\% - 0.005(2)(14.25^2) = 6.72\%$

3. **C** Asset classes have been appropriately specified if:
    - Assets in the class are similar from a descriptive as well as a statistical perspective.
    - They are not highly correlated so they provide the desired diversification.
    - Individual assets cannot be classified into more than one class.
    - They cover the majority of all possible investable assets.
    - They contain a sufficiently large percentage of liquid assets.

    Robinson was incorrect to not include a majority of all possible investable assets in a given portfolio. This was evident in his choice to not consider an international asset class during his development of client portfolios.

4. **B** Mean-variance optimization uses a static approach as opposed to a dynamic approach. Also, the primary drawback to mean-variance optimization is the overwhelming number of estimates needed (e.g., expected returns, standard deviations, correlations).

5. **C** An expected return of 7.5% lies between Corner Portfolios 2 and 3, with expected returns of 7.25% and 8%, respectively. First, determine the weight that should be invested in these two corner portfolios to achieve the expected return.

    $7.5\% = w_2 \times 7.25\% + (1 - w_2) \times 8\%$

    $w_2 = 67\%$, therefore $w_3 = 33\%$

    The standard deviation of the portfolio is the weighted average of the standard deviations of Corner Portfolios 2 and 3.

    $\sigma_P = (0.67)(0.083) + (0.33)(0.1115) = 9.24\%$

6. **C** With no constraint against borrowing the expected return is the weighted average of the risk-free asset and the tangency portfolio. The tangency portfolio is the portfolio with the highest Sharpe ratio which happens to be Portfolio 1. The expected return of Portfolio 1 is 6.5%. The weights in the risk-free asset and the tangency portfolio are as follows:

$7.5\% = w_{RF} \times 2.5\% + (1 - w_{RF}) \times 6.5\%$

$w_{RF} = -25\%$, therefore $w_T = 125\%$

In order to achieve the desired expected return of 7.5% with no constraint against leverage, 25% should be borrowed at the risk-free rate and 125% should be invested in the tangency portfolio.

FORMULAS

endowment spending rules:

$$\text{spending}_t = S\left(\text{market value}_{t-1}\right)$$

$$\text{spending}_t = \left(\text{spending rate}\right)\left(\frac{\text{market value}_{t-1} + \text{market value}_{t-2} + \text{market value}_{t-3}}{3}\right)$$

$$\text{spending}_t = \left(R\right)\left(\text{spending}_{t-1}\right)\left(1 + I_{t-1}\right) + \left(1 - R\right)\left(S\right)\left(\text{market value}_{t-1}\right)$$

leverage-adjusted duration gap: $\text{LADG} = D_{\text{Assets}} - \left(\dfrac{L}{A}\right)D_{\text{Liabilities}}$

asset beta: $\beta_a = w_d\beta_d + w_e\beta_e$

total asset beta: $\beta_{a,T} = w_{a,o}\beta_{a,o} + w_{a,p}\beta_{a,p}$

market volatility: $\sigma_t^2 = \theta\sigma_{t-1}^2 + (1-\theta)\varepsilon_t^2$

factor model based market return: $R_i = \alpha_i + \beta_{i,1}F_1 + \beta_{i,2}F_2 + \varepsilon_i$

factor model based market variance: $\sigma_i^2 = \beta_{i,1}^2\sigma_{F_1}^2 + \beta_{i,2}^2\sigma_{F_2}^2 + 2\beta_{i,1}\beta_{i,2}\text{Cov}\left(F_1,F_2\right) + \sigma_{\varepsilon,i}^2$

covariance of two markets:

$$\text{Cov}\left(i,j\right) = \beta_{i,1}\beta_{j,1}\sigma_{F_1}^2 + \beta_{i,2}\beta_{j,2}\sigma_{F_2}^2 + \left(\beta_{i,1}\beta_{j,2} + \beta_{i,2}\beta_{j,1}\right)\text{Cov}\left(F_1,F_2\right)$$

price of a stock at time 0: $P_0 = \dfrac{\text{Div}_1}{\hat{R}_i - g} \Rightarrow \hat{R}_i = \dfrac{\text{Div}_1}{P_0} + g$

Grinold-Kroner expected return on equity: $\hat{R}_i = \dfrac{\text{Div}_1}{P_0} + i + g - \Delta S + \Delta\left(\dfrac{P}{E}\right)$

expected bond return:

$\hat{R}_B =$ real risk-free rate + inflation risk premium + default risk premium + liquidity risk premium + maturity risk premium + tax premium

ICAPM: $\hat{R}_i = R_F + \beta_i\left(\hat{R}_M - R_F\right)$

beta for stock i: $\beta_i = \dfrac{\text{Cov}\left(i,m\right)}{\sigma_M^2}$

correlation of stock i with the market: $\rho_{i,M} = \dfrac{\text{Cov}\left(i,m\right)}{\sigma_i\,\sigma_M} \Rightarrow \text{Cov}(i,m) = \rho_{i,M}\sigma_i\sigma_M$

equity risk premium for market i: $ERP_i = \rho_{i,M}\sigma_i\left(\dfrac{ERP_M}{\sigma_M}\right)$

target interest rate to achieve neutral rate:

$$r_{target} = r_{neutral} + \left[0.5\left(GDP_{expected} - GDP_{trend}\right) + 0.5\left(i_{expected} - i_{target}\right)\right]$$

Cobb-Douglas function (% change): $\dfrac{\Delta Y}{Y} = \dfrac{\Delta A}{A} + \alpha\dfrac{\Delta K}{K} + (1-\alpha)\dfrac{\Delta L}{L}$

Solow residual = $\%\Delta TFP = \%\Delta Y - \alpha(\%\Delta K) + (1-\alpha)(\%\Delta L)$

H-model: $V_0 = \dfrac{D_0}{r - g_L}\left[\left(1 + g_L\right) + \dfrac{N}{2}\left(g_s - g_L\right)\right]$

constant growth model: $P_0 = \dfrac{D_1}{r - \overline{g}}$

Fed model: $\dfrac{\text{S\&P earnings yield}}{\text{Treasury yield}}$

Yardeni model: $\dfrac{E_1}{P_0} = Y_B - d\left(LTEG\right)$

P/10-year MA(E): $\dfrac{\text{current level of the S\&P}}{\text{average S\&P earnings over last ten years }\left(\text{adjusted for inflation}\right)}$

Tobin's q: $\dfrac{\text{total asset value}}{\text{total replacement cost}} = \dfrac{\text{MV debt + MV equity}}{\text{total replacement cost}}$

equity q: $\dfrac{\text{MV equity}}{\text{MV of net worth}} = \dfrac{\text{\# shares outstanding} \times \text{price per share}}{\text{MV assets} - \text{MV liabilities}}$

$U_P = \hat{R}_P - 0.005(A)\left(\sigma_P^2\right)$

$RSF = \dfrac{\hat{R}_P - R_{MAR}}{\sigma_P}$

return from a foreign asset: $R_\$ = R_{LC} + S + (R_{LC})(S)$

variance of the returns on the foreign asset in U.S. dollar terms:

$$\sigma_\$^2 = \sigma_{LC}^2 + \sigma_S^2 + 2\sigma_{LC}\sigma_S\rho_{LC,S}$$

contribution of currency risk = $\sigma_\$ - \sigma_{LC}$

$\hat{R}_P = w_A\hat{R}_A + w_B\hat{R}_B$

$\sigma_P^2 = w_A^2\sigma_A^2 + w_B^2\sigma_B^2 + 2w_Aw_B\sigma_A\sigma_B\rho_{A,B}$

INDEX

Notes

Notes

Notes

Notes

Notes

Notes

Notes

Notes

Notes

Notes